Restoration Plays and Players

An Introduction

DAVID ROBERTS
Birmingham City University

CAMBRIDGE
UNIVERSITY PRESS

CAMBRIDGE
UNIVERSITY PRESS

University Printing House, Cambridge CB2 8BS, United Kingdom

Cambridge University Press is part of the University of Cambridge.

It furthers the University's mission by disseminating knowledge in the pursuit of education, learning and research at the highest international levels of excellence.

www.cambridge.org
Information on this title: www.cambridge.org/9781107617971

First published 2014

Printed in the United Kingdom by Clays, St Ives plc

A catalogue record for this publication is available from the British Library

Library of Congress Cataloguing in Publication data
Roberts, David, 1960–
Restoration plays and players : an introduction / David Roberts, Birmingham City University.
    pages   cm
ISBN 978-1-107-02783-1 (Hardback) – ISBN 978-1-107-61797-1 (Paperback)
1. English drama–Restoration, 1660–1700–History and criticism.   2. Theater–
England–History–17th century.   3. Theater and society–England–History–17th century.
4. Actors–England.   I. Title.
PR691.R58 2014
822'.409–dc23   2014023641

ISBN 978-1-107-02783-1 Hardback
ISBN 978-1-107-61797-1 Paperback

Contents

Figures

Preface

Why *Restoration Plays and Players*? This book might have been called *Restoration Drama*, in reference to the body of plays written between 1660 and 1714; or *Restoration Theatre*, the performance practices that animated them, or occasionally failed to. Instead, *Restoration Plays and Players* treats reading and performance (institutionally, 'literature' and 'theatre') as mutually fruitful means of approaching late seventeenth-century drama, recognizing that Restoration people themselves experienced drama in print as well as in the theatre. The title harbours a further distinction. *Restoration* is nothing if not political. For the past twenty years studies of the period's plays have devoted a lot of space to the collective experience of shifting ideologies or factional politics. *Players* signals a counterbalancing curiosity about the theatre people who were agents or victims of that experience. Actors, writers, managers and even critics variously innovated, succumbed, resisted or simply carried on as the world changed around them.

So to the subtitle: *An Introduction*. The contexts for Restoration plays are manifold and complex, whether in original performance, reading or recent revival, and it is the job of an introduction to unpick them. Context means little without text, however, and many readers will be unfamiliar with more than a small proportion of the works discussed here. In addition to thumbnail narratives of political and dramatic history, this book therefore reproduces and briefly examines key passages from two dozen or so of the most distinctive Restoration plays, in the hope of conveying something of their individual colour and impact, as well as their relationship to contextual themes and critical controversies: a primer in the primary material, so to speak. There is no attempt at – and no room for – a comprehensive review of recent criticism, but there is a discursive guide to further reading for those who wish to take the subject further.

While *Restoration Plays and Players* seeks to harmonize literary and theatrical approaches, its structure highlights plays' 'life cycle', from writing to performance to print to revival. The chronology of literary history is served by two complementary chapters that describe parallel trajectories for Restoration plays. First there is a survey of the various kinds of political, cultural and dramaturgic change that characterize the period, starting with an account of one its best-known plays; this forms a sketch of what is described as 'regime change theatre'. Then there is a chapter outlining key theatrical innovations, followed by an account of the life cycle of the Restoration play, which serves as a rehearsal for seven subsequent chapters on key components of the process: writers, companies, actors, playhouses, audiences, booksellers and revivals. Each of the total of nine chapters contains case studies of plays and/or people. Discussion of each play is informed, rather than limited (or such is the intention), by the theme of the chapter in which it appears, one of the premises of the book being that Restoration plays tend to refer to the circumstances of their appearance in the world as much as to surrounding events and ideas. The index indicates where in the book discussions of individual plays are to be found, while a timeline at the end of the book supplements the chronology provided in the opening chapter.

References to plays are to the first editions, as available in Early English Books Online (EEBO) and Eighteenth-Century Collections Online (ECCO). The notes also give act/scene/line references as presented, where possible, in David Womersley's *Restoration Drama. An Anthology* (Oxford: Blackwell, 2000). For texts not in Womersley's anthology, an alternative modern edition is cited. Spelling and punctuation have been modernized for the sake of accessibility, except where the verse demands an abbreviated form; where it occurs in titles of plays (*The Luckey Chance, Venice Preserv'd*), old spelling is retained for the sake of recognition.

Thanks are due to Sarah Stanton at Cambridge University Press for proposing the idea of a new introduction to Restoration plays, to Rosemary Crawley for her diligent support during the production process and to Mike Richardson for the copy-editing. Izabela Hopkins chased picture permissions with extraordinary tenacity. I am grateful to the anonymous readers whose wise counsel has improved the book. My thanks also go for Bloomsbury and to Houghton Mifflin, for permission to reproduce the extract in Chapter 3 from Richard Wilbur's translation of *L'Ecole des Femmes*, and to Methuen and Edward Bond, for allowing me to quote from his *Restoration* in Chapter 9.

Somewhat to my surprise, it has been possible to complete this work on schedule in the face of growing administrative duties, and I owe a debt to colleagues at Birmingham City University for allowing me the time I have needed. Maddy Shaw Roberts read an early draft and hunted down citations. Fiona Shaw Roberts has, as ever, been the most patient, kind and loving interlocutor during every problem or breakthrough. Because this book reflects decades of teaching seventeenth-century drama, this preface is a good place to acknowledge the generations of students at Bristol, Oxford, Kyoto, Osaka, Worcester, Warwick and Birmingham who have helped me hone my thoughts.

1 | Regime change theatre

A little before one o'clock in the afternoon two men play cards over that relatively novel luxury, hot chocolate. A servant hovers. The game finishes, they get up, and the loser ventures a comment:

You are a fortunate man, Mr Fainall.

Until the name, it could be a routine quip (*lucky!*). But it's hard to feign all and be thought entirely honest, even at cards. Perhaps used to such banter, Fainall only expresses surprise that the game is done, with a dose of frustration that his companion has been playing 'negligently'. A walkover, it seems, is unsatisfying; he wants to play hard.

By normal standards this Fainall, though competitive, looks the more engaging of the two; the other man is evidently 'reserved', 'out of humour', needing to be coaxed into companionship. What's troubling him, it turns out, is an affair of the heart: a quarrel with the heiress he's in love with, Millamant (her name says she has a thousand other options), and her meddlesome aunt, Lady Wishfort (hers needs no explanation). The discovery underlines the emerging difference between the two card players: one skims across the surface of conversation, the other broods on what lies beneath. Audiences may be surprised to find, nearly a hundred lines in, that the moody man's own name shimmers with success. He may lose to a fortunate Mr Fainall, but 'Mirabell' assures him of his ultimate reward.

Fast-forward three hours, and he gets it. An endgame is in motion, with a different deck and the ultimate trump card. A servant brings in a black box. Out of it emerges a legal deed to prove that Fainall's estranged wife has left all her money in trust to her former lover, none other than Mirabell. Defeated by law, Fainall resorts to cruder weaponry. He draws a sword on Mrs Fainall, but is disarmed before leaving with a remark as ambiguous as the one that had introduced him over cards and chocolate. Is it to be an action at court or swords at dawn when he growls 'Mirabell, you shall hear of this, sir'? We never find out.

Like many fictions before and since, from Terence's *Brothers* (160 BC) to Willy Russell's *Blood Brothers* (1983), William Congreve's *The Way of the World* (1700) employs rival heroes to explore rival values. Usually the rivalries are hard to mistake: nurture against nature, class against class. What makes *The Way of the World* distinctive are the obstacles Congreve puts in the way of telling just how different the rival heroes and their values really are. For all their contrasting cheerfulness at cards, Mirabell and Fainall are of a type. Their pasts are not so much intertwined as intertwinned. They have shared the same woman; they exhibit the same sharp tongue and the same contempt for the same people. In conniving they are all but equal. When they unfold their common network of social relations they understand each other better than anyone else could hope to understand *them*. Mirabell describes Lady Wishfort to Fainall as 'your Wife's Mother, my evil Genius', while country cousin Sir Wilful Witwoud is introduced by Fainall as though to establish the man's claim to some unnamed bequest: '[H]e is half Brother to this Witwoud by a former Wife, who was sister to my Lady Wishfort, my Wife's Mother.'

Still, inch by inch, confidence grows that these men's names – star versus cheat – really mean what they say. Listen to how they talk about themselves. Increasingly, Fainall brings chilly, forensic certainty to his cuckold's situation, as if preparing a legal brief:

I am married already; so that's over. My wife has played the jade with me – well, that's over too. I never loved her, or if I had, why that would have been over too by this time. Jealous of her I cannot be, for I am certain; so there's an end of jealousy. Weary of her, I am, and shall be. No, there's no end of that; no, that were too much to hope. Thus far concerning my repose; now for my reputation. As to my own, I married not for it; so that's out of the question. And as to my part in my wife's – why she had parted with hers before; so bringing none to me, she can take none from me...[1]

Using reason to cheer himself up, he merely demonstrates how darkly unhappy he really is. Mirabell, by contrast, speaks a language of what has been described as 'enlightened ruthlessness', allowing room for self-interest in the pursuit of greater good.[2] Justifying his cynicism in marrying off a former lover to a man neither he nor she could trust, he sounds as much novelist as lawyer, arranging the pieces in a narrative to give each person their just deserts:

Why do we daily commit disagreeable and dangerous actions? To save that idol, reputation. If the familiarities of our loves had produced that consequence, of which you were apprehensive, where could you have fixed a father's name with credit, but on a husband? I knew Fainall to be a Man lavish of his Morals, an interested and professing friend, a false and designing Lover; yet one whose wit and outward fair behaviour have gained a reputation with the town, enough to make that woman stand excused, who has suffered herself to be won by his addresses. A better man ought not to have been sacrificed to the occasion; a worse had not answered to the purpose. When you are weary of him, you know your remedy.[3]

It is hardly edifying. Content to dump his unhappy ex onto a 'false and designing Lover', Mirabell thinks nothing of the prospect of his own (imagined) child growing up with 'a Man lavish of his Morals' for a father. But it is what he offers for her future that really distinguishes him: a remedy for marital misery and security against the financial threat of her husband's recklessness, in prose that envelops past and future options as though there were no others. Out of the terminal black box pops more than a piece of paper. It's the fine difference between the rival heroes: Fainall talks like a lawyer; Mirabell acts like one.

In some ways *The Way of the World* confirms popular stereotypes of Restoration Drama: clever young man, GSOH, colourful past, foppish acquaintances, seeks beautiful heiress for sizzling conversation and life-time freedom from debt. But the games Congreve plays with audiences and readers are as complex as the games the heroes play with each other. This is a 'late' work for its author, its genre and for the period usually thought of as the 'Restoration': a work that stands at the horizons of individual and collective achievement. A minority contribution to a co-authored farce aside, Congreve did not write another comedy.[4] The technical refinement of this one could not be matched nor its transformations of comic conventions repeated. Its enigmatic plotting asks serious questions. Does Mirabell really step out, bright and distinct as his name, from Fainall's shadow? Was Congreve entirely in command of the games he played with his audience? He was himself both lawyer and, by virtue of his 1692 *Incognita*, novelist. It might be speculated that the rival heroes of *The Way of the World* play out a struggle for writerly self-definition. Peter Brooks deploys Freudian terms to express the bipolar nature of life writing:

How we narrate a life...is at least a double process, the attempt to incorporate within an orderly narrative the more devious, persistent and powerful plot whose logic is dictated by desire.[5]

Karl Miller's 1987 study of Victorian fiction, *Doubles*, examines narratives in which heroes try fruitlessly to escape from others they can't
help resembling.[6] No matter how hard we try to distinguish Mirabell
from Fainall, their outlines blur. If Mirabell succeeds, it is largely
because he is a 'more devious, persistent and powerful' plotter than
the rival whose sordid values he endeavours to suppress.

Congreve's 'double process' gives voice to more than a hypothesized
inner struggle. It refracts its historical moment. The carefree young
men of Restoration Comedy are often likened to that brilliant conver-
sationalist and bed hopper King Charles II. But Charles had died
in 1685, fifteen years before *The Way of the World*. Succeeding him,
his Catholic brother, James, lasted only three years before being ousted
by parliamentary action in favour of his son-in-law, the Protestant
Prince William of Orange, who duly became King William III. The
shadow cast by Fainall is that of a dynasty, the Stuarts, recently
departed and little mourned. Mirabell's way with the world seems
to embody a new outlook on human nature: naturally resistant to
tyranny, guided by law and, in its pragmatic regard for the greater
good, fundamentally sociable.

Two philosophers gave formal definition to this outlook. In 1690 John
Locke defined freedom as 'not to be subject to the inconstant, uncertain,
unknown, arbitrary will of another man'. '[I]f we consider the nature of
mankind,' wrote James Tyrrell two years later,

in the whole course of their lives, it ought to be considered as one entire
system of bodies, consisting of several particular parts; so that nothing can be
done in relation to any man's life, family, or fortune, which does not in some
way or other, either benefit or prejudice those things which are most dear
to others also...[7]

It is a benign sentiment sitting at the top of a slippery slope. Conspicuously virtuous conduct might accidentally 'prejudice' someone else,
so surely it is important to perform actions that are not somehow
good in themselves but likely to have the least bad effects. There is the
catch. Might it not be better to act badly if better consequences follow
than from always acting well? In 1714 Bernard Mandeville's *Fable
of the Bees* argued that arrant selfishness might be the best route to
public good:

It is not only the desire of company, good nature, pity, affability and other
graces of a fair outside which make a man sociable... [H]is vilest and most

hateful qualities are the most necessary accomplishments to fit him for the largest and...the happiest and most flourishing societies.[8]

Mandeville might have been describing Congreve's Mirabell.

Political, ethical and stylistic complexity may explain why *The Way of the World* was not a runaway success in the theatre. Five performances are recorded for March 1700. Congreve claimed he never thought of the play as a crowd-pleaser. Like the plays of the Roman Terence ('the most correct writer in the world'), this was intended to advance 'Beauties which the greater part of [the] Audience were incapable of tasting'.[9] But, if Congreve looked to the past for justification, the complex form of *The Way of the World* ushered in the future. Congreve had written that his novel *Incognita* was designed to capture in a prose tale the 'design, contexture and result' of a drama; in his last comedy, he explored a theatrical language that seems more at home in the novel.[10] Peter Conrad argues that *The Way of the World* rewards behaviour 'which is of necessity untheatrical'; the good nature that Congreve asks audiences to accept fails to show itself in the form he is using. It would take a novel, Conrad proposes, to show how the more devious, persistent and powerful Mirabell might be vouched for 'from within'.[11]

How much good nature is manifest in the most memorable passage of the play is seriously open to question. Mirabell and Millamant agree terms for their marriage in the so-called 'proviso scene'. She demands a life free from early mornings, pet names and overfamiliarity, and insists on control of her social circle. As long as he knocks at her door before coming in, she will be content. Those conditions agreed, she admits that she may, perhaps with teeth clenched in prescience, by degrees dwindle into a wife. But, where she sets out to protect her narrowing sphere, he envisages himself already in the room, shaping her conduct and person. She is to have no best friend, no make-up, no gossip and no alcohol. On no account must she over-coddle the child of their marriage, who will, of course, be a son. It is a change of regime contemplated in the most polite terms, but no less assertively for that; not for nothing is Congreve sometimes thought of as the least feminist of the major Restoration dramatists. In marriage as in law, Mirabell is simply more devious, persistent and powerful.

Standing at multiple thresholds, *The Way of the World* is therefore a many-sided response to regime changes that were personal and political, stylistic and generic; it begins this book because it crystallizes like no other work the preoccupations of Restoration Drama. Defining the previously undefined genre of regime change *fiction*, the novelist Patrick McGuinness writes of its tendency to record the cusp of history from the slipstream rather than on the wave of events:

[Y]ou can have the weight of history crushing the characters, but you can also have the characters' daily travails trumping the world-changing events around them.[12]

From Stendhal to the contemporary Egyptian novelist Naguib Mahfouz, regime change fiction sees events through the Rosencrantzes and Guildensterns of the world rather than its Hamlets and Claudiuses. Drama has traditionally favoured the heroic figures who help create and then ride the waves of history. Restoration Drama has its share of those, but its most nuanced responses are often found in 'daily travails' or, more often, daily leisure: in a man rising from cards, for example, and wondering when the secrets of a black box might finally allow him to prevail over his uncanny double, the *un*fortunate Mr Fainall.

The year of *The Way of the World*, 1700, is often taken to mark the end of the period called 'the Restoration'. In fact, this year is only one of any number of possible endings, depending on one's discipline and choice of death. Literary histories often cite 1700 because that is when the period's most prolific writer, John Dryden, died; theatre scholars may prefer 1710, when the most prominent Restoration actor and his friend, Thomas Betterton, followed him. Political historians usually opt either for 1688, the year James II's escape to France made way for William III, or 1714, when James's daughter (and William's sister-in-law), Queen Anne, succumbed to the toll taken by seventeen pregnancies.

When the period began is less controversial. There is little argument, either, over which monarch best embodies its excitements and failures. On 25 May 1660 he stepped from a barge at Dover to reclaim an inheritance lost eleven years before with his father's head. Four days later John Evelyn was in the huge crowd that saw him process through London. Evelyn was a man of unwavering royalist principles at a time when many found it prudent to waver. In the restoration of the thirty-year-old Charles II he saw a grand mythical homecoming that inspired this, the last word in street theatre:

[A] triumph of above 20,000 horse and foot, brandishing their swords and shouting with inexpressible joy; the ways strewed with flowers, the bells ringing, the streets hung with tapestry, fountains running with wine; the Mayor, Aldermen, and all the Companies in their liveries, chains of gold, and banners; Lords and Nobles clad in cloth of silver, gold, and velvet; the windows and balconies well set with ladies; trumpets, music, and myriads of people flocking, even so far as from Rochester, so as they were seven hours in passing the City, even from 2 in the afternoon till 9 at night.

I stood in the Strand and beheld it, and blessed God. And all this was done without one drop of blood, and by that very army which rebelled against him; but it was the Lord's doing, for such a Restoration was never mentioned in any history ancient or modern, since the return of the Jews from the Babylonish captivity...[13]

It was not all adulation. Amid the spectacle, even Evelyn felt bound to ask an awkward question. Whose work was this, exactly? That 'very army' that had sent Charles I to the executioner's block? Or 'the Lord's doing'? Miraculous or natural? The same question would be asked between 1660 and 1714 of a host of phenomena, not least the plague that would empty the Strand five years later. Evelyn, confident that the answer was 'both', still needed to remind himself. Seldom has the word 'but' been made to work harder ('but it was the Lord's doing'), quelling the suspicion that the biblical epic might be only a U-turn by armed men. Over the succeeding decades many others would reawaken the suspicion in pamphlets, poems and, especially, plays. Few were able to suppress their doubts as swiftly as Evelyn.

So, while the reach of the term 'Restoration' may vary among academic disciplines, Restoration Drama is steeped in the discipline of political history: specifically, in that of the Stuart dynasty, its principal sponsor, patron, regulator and, obliquely, even in its exile or death throes, subject. No country – and no theatre – survives on ceremony. Triumph it may have been, but Evelyn's day in the Strand was also a bandage on old wounds. As Ronald Hutton puts it,

In the period 1638–42, the tensions between executive and legislature, Church and dissenter, and court and country, had developed to the point of bloodshed. They were to remain a cause of this during every decade until 1690. In this sense, whatever had ended in 1660–2, it was not the English Civil War.[14]

The plays of Restoration London might be described as attempts at defusing, resolving, aggravating and skating over these tensions, sometimes all in the space of three hours.

Foreign wars performed a not dissimilar function. Periods of alliance with Catholic France led to aggression against the Protestant Dutch; when diplomacy with Paris wobbled, The Hague became the partner of choice. Restoration politics up to 1688 was in part a heated argument over who the country's more natural ally was, and Restoration plays and players maintained the temperature with stereotypes that progressively helped define what it meant to be English. Flouncing Francophone fops and boorish Dutch burghers supplied measures of indigenous manliness; frightening images of state repression, whether of Dutch merchants inflicting atrocities overseas or torture chambers reminiscent of the Inquisition, argued equally for the rule of English law.[15] Both the fear and the glamour of royal dictatorship found expression in a succession of stage potentates from the Near East, and there was no more vivid ghost of civil war than the fearless outsider who, acting upon will rather than birthright, encapsulated the alluring danger of the Cromwellian revolutionary.

Erasing the past was a prime directive for the most enduring, protean type of all, whose contours can be traced with only a little more definition in Fainall than in Mirabell. The libertine: a young man of healthy appetites, smart patter and little cash. He drew confidence and danger from many sources: from Irish rogues held to represent either royalists or republicans during the civil war, depending on the allegiance of the reporter; from free-thinking pamphleteers of the 1640s and 1650s (even John Milton was described as a libertine); and from aristocrats such as Sir Charles Sedley, whose exploits included standing naked on the balcony of a tavern while 'acting all the postures of lust and buggery that could be imagined, and abusing of scripture'.[16] Sedley's final gesture that day shows where he thought the ultimate sanction for his behaviour lay: washing his penis in a tumbler, he toasted the king.

When the Earl of Halifax wrote a 'Character' of Charles II, he might have had in mind any number of libertine heroes in his chapters on 'Dissimulation', 'Wit and Conversation' and 'Amours and Mistresses' ('[H]e lived with his Ministers as he did with his Mistresses,' Halifax drily observed; 'he used them, but he was not in love with them').[17] Portraits of the king, such as the one by John Michael Wright presented

Figure 1.1 King Charles II, by John Michael Wright

as Figure 1.1, suggest a charming languor that concealed, as for many a stage libertine, boundless reserves of cunning and deceit.

Dramatic stereotypes necessarily moved with changing times, and it is useful at this point to establish in a little more detail what these changes were. For the sake of convenient introduction, the period from 1660 to 1714 is divided into three phases of regime change. Broadly, the eighteen years until 1678 saw a slow wearing down of the optimism that had greeted Charles II's homecoming. For the next nine years the fear and reality of Catholic succession dominated political debate. Then, from 1688, the country began to establish itself as a newly reformed, Protestant nation, a nascent imperial power and an unequivocal enemy of France. Taken together, these phases of political life constituted a revolution more profound – and certainly more lasting – than the one symbolized by the beheading of Charles I. Indeed, it is often said that 1688 saw the revolution that was attempted but squandered in 1649.

Political revolutions

1660–1678

It was in matters of royal succession and religious faith that anxiety about the nation's past and future found vital sustenance. Charles II and his Portuguese wife, Catherine of Braganza, produced no heir. Second in line was Charles's brother, James, Duke of York, who evoked memories of an older national trauma, reaching back beyond the English Civil War to the 1550s, when English Protestants were burned at the stake in the reign of Mary Tudor. Suspected of Catholic inclinations soon after the Restoration, ten years on James made a public conversion to the old faith at the very time when a treaty was being negotiated with France. It was not just music, drama and cash that set France apart; the country was a standing exhibition of how absolute power could be wielded by a charismatic Catholic monarch.

Charles II ruled in the deep shadow cast by his cousin, Louis XIV, the 'Sun King', craving a French style of monarchy without the means to achieve it. Accordingly, he also ruled in Louis's pocket. Through a highly efficient diplomatic network, the French king ensured that selected parliamentarians and courtiers were, in the parlance of the day, 'pensioners of France'. The arrangement helped smooth the passage to occasional war with the Dutch, and Louis's generosity extended to the English throne. In 1670 Charles II committed one of the most treasonous acts ever devised by an English monarch, emulating even his own father's intention to deploy Irish mercenaries against the forces of Parliament in 1641. Signing the secret Treaty of Dover in May 1670, he accepted a huge subsidy from Louis on the promise of converting to Catholicism himself and then persuading his people to follow suit. In the event of resistance, French troops would come to his aid.

Yet he pulled back. His motives were obscure: was it weakness, fear of conflict or an acknowledgement that his ambition to rule like his cousin was futile? By 1672 Charles was passing anti-Catholic legislation to appease Parliament, so excluding his own heir and brother from public office (James had been head of the navy), though not from the succession. Duly encouraged, James's opponents began to congregate around an alternative candidate. James Scott, Duke of Monmouth, was the offspring of an affair Charles had had in the 1650s with a woman called Lucy Walters. The young duke shared many of his father's qualities, and he had one great advantage over Uncle James. Charming, funny, popular with women and fond of the theatre, Monmouth was a Protestant. Support for him saw the birth of party politics, at least in the matter of names. Monmouth's backers were nicknamed 'Whigs', an insulting abbreviation of a 1640s word for Scots horse rustlers. More threatening was the name given to followers of Uncle James: *toraighe*, Irish brigands it was more convenient to call 'Tories'.

1679–1688

The succession crisis threatened to overwhelm the whole country in 1678, thanks to the claims of a deranged vicar and his singular friend. The Reverend Ezerel Tonge had lost church and living in the Great Fire of 1666, spending a brief period of exile as chaplain to the garrison city of Tangier, which had been part of Catherine of Braganza's dowry. Even as the forces of Islam mustered across the Mediterranean, Tonge began to give shape to his view that the Great Fire and all his worldly woes could be laid at the door of a more dangerous conspiracy whose heart was Rome. Returning to London, Tonge chanced upon someone who, for every sentence of conspiracy theory, promised a dense footnote of fact. He was an oddity, this new acquaintance: built like an overgrown dwarf with, wrote one observer, the voice of a guinea pig.[18] He called himself Father Ambrose, and he claimed to have spent time in the training camps and intellectual seedbeds of international terrorism: at Salamanca and Valladolid, and at the seminary of St Omer, where the armies of Jesuit spies and poisoners were thought to receive instruction in their hellish mission. When Tonge became more familiar with his new friend he learned to call him by the name of Mr Oates: Titus Oates, who led him and half the country to believe that the international Catholic conspiracy had taken a new turn. There was, claimed Oates, a plot to install James, Duke of York, as the king of England, by the convenient means of assassinating Charles II.[19] Across the country, he swore, a secret Catholic militia was arming itself for a takeover. Narrating his case before endless meetings of the

Privy Council, he showed powers of memory and imagination that must have been the envy of many playwrights.

Like them, he was to a significant degree making it all up. When the alleged weapons of mass destruction were produced in court, they consisted of such terrors as 'a fowling piece, a musket, . . .one great sword' and, from a Widow Platt, 'an old gun'.[20] Even so, incriminating evidence did emerge. James's chaplain, Edward Coleman, was convicted of treason on the basis of actual correspondence with the French, and everyone knew of the wish among the Catholic powers of Europe to see England reconvert. Oates, one of the more successful conspiracy theorists in world history, was eventually imprisoned and whipped round the streets of London. But the nightmares this largely phantom 'Popish Plot' had evoked soon resurfaced and began to seem real. In 1685 James did finally succeed his brother Charles, who made a deathbed conversion to Catholicism. Ironically, the same year saw an influx of French Protestants fleeing Louis XIV's revocation of laws that gave them protection. Migrants such as the playwrights Peter Anthony Motteux and Abel Boyer duly made their own distinctive contribution to London's cultural life.

Monmouth attempted a revolt against James's succession but was defeated at Sedgemoor, and his supporters were tried at the Bloody Assizes. But James's victory would leave no legacy longer than the bitter memory of those trials, presided over by Judge Jeffreys. The new king's subsequent programme of Catholic reform, which threatened to de-nature government, the Church and the universities, was opposed so vigorously and successfully that by 1688 he was in flight from a country that had declared allegiance to his own son-in-law, the Dutch Protestant Prince of Orange, who duly became William III. Though officially 'Glorious', or, as Evelyn had put it in 1660, 'without one drop of Blood', this latest revolution was the most violent of any since the English Civil War, not least for the Jacobite loyalists massacred at the Battle of the Boyne in 1690 by King William. Like Mirabell, the new Dutch king was simply the more powerful and persistent of the two adversaries.

1689–1714

William's accession marked a final turning away not simply from state Catholicism but from the idea of absolute monarchy that had, since James II's grandfather James I pitched it to Parliament in 1610, been something of a Stuart family obsession. A new deal had to be brokered. It took the form of a Bill of Rights: the king could not raise taxes without the will of Parliament; voting rights were established for property owners; monarchy was redefined not as absolute or divine, but constitutional and legal. As Stuart values were slowly expunged from the state and inscribed afresh on the faces of the new enemy – the Jacobite rebels who declared allegiance to successive pretenders – Stuart people managed the transition as best they could. William's wife Mary, who had acted at court in the heyday of Charles's reign and found herself in the awkward position of supplanting her own father, died in December 1694. After William's death, just over seven years later, her sister, Anne, assumed the throne. When she died in 1714 there was no question that another of her immediate family would follow her. The age of the Stuarts was over.

The progressive exorcism of their values was one symptom of a broader preoccupation: defining what it meant to be genteel, and what it meant to be English. Manners began to displace blood as the sign of 'good breeding'.[21] New models of national identity were forged from the study of history, politics, theology, literature and drama. France became less a point of reference and more a point of departure for cultural norms and ideals; as global trade developed, it assumed the role of imperial competitor. Here lie the seeds of the most powerful regime change of all: for the death rattle of the Stuart dynasty, the lusty birth cries of the British Empire.

Metropolitan revolutions

In outline, such is the historical basis for a 'Whig' view of history, in which parliamentary democracy asserted itself over royal privilege. Yet Restoration plays and players contended with and inflected other revolutions – ones of style, management and space. London is the setting for scores of Restoration comedies; its spaces, manners, social structures and even history are woven into their subtexts. Characters new to the city tend to be dazzled by it; those in exile verge on depression. Staged encounters in coffee houses, parks and trading places borrow and enhance the cultural symbolism of their originals. But the sign system was not fixed. Marked by the political revolutions it witnessed, the teeming, filthy, industrial capital that was Restoration London was in a process of continual transformation.

A major influx of people after the Restoration took the population to about 300,000, compared with 200,000 in 1650; by 1700 London had overtaken Paris, at 500,000. Gregory King, engraver turned government statistician, wrote a series of reports on the nation's people, from lords temporal and spiritual to 'Gipsies, Thieves, Beggars, etc.'. London's growth meant that King had constantly to revise his social taxonomy; ideas about class were as much subject to change as everything else. He started with twenty-six levels of society, and over the years narrowed them down to two, reserving particular scorn (like many government officials since then) for those who 'decrease the wealth of the kingdom'.[22] The city spread rapidly westwards from its Roman origins around the Tower of London, and the stylish phenomenon called the West End came into being: a series of fashionable streets where money and leisure could be indulged.[23]

Rather than be restrained by it, urban growth seemed to thrive on disaster. The Great Plague of 1665 killed between a fifth and a quarter of the population (perhaps caused by the mass arrival of 'virgin' populations after 1660 who had never been exposed to the disease beforehand); the Great Fire of the following year prompted a mass rebuilding programme, with fresh generations of craftsmen and labourers arriving to find work, and charging handsomely for it. Even the third London disaster of the 1660s, the humiliating appearance of a hostile Dutch fleet up the Thames in 1667, did not restrain growth.

Economic expansion also enlarged the appetite for novelty. Restoration London was an innovative city that imported new kinds of food, clothing and luxury goods. It saw the founding of institutions that embodied more rational approaches to science, such as the Royal Society, and those that formalized increasingly mysterious models of finance, such as the Bank of England. The complex share dealings that helped keep Restoration theatres running show how money itself was becoming a more elusive entity; numerous court cases from the period were devoted to finding out who actually owned what in theatre land, or whose shares had been transferred to whom. An obsession with novelty might be traced to fear of the political past, but it also manifested the logic of newly aggressive consumerism: the more you produce that seems new, the more you fear it merely looks the same as the old.

Political revolutions and theatre

The Way of the World is one example of how the theatre engaged with political change even when it appeared to be concerned with the less portentous business of wills and marriage settlements. In their different ways, all the plays discussed in this book are to a greater or lesser extent steeped in Restoration politics. Yet they are sufficiently diverse in genre and effect to threaten the integrity of the very term 'Restoration Drama'. Robert D. Hume defines five phases of late seventeenth-century dramatic history, each responsive to evolving ideologies and events.[24]

(i) Carolean Drama (1660–9); note the difference from 'Caroline', which refers to drama in the time of Charles I.
(ii) Satirical/Violent Drama (1670–77).
(iii) Popish Plot Drama and its aftermath (1678–87).
(iv) Sentimental Drama (1688–97).
(v) Augustan or Classical Drama (1698–1714).

The definitions are no less valid for being elastic, not least when we consider how revivals took on a different colour according to the decade in which they surfaced. So how do the major plays of the period discussed in this book fit into Hume's five-part division of Restoration Drama?

(i) The Carolean Drama of the 1660s promoted the levity and high ideals of the Restoration itself. Its defining form is heroic tragedy, influenced (though not exclusively) by the French classical drama Charles II had seen in exile during the 1650s, and not necessarily tragic in a sense recognizable from William Shakespeare. Heroic plays tended towards compression of time, place and action even as they strained after rhetorical excess in pursuit of generic conflicts of love and honour besetting high-minded men who strive to do the right thing in impossible circumstances. The work of Pierre Corneille (1606–84) was an obvious model, preferable in tone and valour to the more inward ruminations of Jean Racine (1639–99), whose plays achieved greater prominence in the disenchanted 1670s. Corneille's *Pompée* was translated by two different writers in the 1660s; his shadow fell over the early work of dramatists such as John Dryden and Roger Boyle even as they distanced themselves from it. *The Indian Queen* (discussed below at pp. 56–61) by **Dryden and Sir Robert Howard** is a fine example of the heroic play that, for all its verbal inflation, hits the rawest nerve of Restoration England in its depiction of a brilliant general, Montezuma, with pretensions to royalty. Revived with a superb musical score in the 1690s, its politics became even more pointed; like the English court, it showed an outsider marrying a royal princess.

Carolean Drama is not just the story of high-minded heroes imitating their French cousins. Shakespeare struggled for supremacy with Ben Jonson and John Fletcher in a series of revivals. Tragicomedy became a nimble way of reconciling London to the mixed fortunes of its ruling family. Popular comedies such as **Sir Samuel Tuke's** *The Adventures of Five Hours* (1663) **and Dryden's** *Sir Martin Mar-All* (1667), both discussed below at pp. 47–9, exploited and helped create the mood of joyous innocence Evelyn had enjoyed in the Strand.

(ii) Dryden had drawn on another French writer whose work would be endlessly plundered and critiqued during the 1670s. Jean-Baptiste Poquelin (1622–73), better known as Molière, combined physical farce and intellectual satire in proportions that appealed to a public newly conscious of the hypocrisies of regime change politics. **William Wycherley's 1675** *The Country Wife* (discussed below at pp. 69–74) is in part an adaptation of Molière's *L'Ecole des Femmes* (*The School for Wives*), whose hero mistakenly believes he can groom a young girl to be his wife. With **Sir George Etherege's 1676** *The Man of Mode* (see pp. 52–6), Wycherley's play stands as one of the finest examples of 'libertine' or 'rakish' comedy – in other words, drama that appears to celebrate the antics of verbally and amorously dexterous young men, such as his hero, the aptly named Horner. The trend demanded a response, and got it. In the comedies of Aphra Behn, whose first play was performed in December 1670, a bright light shines on the miseries of male dominion, even though the libertine heroes of works such as *The Rover* (1677, discussed below at pp. 134–7) turn out to be curiously desirable.

Attempts to consolidate the tradition of heroic drama encountered the ugly realities of contemporary politics, or exploited their potential for horror. **Thomas Otway's** hugely successful **1676** *Don Carlos* (discussed below at pp. 77–9) was timed as a compliment to the Duke of York at precisely the moment when news broke of the heir to the throne's total abandonment of the Anglican communion. Its portrayal of bloody suicides and scheming Catholic courts can hardly have calmed anxieties about what would happen when Charles II died. **Dryden's 1670–1** *The Conquest of Granada* (discussed below at pp. 19–23) is a sprawling two-part epic that straddles the crossroads between the highfalutin optimism of *The Indian Queen* and a sense of imminent national conflict. The pretensions of the heroic tradition it encapsulates were vividly satirized by the **Duke of Buckingham's 1671** *The Rehearsal* (see below, pp. 156–8).

(iii) The Popish Plot and Succession Drama of the years 1678 to 1687 frequently saw the theatres in conflict with authority. Questions of succession had loomed over the stage years before Titus Oates began weaving his tales to the King's Council, but they reached a particular pitch from 1678 onwards, during a period when the theatres were often closed as a result either of violent disturbances or seditious content. **Nathaniel Lee's 1680** *Lucius Junius Brutus* (see below, pp. 23–6) appeared to champion republicanism and was banned. **Dryden's** *The Spanish Fryar* of the same year (see pp. 75–6 and 209–11) made mockery of the Catholic Church and proved too strong for its royal audience, even on revival for a royal audience after the Glorious Revolution. **Dryden's 1678** *All for Love* and **Lee's 1677** *The Rival Queens* (see pp. 105–10 and 138–40 respectively) both reflected askance on Charles II himself, with dying heroes pulled this way and that by the rival claims of wives and mistresses. In the most infamous Shakespeare adaptation of the period, Nahum Tate underlined Shakespeare's bastard Edmund as the root of all evil in *King Lear* at the very time when the Whigs were noisily promoting the claims of the Duke of Monmouth (see below, pp. 49–52). **Thomas Otway's** *Venice Preserv'd*, almost the only Restoration tragedy to be performed regularly in modern times, provided in 1682 the most complex and ambiguous response to the Popish Plot of any play in the period (see below, pp. 128–34). **Aphra Behn's late comedy of 1686,** *The Luckey Chance* (see below, pp. 79–83), addresses the now enthroned Catholic James II in terms that seek to re-establish his appeal through a return to familiar comic conventions.

(iv) The Sentimental Drama that emerged between 1688 and 1697 exhibited, among other things, the benefits of having a soft heart rather than (but quite often as well as) a hard penis. In a world of post-Stuart masculinity, comic heroes are sympathetically mindful of the way right feeling led to right social living; heroines are increasingly preoccupied with analysing the shortcomings of their own situation in life and insisting on greater respect. **Thomas Southerne's 1691** *The Wives' Excuse* and **Sir John Vanbrugh's 1697** *The Provok'd Wife* (pp. 172–6 and 158–61 respectively) both involve women who have every reason to get even with their boorish, play-away husbands but decline the opportunity; **Colley Cibber's 1696** *Love's Last Shift* and **George Farquhar's** *The Constant Couple* (below, pp. 176–9 and 179–80 respectively) feature the reformation of old-style libertines into new-style men of feeling, a journey already forged by **Congreve's** *Love for Love* (see below, pp. 102–4) and reinflected, as we have seen, in *The Way of the World* (see above, pp. 1–5). The impetus for such reformation lay not just in politics or philosophy but in the righteous indignation of the **Reverend Jeremy Collier** (see below, pp. 180–4), who saw in Restoration Theatre a sewer of iniquity. No such charge could be levelled against another significant trend of the 1690s, when increasing sophistication in stage technology and the growth of concerts around the capital led to large-scale musical works such as the adaptation of *The Indian Queen* and *The Fairy Queen* (see below, 152–5), a baroque extravaganza based on Shakespeare's *A Midsummer Night's Dream*.

(v) Augustan Drama, a period loosely defined as beginning in the late 1690s and continuing at least to Queen Anne's death in 1714, develops a renewed interest in mythical and historical heroes. Nicholas Rowe's retelling of the glorious deeds of Tamburlaine the Great (*Tamerlane*, 1702) compared him explicitly to William III, turning Marlowe's savage outsider into an ideal immigrant who has picked up local manners more perfectly than the locals. Ideals of classical clarity and compression resurfaced in a new wave of translations of French Drama. By far the most distinctive plays of this period, however, were written with a dogged sense of allegiance to personal experience by another migrant, George Farquhar, who had left Dublin for London. His two masterpieces, *The Recruiting Officer* **and** *The Beaux' Stratagem* (see below, pp. 222–8 and 110–14 respectively), break the mould of Restoration Comedy, often thought to be the preserve of urban sophisticates. Set in Shrewsbury and Lichfield, the plays convey with extraordinary poignancy the textures of both provincial and migrant life.

Theatre and regime change politics: two case studies

The Way of the World shows how Restoration playwrights engaged with current affairs through the minutiae of daily life and manners. The two case studies that close this chapter illustrate what happened when they sailed closer to the wind, seeking parallels of history and dramatic form for the turbulent political world around them, and with very different degrees of disjunction.

The apex of heroic drama? Dryden and *The Conquest of Granada* (1670–1)

The Conquest of Granada looms over the 1670s as both a memorial and a portent; like *The Way of the World*, it stands at a threshold. Its two five-act parts make it one of the longest entertainments devised for the Restoration Stage, and with scale comes ideologically inclusiveness. With foundations in the high-minded Carolean style of the 1660s, it looks back to less politically anxious times. Yet its fulsome dedication to James, Duke of York ('Heroic poesy has always been sacred to princes, and to heroes,' begins Dryden's introductory epistle), propelled readers and audiences forward to the succession crisis of the early 1680s, for James's religious affiliation was already widely known. Like many other heroic plays of the period, it is about the conflict of love and honour under the cloud of war; Dryden took the opportunity to return to the territory he had explored in *The Indian Queen* and reinflect it for changing times. Almanzor fights for the Moors against the besieging forces of Castile and Aragon. He falls for Almahide, fiancée to the Moorish king Boabdelin, who is angered but knows he needs his warrior-hero if Granada is to stand firm. When Boabdelin dies, the lovers are united, and Almanzor is revealed to be the child of a Spanish duke: birthright joins efficacy in a perfect political resolution. Two subplots of crossed lovers divided by the Moorish factions fill the remainder of this sprawling epic.

The play shows how the most unlikely act of succession may be necessary for the ship of state to survive. Almanzor, a dubious outsider in the mould of Montezuma from *The Indian Queen*, is a romanticized Bolingbroke: a threat to natural succession who is also, by virtue first of natural gifts, the only possible successor. Unlike the wobbly heroes of Dryden's contemporary, Thomas Otway, he is strengthened by love rather than undermined by it. This makes him an ambiguous stage presence, as though Coriolanus had been smitten by Cleopatra and decided to fight harder as a result; and, like Coriolanus's, Almanzor's heroism seems decidedly double-edged. Through Dryden's measured couplets, the classic medium of heroic drama, it is Coriolanian defiance we hear in the last act of Part One, when Boabdelin gives in to jealousy and Almanzor accepts banishment on his own terms:

> Where'er I go, there can no exile be;
> But from Almanzor's sight I banish thee:
> I will not now, if thou wouldst beg me, stay;
> But I will take my Almahide away.
> Stay thou with all they subjects here, but know,
> We leave thy city empty when we go.[25]

Introducing the essay 'Of Heroic Plays' that prefaces the first edition, Dryden argued that 'heroic verse' (the couplet form) was then 'so much in possession of the stage' that it had become uncontroversial, and that those who complained of its unnaturalness should remember that 'serious plays ought not to imitate conversation too nearly'.[26] It is easy to misinterpret this as a signal that Dryden was indifferent to the way couplets can, in the right hands, exploit and enhance the expressive potential of speech. The pattern of masculine rhymes in the passage just quoted gives the actor the opportunity to stress the rhyming word as a weapon ('I banish *thee*') or subdue it to achieve a kind of melodic serenity ('But I will take my Almahide away'). The end-stopping of lines creates space for the actor/character to impose himself through gradations of thought and threat: Dryden's initial 'But' – slightly overused throughout the two plays, and symptomatic of the writer's instinct for symmetrical qualification – holds the floor and keeps the argumentative and emotional structure of the speech intact.

On one spectator, at least, the effect was to take her out of the present moment entirely. To John Evelyn's wife it was a blend of 'love...so pure, and valour so nice, that one would image it designed for an Utopia rather than our stage'. She marvelled that a writer 'born in the decline of morality should be able to feign such exact virtue'.[27] We might imagine this 'exact virtue' to derive from French neoclassicism, but Nancy Klein Maguire argues that it is to the Caroline masque that we should turn for the origins of Dryden's theatrical glorification of a Stuart monarch-in-waiting; only, however, for its origins: what *The Conquest of Granada* gives us, she contends, is a 'demysticized and *de facto* presentation of monarchy' in which 'masque characters have a developed inner life'.[28] In this sense, the play lies at the opposite end of sophistication – and lavishness – from Dryden's final masque-like celebration of the Stuarts, *Albion and Albanius*, which in 1685 became both a memorial for Charles II's death and a fanfare for his brother James's accession. So, is the self-professedly heroic *Conquest of Granada* a celebration of heroism or an interrogation of it? Does it refine contemporary politics out of existence in its reference back to the ideals of 1660s heroic drama, or meet them head-on?

Consider the dialogue between Almanzor and Almahide at the end of Act Four of Part One, in which he unfolds his love for her.

ALMANZOR: If not a subject then, a ghost I'll be;
  And from a ghost, you know, no place is free.
  Asleep, awake, I'll haunt you everywhere;
  From my white shroud groan love into your ear:
  When in your lover's arms you sleep at night,
  I'll glide in cold betwixt, and seize my right:
  And is't not better, in your nuptial bed,
  To have a living lover than a dead?
ALMAHIDE: I can no longer bear to be accused,
  As if what I could grant you, I refused.
  My father's choice I never will dispute
  And he has chosen ere you moved your suit.
  You know my case; if equal you can be,
  Plead for yourself, and answer it for me.
ALMANZOR: Then madam, in that hope you bid me live;
  I ask no more than you may justly give:
  But in strict justice there may favour be,
  And may I hope that you have that for me?
ALMAHIDE: Why do you thus my secret thoughts pursue,
  Which, known, hurt me, and cannot profit you?
  Your knowledge but new troubles does prepare,
  Like theirs who curious in their fortunes are.
  To say, I could with more content be yours,
  Tempts you to hope; but not that hope assures.
  For since the King has right,
  And favoured by my father in his suit,
  It is a blossom which can bear no fruit.
  Yet, if you dare attempt so hard a task,
  May you succeed; you have my leave to ask.

ALMANZOR: I can with courage now my hopes pursue,
  Since I no longer have to combat you.
  That did the greatest difficulty bring;
  The rest are small, a father and a king.
ALMAHIDE: Great souls discern not when the leap's too wide,
  Because they only view the farther side.
  Whatever you desire, you think is near;
  But with more reason the event I fear.
ALMANZOR: No, there is a necessity in fate,
  Why still the brave bold man is fortunate:
  He keeps his object ever full in sight,
  And that assurance holds him firm and right.
  True, 'tis a narrow path that leads to bliss,
  But right before there is no precipice:
  Fear makes men look aside, and then their footing miss.[29]

The heroic register is achieved through a language of abstraction (justice, favour, hope, courage) moderated by familiar metaphors (the leap, a narrow path, no precipice). Almahide's 'Great souls' is both didactic and a challenge: a truth imparted to an admiring audience and a critique of Almanzor that consciously echoes Macbeth's 'vaulting ambition'. We might hear it as a yearning for religious authority that pumps up the merely natural. The whole exchange verges on the musical. Each performer is given space to articulate emotion almost independently of the other. Dryden's confidence with the dramatic verse form is such that he can afford himself a joke with the last line, whose poetic 'foot' goes wrong just like the real one of the fearful man Almanzor describes. Presumably his actors – in this case Charles Hart – were alert to the subtle changes in rhythm and used them to signal changes of mood. The dialogue pays Almanzor the tribute that Dryden's dedication paid to James; this scene concludes with the hero declaring himself 'Born...still to command, not to sue', but presenting an image of power that by the late 1670s would, if associated with the Catholic James, seem terrifying:

The best and bravest souls I can select,
And on their conquered necks my throne erect.[30]

Almahide seems less a distraction from politics than the political issue itself: the goal that, like the crown, the hero must attain. In situational terms the scene might be from almost Restoration Comedy: lusty young man tries to talk his way into the bed of vital young

women betrothed to aged patriarch. One difference is the quality Mary
Evelyn identified: Almanzor asks 'no more than [Almahide] can justly
give'. But his self-confessed 'haunting' is the cultural nightmare represented by James, a problem that had recently emerged from the mists
of rumour into hard, unmistakable definition. Prescribing the terms
of his hero's courage in outfacing doubts, Dryden does not diminish
the frightful impact of his very presence. If this is, as Nancy Klein
Maguire suggests, a celebration of 'political expediency', it is thoroughly double-edged: stylistically and morally rarefied to a degree that
betrays a profound cultural anxiety about the historical moment.[31]

What happens when political anxiety loses its rarefied register is
illustrated by the next play.

The Nadir of heroic drama? Nathaniel Lee's *Lucius Junius Brutus* (1680)

Shakespeare's Cassius warms Brutus to Caesar's assassination with
a reminder of his illustrious namesake:

> O, you and I have heard our fathers say,
> There was a Brutus once that would have brook'd
> The eternal devil to keep his state in Rome
> As easily as a king.[32]

Reference to this former Brutus is couched in the form of an anti-
Catholic joke; as far as many of Shakespeare's countrymen were concerned (or Nathaniel Lee's, for that matter), the eternal devil did keep
his state in Rome under the *baldacchino* of St Peter's Basilica. Lucius
Junius Brutus was the legendary founder of the Roman Republic. He
expelled the Etruscan king Tarquin (father of Lucrece's rapist) and
condemned to death his own sons for joining an insurrection to restore
the Tarquinian dynasty: as a subject, he was Abraham and Cromwell
rolled into one. It is hard to think of a more contentious subject for the
Restoration Stage, especially in December 1680, when the play opened
right at the heart of the succession crisis; and hard to think of any who
more aptly condensed popular feeling against state (or, indeed, any)
Catholicism. The devil might keep his state in London once Charles II
was dead.

Yet Whig poets and pamphleteers had already lighted on Lucius
as a hero for the times, and usually without penalty, which may have

led Lee and the Duke's Company to express surprise when they received, after the third performance, this order from the Lord Chamberlain:

Whereas I am informed that there is acted by you a play called Lucius Junius Brutus...wherein are very scandalous expressions & reflection upon the Government, these [papers] are to require you not to act the said play again.[33]

Stage censorship was sporadic and often dictated by events; it was hard to predict when the axe might fall, and *Lucius* was probably the first play to be banned during the Popish Plot crisis.[34] A month later the King's Company was prevented from performing Nahum Tate's version of *Richard II*. Charles Gildon, who knew the Duke's Company manager, Thomas Betterton, later said that *Lucius* was banned because it was thought 'anti-monarchical'.[35]

Modern critics distance Lee from any intention simply to stage a political agenda. Brutus himself is a noble archetype of the republican hero, a part for the company's leading tragic actor, Betterton; but no Tory satirist could have framed a more reductive satire of low Whiggish conniving than his collaborator Vinditius, who was played by the company's simian clown, James Nokes. The trouble is, Vinditius's outbursts are prone to prompt a guilty laughter that must have seemed seditious. Here he is, leading a group of 'Plebeians' into the forum:

Sirs, I am a true Commonwealths-man, and do not naturally love kings, though they be good; for why should any one man have more power than the people? Is he bigger, or wiser than the people? Has he more guts, or more brains than the people? What can he do for the people, that the people can't do for themselves? Can he make corn grow in a famine? Can he give us rain in drought? Or make our pots boil, though the Devil piss in the fire?[36]

Writing like this suggests a dramatist deliberately sailing close to the wind, perhaps trusting to the erratic attentions of the censor. When he came to pen his dedication of the play to the Earl of Dorset, Lee reflected on the task facing the adapter of the Brutus story with what looks like extreme disingenuousness:

The poet must elevate his fancy with the mightiest imagination, he must run back so many hundred years, take a just prospect of the spirit of those times without the least thought of ours...[37]

Yet perhaps that is what Lee, and the Duke's Company, thought he was really doing. He added a romantic subplot that makes republican idealism seem a terrifying prospect for anyone with normal human feelings; in this respect there are moments when, for all his inflated rhetoric, he thinks like Henrik Ibsen. Brutus himself wrestles to subdue his tender instincts at a time when 'honour, / When Rome, the world and the Gods come to claim us'.[38] Overall, there is some foundation for David Womersley's claim that the play is very far from a piece of Whig propaganda and more a 'dispassionate inspection of a Whig moment in history'.[39]

But there is passion aplenty in the extraordinary scene in which the sons of Brutus reveal a scene of ritual sacrifice to celebrate the return of the Tarquins and the prospect of the 'Traitor Senate' and the 'foul Hydra multitude...frying with their fat'. Here, violent pagan imagery draws on the popular association of Catholics with cannibals who literally eat their lord's flesh and drink his blood, and wish to do the same to good Protestants.

The Scene draws, showing the Sacrifice: one burning, and another crucified: the priests coming forward with goblets in their hands, filled with human blood.

1ST PRIEST: Kneel all you heroes of this black design,
  Each take his goblet fill'd with blood and wine;
  Swear by the Thunderer, swear by Jove,
  Swear by the hundred Gods above...
2ND PRIEST: To keep it close till *Tarquin* comes,
  With trumpets sound and beat of drums:
  But then to thunder forth the deed,
  That Rome may blush, and traitors bleed.
  Swear all.
ALL: We swear.
1ST PRIEST: Now drink the blood,
  To make the conjuration good.

Tiberius, rebellious son of Brutus, feels the 'exalted blood' warm his heart and give 'new fierceness to the King's revenge'. Characteristically, Lee deploys sensational imagery while seeking to balance it with low comedy that, far from being satirical of Whiggish anti-Catholic frenzy, threatens to whip it up further. 'Oh the Gods!' cries the clownishly hysterical Vinditius. 'What, burn a man alive! Oh cannibals, hell-hounds! Eat one man, and drink another!'[40] Overall, the scene borrows something from the masque conventions that also inform the witch scenes from *Macbeth*: stark oppositions, incantatory language and, in this case, the use of violently suggestive scenography to generate political fear and loathing.

It was at those very moments when Lee tried hardest to 'take a prospect of the spirit' of past times that he took the biggest risks; such is the paradox of writing self-consciously about the past. Addressing the Senate in Act V, Brutus offers a political vision that, in its lofty classical oratory, strikes directly against the excesses of the Stuart court and even manages to sound like a manifesto for the Glorious Revolution to come:

> Thus shall we stop the mouth of loud sedition,
> Thus show the difference betwixt the sway
> Of partial tyrants, and of a free-born people,
> Where no man shall offend because he's great,
> Where none need doubt his wife's or daughter's honour,
> Where all enjoy their own without suspicion,
> Where there's no innovation of religion,
> No change of laws, no breach of privilege...[41]

'Scandalous expressions' indeed. But the greater scandal for anyone looking to idealize Brutus is the massacre that surrounds him: his 'Thus' at the start of the speech refers to 'the bodies of the Roman youth / All headless by [his] doom'.[42] Change your regime, the play seems to say, but don't expect the process to be glorious or bloodless.

Endnotes

1 William Congreve, *The Way of the World* (London, 1700), 50 (III.i.782–96).

2 Robert D. Markley, *Two-Edg'd Weapons: Style and Ideology in the Comedies of Etherege, Wycherley and Congreve* (Oxford: Clarendon Press, 1988), 237.

3 Congreve, *The Way of the World*, 24 (II.i.310–26).

4 *Squire Trelooby*, a version of Molière's *Monsieur de Pouceaugnac* co-authored in 1704.

5 Peter Brooks, *Reading for the Plot* (Oxford: Clarendon Press, 1984), 19.

6 Karl Miller, *Doubles* (Oxford University Press, 1987).

7 John Locke, *Two Treatises of Government* (London, 1690); James Tyrrell, *A Brief Disquisition of the Law of Nature* (London, 1692), 50.

8 Bernard Mandeville, 'Preface', *The Fable of the Bees* (London, 1714), np [i.e. no page number given in the edition].

9 John Downes, *Roscius Anglicanus*, ed. Judith Milhous and Robert D. Hume (London: Society for Theatre Research, 1987), 95; William Congreve, 'To the Right Honourable Ralph, Earl of Montague, &c.', *The Way of the World*, np.

10 Congreve, 'Preface to the Reader', *Incognita* (London, 1692), np.

11 Peter Conrad, *The Everyman History of English Literature* (London: Dent, 1985), 309.

12 Patrick McGuinness, 'Regime change fiction – a genre without a name (yet)', *The Guardian*, 5 September 2011.

13 *The Diary of John Evelyn*, ed. E. S. de Beer, 6 vols. (Oxford: Clarendon Press. 1955), 29 May 1660.

14 Ronald Hutton, *The Restoration: A Political and Religious History of England and Wales 1658–1667* (Oxford University Press, 1985), 290.

15 Compare two plays performed within days of each other in the summer of 1673: Dryden's *Amboyna, or, the Cruelties of the Dutch to the English Merchants*, and Settle's *The Empress of Morocco*.

16 *The Diary of Samuel Pepys*, ed. Robert Latham and William Matthews, 11 vols. (London: Bell & Hyman, 1971–83), 1 July 1663. For libertines, see James Grantham Turner, *Libertines and Radicals in Early Modern London: Sexuality, Politics, and Literary Culture, 1630–1685* (Cambridge University Press, 2002).

17 George Savile, Marquess of Halifax, 'A Character of King Charles the Second', in *Halifax: Complete Works*, ed. J. P. Kenyon (Harmondsworth: Penguin Books, 1969), 245–67.

18 Anon., *A Hue and Cry after Dr T.O.* (London, 1681).

19 For a brilliant study, see J. P. Kenyon, *The Popish Plot* (Harmondsworth: Pelican Books, 1974).

20 Ibid., 124.

21 See Felicity Heal and Clive Holmes, *The Gentry in England and Wales, 1500–1700* (Stanford University Press, 1994).

22 Gregory King, *Scheme of the Income and Expense of the Several Families of England* (London, 1688).

23 Lawrence Stone, 'The residential development of the West End of London in the seventeenth century', in Barbara C. Malament, ed., *After the Reformation* (Manchester University Press, 1980), 167–212.

24 Robert D. Hume, *The Development of English Drama in the Late Seventeenth Century* (Oxford: Clarendon Press, 1976).

25 John Dryden, *The Conquest of Granada, Part One* (London, 1672), 60 (V.i.277–82).

26 Dryden, 'Of Heroic Plays', *The Conquest of Granada, Part One*, sig a2.

27 In *The Diary and Correspondence of John Evelyn*, cited in William van Lennep, ed., *The London Stage Part 1: 1660–1700* (Carbondale:

Southern Illinois University Press, 1965), 177 [hereafter this volume is cited as 'LS1'].

28 Nancy Klein Maguire, *Regicide and Restoration: English Tragicomedy, 1660–1671* (Cambridge University Press, 1992), 210.

29 Dryden, *The Conquest of Granada, Part One*, 50 (IV.ii.418–62).

30 Ibid., 51 (IV.ii.478–9).

31 Maguire, *Regicide and Restoration*, 214.

32 Shakespeare, *Julius Caesar*, ed. T. S. Dorsch (London: Methuen, 1955), I.ii.156–9.

33 Lord Chamberlain's papers, 5/144, p. 28, referenced in Judith Milhous and Robert D. Hume, eds., *A Register of English Theatrical Documents 1660–1737*, 2 vols. (Carbondale: Southern Illinois University Press, 1991), no. 1117 [hereafter this volume is referred to as '*Register*', followed by the document number; Lord Chamberlain's papers are referred to as 'LC', followed by the reference numbers]. For the character of Lucius in other literature of the period, see Susan J. Owen, '"Partial tyrants" and "Freeborn people" in *Lucius Junius Brutus*', *Studies in English Literature* **31** (1991), 463–82.

34 See Robert D. Hume, '*The Maid's Tragedy* and censorship in the Restoration theatre', *Philological Quarterly* **61** (1982), 484–90.

35 Charles Gildon, 'Preface', *The Patriot* (1703); for Tate's play, see LS1, 293.

36 Nathaniel Lee, *Lucius Junius Brutus* (London, 1681), 15 (II.i.44–53).

37 Lee, 'To the Right Honourable Charles, Earl of Dorset and Middlesex', *Lucius Junius Brutus*, 2.

38 Lee, *Lucius Junius Brutus*, 24 (II.i.403–4).

39 David Womersley, ed., *Restoration Drama: An Anthology* (Oxford: Blackwell, 2000), 430.

40 Lee, *Lucius Junius Brutus*, 47–8 (IV.i.105–29).

41 Ibid., 67 (V.ii.42–9).

42 Ibid., 68 (V.ii.116–17).

2 | *The life cycle of the Restoration play*

Managerial revolutions

In the midst of political regime change, theatre people contended with their own upheavals of leadership and culture. Competing managerial ideologies and practices, and financial success and failure, made Restoration Drama rich in allusions to what was, for all the comforts of royal patronage, a cut-throat business environment. 1660 saw the restoration not just of monarchy but of state-sponsored theatre, which had languished since the outbreak of civil war. A surprising amount of semi-official theatre survived during the 1650s amid the demolition of playhouses and army raids on unlicensed performances, but it was not until Charles II's return that actors could work again under the sort of protection they had enjoyed during his father's reign.[1] Even so, opportunities were restricted, and deliberately.

Two licensed companies operating under the names of the king and the Duke of York maximized the chances of official control, and the managers who ran them did not flinch from using their duopoly to suppress unofficial competition. **Sir William Davenant of the Duke's Company** (see below, pp. 93–6) and **Thomas Killigrew of the King's** (see below, pp. 96–9) were genial rivals, charged with implementing Charles II's Francophile tastes in theatre, but equally concerned with making their businesses profitable at a time when the total audience for London theatre probably numbered fewer than 30,000.[2]

Davenant was the more successful and innovative of the two, but his greatest success was in the legacy of business nous, stage technology and company discipline he bequeathed to his two leading actors on his death in 1668. His widow, Mary, was left nominally in charge – remarkably, the first instance in English theatre history of a woman running a theatre company – but she was canny enough to delegate. Thomas Betterton and Henry Harris were paid to determine artistic policy and manage the egos of the actors who had been their peers.

As performers and managers, their contrasting gifts made them a good team. Smooth of tongue and conventionally handsome, Harris was at ease in high society: 'I do not know another better qualified for converse,' remarked his friend Samuel Pepys, on whom Harris regularly sponged.[3] Betterton, by contrast, cut a squat figure and seemed gravely industrious; Pepys thought of him as 'studious', an accumulator of expertise and cash.[4] Predictably, it was Harris who gradually took the opportunity to step aside from the rigours of daily performance and Betterton who kept up a daunting personal regime of acting and management, as they worked together to secure not just a successful company but a new building.

In 1660–1 Davenant and Killigrew had adapted real tennis courts, an example of which survives at Hampton Court, to suit their purposes. In 1671 Betterton and Harris opened the purpose-built Dorset Garden Theatre, fronting the Thames just south of Fleet Street, as a vehicle for the very latest in multimedia performance. Their rivals jibed that it was a place for glitzy, bourgeois trash, and the new theatre duly proved a commercial success. During the 1670s the King's Company suffered the consequences of not inheriting the Davenant legacy of tight discipline, capital investment and stylistic innovation. Under the increasingly distant Killigrew, the company imploded amid a flurry of recrimination, petty theft and sword fights. By 1681 Killigrew had long surrendered to his son whatever control he had left, and his former leading actors were doing a secret deal with Betterton to secure a merger and protect their pension rights. In the following year the United Company came into being.

The new name declared a shift of priorities. From 1682 onwards the story of Restoration theatre management is dominated by shareholders. Among them, one name stands out: **Christopher Rich** (see below, pp. 99–102), hardbitten Somerset lawyer, zealous business reformer and pantomime villain of British theatre history. Having bought his way into a position of dominance in the United Company, Rich came to view as obsolete and inefficient the entrenched ways of the older actors, with their perks, their rights over roles and, no doubt, their annoying habit of protesting that they were servants of the Crown rather than slaves to commercial management. In the name of that older theatrical ideology, and in a spirit of returning to his Restoration roots, Betterton and a number of senior performers split from Rich's company in 1695, returning to the converted tennis court in Lincoln's Inn Fields at which his career with Davenant had begun.

Bitter theatrical rivalry followed, with burlesque and mimicry filling the space vacated by innovation. Betterton became convinced that expensive French talent was the route to success, paying astronomical fees to a succession of Parisian dancers and singers who embodied, in the words of his prompter, 'the desires and Fancies of the Nobility and Gentry'.[5] But he also gave opportunities to the Restoration's second generation of women playwrights.[6] The company struggled in every way as Davenant's legacy finally eluded his best pupil. New drama fell into decline, scenic invention was constrained by space, and even discipline began to fall apart. Junior actors latched on – not without justification – to Rich's old jibes that Betterton was (to put the matter diplomatically) unduly secretive when it came to keeping accounts. In 1705, at the age of seventy, Betterton ceded his licence to his friends Vanbrugh and Congreve, who founded an impressive new theatre, the Queen's at Haymarket, and made Betterton and company the chief residents. In his farewell performance, given two weeks before his death in April 1710, Betterton had to be held up by two actresses. His gout was so painful that for his final role, the dauntless soldier-hero Melantius in Francis Beaumont and John Fletcher's *The Maid's Tragedy*, he wore slippers.

The new licence harked back to a seismic episode that might have compelled him to take up wearing slippers rather sooner. Vanbrugh and Congreve argued that 'a new Company of Comedians' was needed for 'the better Reforming the Abuses and Immorality of the Stage', which in 1698 had been vigorously prosecuted in their work and Betterton's by the Reverend Jeremy Collier (see below, pp. 180–4).[7] If Christopher Rich mistrusted what he thought of as the Spanish practices of Restoration theatre management, Collier hated the entire institution that was Restoration Theatre with startled ferocity. Of all the private citizens who have tried to instigate action against the theatre in London, from Philip Stubbes in 1583 to Mary Whitehouse in 1980, Collier was arguably the most effective.[8] Networks of informers would sit in the theatres, note down instances of bad language and see some of Collier's targets punished in court. Betterton and eleven of his colleagues were fined £5 each for uttering 'Profane, Vicious & immoral Expressions' in plays by, among others, Vanbrugh and Congreve. The Attorney General went out of his way to explain that the intention was not to suppress the theatre, but Collier had other ideas.[9]

Parallels between the political and managerial history of the Restoration Stage arguably invite a language not of steady progress towards enlightenment but of entropy. Just as the country teetered on the verge of renewed civil conflict, so the theatre, newly restored, was never far from collapse. It is often said that the theatre was remarkably durable under the Commonwealth, but less often observed that it was extremely fragile during the Restoration. Plays would always drop out of fashion as the political climate changed, but there was a more serious list of threats to company well-being. Plague, fire, royal deaths, company indiscipline, slander, public disorder, low attendance, merger, industrial action, moral crusades and, not least, the often vacant summer months: for those reasons and more the playhouses of Restoration London might shut for days, weeks, months or – very nearly – for good. Like London itself, the theatres teemed with novelty, history and waste. Speaking the epilogue to Henry Smith's 1699 *The Prince of Parma*, Anne Bracegirdle voiced her company's darkest fear, specific to the moment of performance but true to the experience of most Restoration theatre people: that the converted structure they acted in might reverberate once more not to the rising arc of Betterton's voice or the violins striking up another dance but to the soft plop of a tennis ball.

Theatrical revolutions

With so much to fear in the past and future, Restoration people were swift to innovate; Restoration theatre people were no exception. They were agents and victims of the thirst for change, with the result that 1660 was a watershed for how plays looked, sounded, felt and read. Four revolutions stand out: the introduction of actresses; the development of painted scenery; the elevation of theatrical taste; and the formation of a canon of drama.

Actresses

By the time Anne Bracegirdle spoke her chilly epilogue in 1699 her entitlement to do so was well established. The professional English actress, arguably the single most significant innovation of the Restoration Stage, probably made her London debut on 8 December 1660 in a production of *Othello* that had featured a male Desdemona only two months beforehand.[10] That so many prologues and epilogues were, like Henry Smith's, spoken by actresses says something important about how this new species of performer was deployed and received. Some recent critics have read the Restoration actress through the cinematic concept of the 'gaze', as though Bracegirdle and her colleagues were nothing but objects of desire in a room oozing testosterone; rehearsing Wycherley's *The Country Wife* at the National Theatre in 1977, Peter Hall thought that Restoration theatres give 'the overwhelming impression of a sex-orientated, fashionable club'.[11] Perhaps: one-quarter of the new plays written between 1660 and 1700 feature rape scenes, not to mention all the other occasions when actresses were required to display legs, arms, shoulders or breasts.[12] But, if that was what Restoration theatre managers and audiences demanded, they were slow to impose their will, since scenes of sexual violence were rare before the 1670s. Moreover, the freedom enjoyed by actresses to 'talk back' to the audience through prologues and epilogues (albeit ones written for them largely by men) suggests that actresses were understood not just as sex objects but as feisty professionals capable of reversing the gaze to put their audience – not by any means all male – in the spotlight.[13]

Charles II had other aims in mind when, issuing Davenant and Killigrew with their patents, he required them to employ women to act. Not that he merely fancied his chances with Nell Gwyn, Moll Davis and others who were duly beckoned to the royal bedchamber, or that he wanted London to be more like Paris, where actresses had been around at least since the days of Henry VIII.[14] Officially the actress was there to purge the 'sex-orientated, fashionable club' of a grosser trangression. 'Some have taken offence,' reads Killigrew's patent, at female roles being 'acted by men in the habit of women'.[15] How many puritans would be pacified by seeing (in their view of such things) a drag queen supplanted by a pole dancer is open to doubt, but Killigrew's patent helps explain why it took ten years for the actress's professional dignity to be threatened by the rape scenes that multiplied in the 1670s. By then there was no turning back, politically or performatively.

What difference did they make to performance style, these actresses? In Richard Eyre's 2004 film *Stage Beauty*, 1660 winds forward to 1898, when Konstantin Stanislavski and Vladimir Namirovich-Danchenko founded the Moscow Arts Theatre and the style of acting we now call 'the Method'. Actors trained in the ponderous rhetorical school of patterned gesture and enunciation acquire in the later scenes of *Stage Beauty* a new emotional dynamism. Once a parade of monumental alabaster, *Othello* with actresses trembles with all the immediacy and inner anguish of a soap opera. It makes for a good film, but the idea is, disappointingly, fanciful. Audiences evidently experienced the 'rhetorical school' as natural and exciting, and actresses, paid shillings to their fellow actors' pounds, were coached to fit in with the prevailing company style.[16]

Scenes

Although the theory of the 'gaze' has been applied to the Restoration Stage, this was precisely the time when the performer's body as signifier-in-chief fell into decline. Dialogue would still refer to a park when a playwright wanted the audience to believe that his characters were strolling in one, and the actor could still walk in imitation of the fashionable denizens of the capital, but from 1661 onwards they could rely on movable painted scenery to sustain the illusion. The more spectacular the scenery, the more actors had to fit in with the *mise-en-scène*, to blend into rather than disrupt the stage picture. Playwrights began to write not just for a company of specific performers but for a set of stock visual backgrounds. Rapid topographical transitions such as the ones Shakespeare deployed in the Battle of Actium scenes in *Antony and Cleopatra* became hard to manage. The physical parting of scenes that was increasingly used to evoke shock and awe was replicated in a new fashion for narratives of secrecy, as in *The Way of the World*. In Shakespeare's Theatre, writes Peter Thomson, there were no secrets; Shakespeare's own plays have no place, with the possible exception of *The Winter's Tale*, for the sort of startling Act V denouement that can be earned only from an audience's ignorance of what has really happened (and even in *The Winter's Tale* we are left wondering what on earth *has* happened, which is one reason it was not performed in the Restoration period).[17]

The high art of theatre

Amid this hurtling atmosphere of innovation emerged, by the natural laws of consumerism, an appetite for refinement. The actress and the scene were partners in a broader cultural endeavour. As the audience became more addicted to sight, it valued so much more the object that was the actress within the scene. This was a culture of the scopophi-lic.[18] But nowhere was the actress more intensely visualized than in the theatrical form that depended on her ability to transcend sight – to do, in fact, what no transvestite boy could be trusted to do with the conviction and skill required by the third great innovation of the Restoration Stage. Actresses did not only speak and move and occasionally bare their bodies. Like many of their male counterparts, they sang, and the riches of vocal and visual splendour combined to give birth to what Wagner would describe a century and a half later as the ultimate art form. John Evelyn's was, according to the *Oxford English Dictionary*, the first recorded use of the word 'opera' in our language, and he deployed it with the nervousness of someone who had just encountered something so thrillingly strange and virtuosic. In 1644, recalling a visit to St Peter's in Rome, he described an occasion that was as much architectural as musical:

Bernini, a Florentine sculptor, architect, painter and poet…gave a public Opera (for so they call shows of that kind) wherein he painted the scenes, cut the statues, invented the engines, composed the music, writ the comedy, and built the theatre.[19]

If opera, scenery and the wonders of the human voice in all its diversity were natural companions, it took time for theatre people to understand that so magnificent a concoction could flourish apart from the world of words and five-act dramas. 'Dramatic opera' is the preferred term for the leviathan shows that straddled the stage from the 1670s, inserting elaborate musical interludes into mythical or historical entertainments. 'One wonders how audiences of the time could possibly have endured the thing,' mused *The Times* critic after a 1984 revival of the Purcell/Dryden *The Indian Queen*, in which the present author had the mixed pleasure of playing a lead role.[20] Davenant had begun the trend in 1656. For its Restoration revival this first English 'opera' was known as *The Siege of Rhodes*; as performed to a private audience at Rutland House, it was more politic to describe it as *The First Day's Entertainment*, lest anyone puritanically inclined should think it had anything to do with theatre. Not until the 1680s, with John Blow's *Venus and Adonis* and Henry Purcell's *Dido and Aeneas*, did opera soar free above the spoken word, although in its pure form it tended to do so in private venues rather than public theatres.[21] Dramatic opera, mustering all the innovations of the

Restoration Theatre, marked a kind of revolution whose legacy remains current, for better or – occasionally – worse: the idea of theatre itself as an object of serious inquiry that transcended the rush of the weekly repertory, as a prized cultural asset, and with a price to match. For the 1685 spectacle *Albion and Albanius*, a box seat cost more than four times the usual figure of five shillings.[22]

Text and canon

Connoisseurial distinction is loudly advertised in the passage some-times described as the first piece of theatre criticism in English, pub-lished some time beyond the Restoration period but on the subject of its foremost actor. Colley Cibber's 1740 reminiscence of the way Betterton's Hamlet greeted his father's ghost turns theatre-going into food for the expert. Sitting next to the father of English criticism, Joseph Addison, Cibber contrasts Betterton's modulated refinement with the ranting vulgarity of lesser actors.[23] The foundations had always been partly Addison's; his journal, *The Spectator*, along with *The Tatler*, had set new standards for discussing what made a good play or a plausible actor. But new kinds of critical discourse were also nurtured by the published play text, which increasingly became a forum for playwrights to account for their work.

Dryden thought of it, half in jest, as a French habit:

The writing of prefaces to plays was probably invented by some very ambi-tious poet, who never thought he had done enough: perhaps by some ape of the French eloquence, who uses to make a business of a letter of gallantry, an examen of a farce; and in short, a great pomp and ostentation of words on every trifle. This is certainly the talent of that nation, and ought not to be invaded by any other.[24]

But few welcomed the invasion more expansively than Dryden himself, whose play prefaces form the most impressive body of dramatic criticism in the language. Shaping understanding of individual plays, defining dramatic traditions, promoting theatre as necessary to civil society – such writing also had the simpler effect of drawing attention to the author as chief creator and interpreter. Paulina Kewes has shown how the status of the dramatic author changed during the Restoration period. Pay improved, published texts allowed them to speak in new ways, plagiarism became a matter of concern, and collaboration fell decisively out of favour.[25] In 1600 it had been common for two or three playwrights to work together; by 1700 that was held to be a recipe for muddle. The sole author, that foundation stone of literary heritage, took up residence in the canons of critical thought.

The life cycle of the play

Restoration players and playwrights occupied the slipstream and sometimes the tide of history, but their most immediate concern was the tide of a particular play. Here the perpetual conflict of convention and innovation was at its most acute. However many political and cultural histories are told for the period from 1660 to 1714, the story of how plays came to be written, rehearsed, performed, received, revived and printed was for theatre people the most visible and compelling tale of all, for on the play's life cycle their own living depended. Subsequent chapters explore the roles played by the major components of that process; this one continues with the story of how they all fitted together, or didn't.

The season

The foundation of the play's life cycle, the theatrical season, was largely – if manically – predictable. It followed the social 'season', or the period when the court and high society were generally in residence in London, which lasted from September until June; the terms of the Inns of Court, who supplied a good proportion of the theatre audience, followed the same pattern. For the nine months of the season the theatre companies worked at full stretch: performances on six afternoons a week but for Easter week and Fridays during Lent, with morning and sometimes evening rehearsals thrown in; at first two o'clock was a usual time to begin a performance, but by the end of the century this stretched to four or five o'clock, so accommodating a wider range of working people.[26] Stability was, relative to current practice, in short supply. In May 1669 the Duke's Company performed an adaptation of John Webster's *Appius and Virginia* for eight days in a row, but in January of the same year they had programmed *Twelfth Night*, *The Tempest*, Samuel Tuke's *The Adventures of Five Hours* and William Davenant's *The Wits* across the same period.[27] An average season for a company might see fifty plays, ten of them new, although this pattern varied significantly between 1660 and 1714. In good times there were significantly more new plays; poor trade led to overdependence on safe revivals. Whatever the economic weather, an industrious actor could expect to feature in three-quarters of all productions. Advertising meant posting or distributing playbills, announcements at the end of a performance or just spreading the word.[28]

The season developed its own pattern. New plays or productions might be eased into the repertoire during the autumn, with some of the summer weeks set aside for rehearsal: Betterton first played Hamlet in late August 1661 after prolonged study with Davenant.[29] Christmas and the New Year emerged as favoured slots for lavish spectacle, such as the *Henry VIII* mounted by the Duke's Company in 1663–4. Later, June and July saw more spectaculars such as *The Fairy Queen*, Purcell and Betterton's musical version of *A Midsummer Night's Dream*, a grandiose farewell to gentry about to depart for the summer to their country estates. In some cases, the actors followed them. John Le Neve reports that Richard Jordan MP kept a theatre at his house in Hampshire, where 'the most noted Players in Town have been entertained for Two or Three Months in the Vacation, and acted Comedies and Tragedies'.[30] Lesser performers, or those being trained up to join the company, might tour the provinces.[31] Interruptions to this familiar cycle – outbreaks of plague, censorship, company fallouts, royal deaths and the rest – were endemic commercial risks.

In general, however, there was more stability than before the war. Restoration actors enjoyed a privilege their Shakespearean ancestors did not. In the 1590s it had been common for a company to perform six different plays in a week. After 1660 successful runs became more frequent, with some plays enjoying an initial run of up to two weeks. There are examples from every decade up to 1700. Dryden and Howard's *The Indian Queen* opened on 25 January 1664 and was still playing on 5 February. Otway's *Don Carlos* opened on 8 June 1676 and was still going on 19 June; Shadwell's *The Squire of Alsatia* ran from 3 May to 17 May 1688. Congreve's *Love for Love* premiered on 30 April 1695 and lasted until 14 May. With experience came higher expectations: Dryden's *Albion and Albanius* was a disappointment in 1685 because it ran for only six performances.[32] But *Love for Love* was already something of an exception in the 1690s, and a busier repertory cycle returned from 1700.[33]

Managers had to adapt quickly to circumstances when scheduling, however much they might attempt to plan ahead. Otway's *Venice Preserv'd*, which had done modestly well in February 1682, was revived when the Duke of York, whose enemies it appeared to pillory, returned to the capital in April; when the duchess did the same the following month, a further revival was mounted.[34] Performances at court also had to be scheduled, sometimes at short notice. There were usually eight or nine a year (roughly once a month during the season) and they earned a company £20: an indifferent alternative to a full house but adequate insurance against a poor one. Even so, for the most part the court ventured out to the public theatres and paid half that sum for the privilege, although even then the records show that payment was not necessarily prompt.[35] On a small number of occasions the companies were required to follow the court on its travels. In 1670 the King's and the Duke's Companies were promised no less than £500 each to act at Dover for the signatories of the new treaty with France. The unprecedented figure reflected the need for the actors to abandon London at a potentially profitable time, but also the sensitivity of the occasion.[36]

Plays, companies and playhouses

The term 'Restoration Drama' signifies new plays, but the bulk of what was performed on the Restoration Stage was revived drama subject to legal protection. During the autumn of 1660 the King's and Duke's Companies agreed to divide up existing repertory by legal warrant, and the orders were renewed during the 1668–9 season, after Davenant's death.[37] It is sometimes said that Davenant and the Duke's largely opted for Shakespeare, and Killigrew and the King's for Jonson. Not quite. Commercially, *Hamlet*, *Macbeth*, *The Tempest* and *Henry VIII* were signature successes for the Duke's and continued to be so in adapted form, while *The Alchemist*, *Epicoene* and *Volpone* did well for the King's, although their durability was limited partly by the company's unwillingness to dress them up in new clothes, scenery, language and music. Yet both companies laid claim to plays by Jonson and Shakespeare of which there are no Restoration performance records. Davenant was particularly cautious. He took Jonson's *The Poetaster* but then, so far as we can tell, did nothing with it. By contrast, Killigrew made a point of hoovering up Shakespearean repertory, which did not then see the light of day for decades. His *Julius Caesar* may, like *Hamlet*, have taken advantage of the political atmosphere of the 1660s, and *Othello* may have traded on its status as the first Restoration play to feature real women, but other plays – largely comedies – stayed in the bottom drawer.

This isn't necessarily because Shakespeare's comedies were tested in the theatre and failed. Pepys thought *Twelfth Night* 'a silly play' and *A Midsummer Night's Dream* 'the most insipid ridiculous play that ever I saw in my life', but John Downes reports that the former was a 'mighty Success' for the Duke's Company – his usual code for 'lucrative'.[38] Plays such as *As You Like It*, *Love's Labours Lost*, *The Merchant of Venice* and *The Two Gentlemen of Verona* fell out of the repertory because the King's Company, having elected to own them, did not think them worth reviving. With the publication of the third and fourth folios of Shakespeare's plays in 1663 and 1685, they turned into library pieces, cementing a trend towards the more literary appreciation of his work that had been announced by the 1623 first folio and continued after the Restoration with the third and fourth folios.

Both Davenant and Killigrew naturally claimed the right to their own plays, continued writing for a short period and set about finding new ones for the new age. How easy that was depended on the stability of the companies they ran. A privileged number of playwrights enjoyed a prolonged, fruitful association with the Duke's Company under the management of Betterton and Harris; part of the company's success can be traced to its ability to nurture and retain writing talent. They took all thirteen of Thomas Shadwell's plays from *The Sullen Lovers* in 1668 to *The Lancashire Witches* in 1681; all eight of Thomas Otway's plays between *Alcibiades* in 1675 and *Venice Preserv'd* in 1682; and all thirteen of Aphra Behn's from *The Forc'd Marriage* in 1670 to *The City Heiress* in 1682. In all three cases the relationship continued into the regime of the United Company. By contrast, the King's Company's biggest names – John Dryden, Nathaniel Lee and William Wycherley – all wrote for the Duke's as well, and, when the King's Company started to fall apart in the late 1670s, they abandoned it. Sir George Etherege wrote only for the Duke's; William Congreve followed Thomas Betterton and his small group of favoured actors when they broke away from Christopher Rich in 1695.

Enduring relationships between managers and writers might amount to protection, and even co-authorship. Betterton went to great lengths to keep the spendthrift and psychologically vulnerable Otway on an even keel. Shadwell credited the same genial manager with the idea of writing *Psyche*, while such contrastingly gifted playwrights as Charles Gildon, Elkanah Settle, John Dennis and John Dryden all acknowledged his help with the structure or casting of their plays.[39] Writing for a company meant, of course, writing roles that fitted the established profiles or 'lines' of the actors, although that in turn created scope for the creative disturbance (or, indeed, confusion) that comes of casting against type. The same may be said for the business of writing for a company's stock of scenery and musical resources, which had to be shown off and, as the promise of suitable success presented itself, augmented. Here too Betterton had his say, drafting designs for Dryden's spectacular *Albion and Albanius*, a mind-boggling stage direction for which is to be found below (pp. 147–8).

In the theatre any notion of the author as the start of the 'life cycle' of the text is precarious; in the Restoration Theatre it makes even less sense, given the degree of company collaboration and adaptation needed to sustain the knife-edge theatrical economy. Authors were statistically less busy than their Renaissance counterparts: compare Behn's thirteen plays in as many years with the contract issued to Richard Brome in 1635, which demanded two or three plays a year.[40] But in one respect the idea of the Restoration author as the start of a play's life cycle makes perfect sense, since it was from the author's own lips that the actors first heard a new script.

Readings and rehearsals

Colley Cibber recalled two examples of authors presenting their work to companies. The first was John Dryden:

When [Dryden] brought his Play of *Amphitryon* to the Stage [in 1690], I heard him give it his first reading to the actors... [T]he whole was in so cold, so flat, and unaffecting a manner, that I am afraid of it not being believed when I affirm it.[41]

Actors might need to be persuaded that a play read in such an uninspiring tone could succeed. Dryden's low-key manner could encourage them to believe they were not secondary beings, but instrumental to the play's fortunes – a favourite theme of Cibber's, who was an actor.

Yet this account of the great poet's reading style also highlights the aura that surrounded the author even when the first reading was a disappointment. 'I am afraid of it not being believed,' wrote Cibber, as though people would naturally assume that someone capable of such impassioned writing should also be a fiery reader.

Cibber's second example illustrates the dangers of an author getting too incendiary. Nathaniel Lee,

far [Dryden's] inferior in poetry, was so pathetic [i.e. moving] a reader of his own scenes, that. . .while [he] was reading to Major Mohun at a rehearsal, Mohun. . .threw down his part, and said, 'Unless I were able to play it as well as you read it, to what purpose should I undertake it?'[42]

Like the reading of *Amphitryon*, this gave another reason to resist the authority of the author while admiring it. Taken together, the two examples paint the start of the rehearsal process as an imminent turf war between actor and author. Indeed, there were cases when actors refused to accept a play on the basis of the author's reading, while theatre managers often helped 'theatricalize' scripts presented to them.[43] The practice of an initial reading applied to revivals as well, except that then it was a manager (which often meant a senior actor) who did the business.

The first reading was the actors' best chance of appreciating the overall shape of the play, since they were given only their individual parts to learn, suitably dressed with cues that could be dauntingly brief. The result, nevertheless, was that it became more important to learn the cues than anything else, and it is in the nature of any such technology that a necessary convenience metamorphosed into a short cut that lazy actors, much to the chagrin of authors, learned to take. There was a convention that performers should spend much of the evening in 'study', the lone or tutorial refinement of individual gesture and pronunciation that writers of the time distinguished from 'rehearsal', which was a more collective exercise usually scheduled for the morning. Cibber is warm in his praise of particular actors who would seek out individual instruction, partly to distinguish them from the ones who set out to exploit the turf war of authority begun at first reading, or who were just too fond of a good night out. A passage from Charles Gildon's *Life of Betterton* distinguishes between the discipline of Davenant's management in the 1660s, when 'our Study was our Business', and Betterton's experience in the later 1690s, when 'Rehearsals' were all the preparation there was, and those were too often spoiled by actors 'scarce recovered from their last night's debauch'.[44] The language of education is deployed to emphasize the discipline, and through that the art, of a profession Betterton and his biographer hoped to make more respectable.

'Study' was the more important when an all-cast 'rehearsal' might be limited to a single occasion that, today, would be called a full dress rehearsal, although one can forgive any actor the wish to drown his sorrows faced with the prospect of learning a new role in a matter of hours (fortunately, a fortnight was more usual).[45] A powerful reason for not studying too hard was the well-founded suspicion that a new play might sink after a single performance, which readily became a self-fulfilling prophecy. Aphra Behn's *The Dutch Lover*, plausibly proof that prejudice against women playwrights reached beyond the auditorium and into theatre companies, 'was hugely injured in the acting' because of the 'intolerable negligence of some that acted in it'. Records suggest it failed to see the light of day again. Betterton himself, the model professional, occasionally corpsed, forgot his lines and made unscripted noises off.[46]

Actors who learned to treat first performances as a form of market research also enjoyed the freedom to cultivate signature roles across decades, however. Betterton gave his first known Hamlet in 1661 and his last in 1709. Flying scenery and dancing Danes might intervene at the Dorset Garden production of 1674, but the performance had time to mature until it became, no doubt, a simulacrum of itself. Actors owned their parts – the best way of trying to undermine performers was not to pay them less but to challenge their right to particular roles – and made serious, long-term investment in them. Exclusive focus on the new drama of the period can leave the impression that Restoration acting was merely a frantic dash for new trinkets. The core business of revivals shows, by contrast, that there was also time to polish antiques.

Actors and performance

A rehearsal system founded on individual 'study' had consequences for performance: in theory at least, actors were so focused from the start on their own roles (assuming they learned them properly) that they had little leisure to bestow on the broader effect. Or so the theory goes. Gildon's Betterton magisterially complained of actors 'whispering to one another, or bowing to their Friends in the Pit, or gazing about' – then, their own speeches complete, they blended into the audience.[47] But he was reflecting on the latter stages of his career, and instances of actors being 'out' or negligent are less common than they might seem; Pepys mentions the problem only a few times in a decade of theatre-going. Almost all the surviving evidence of on-stage indiscretions relates to low-tech shows. When it came to lavish scenic productions with music, companies were more careful because they had to be, both financially and technologically.

The same goes for improvisation. Hamlet begs the travelling players that their clowns should 'speak no more than is set down for them', and the joke must have survived well into the eighteenth century. In George Farquhar's *The Recruiting Officer*, Captain Plume asks the Shropshire simpleton Thomas Appletree his name. In the 1706 premiere, Robert Wilks, as Plume, was in for a surprise. 'Why, don't you know my name, Bob?' asked the other actor, William Penkethman. Wilks fed him the line, but Penkethman was having none of it. 'Thomas Appletree? Thomas Devil,' he replied. 'My name is Will Penkethman.'[48] It is too much to expect that the humour of the moment could be captured in an anecdote: it surprised the audience, so it was found funny enough to record. Anecdotes concerning verbal improvisation generally focus on comic actors and performances, although ambitious tragedians such as George Powell might follow the letter of a speech while missing its spirit entirely. Powell gave 'vehemence to words where there was no passion' – what Hamlet might have described as 'tear[ing] a passion to tatters'.[49]

Authors as well as actors accepted, however, that, when it came to the first performance, 'what [was] set down' was hardly the end of the story. A fair proportion of premieres were scheduled for Saturday, partly to maximize the audience but also to allow some time for adjustments to be made either to the script or the production before the second, or Monday, showing.[50] The author's chief hope was that there would be a third, or benefit, performance, and any actor with an instinct for self-preservation also had an interest in securing it. Watching particular actors was as powerful a motivation for going to the theatre as seeing a new play; seeing an established hit, if Pepys was typical, was the most powerful motivation of all.

The audience

The playwright Thomas D'Urfey defined the purpose of a first night as a test of the audience's patience:

[M]y play might be too long, which is a general fault amongst us, and not to be remedied till the first day is over, and...some scenes might seem tedious till it was shortened, which is always the second day's work.[51]

D'Urfey's insouciant generalizations may be the mask for his own chronic long-windedness, but there is plenty of other evidence to suggest that the audience played an active role not simply in sustaining a play or binning it but in editing it. Whole scenes might disappear, and endings change, on the whim of collective or individual will. The conclusion to George Granville's 1698 *Heroic Love* was, in the aggrieved playwright's words, 'murdered [rather] than cut' after a difficult first performance, but it survived its mortal surgery to 'mightily please the Court and City'.[52] There are numerous other instances of playwrights and actors responding to criticism by making substantial changes.[53]

So, centuries before the world of blogging file sharers and dead authors, there was a culture of 'users' of Restoration Theatre. Who were they, these co-creating consumers? There are two long-standing myths about the Restoration audience: that they were largely uppercrust, and often violent. Pepys says otherwise. Although the cheapest seats were beyond the means of some people, they were far from being so expensive as to deter apprentices and others the Navy Office clerk wished had stayed away. Similarly, it would be obvious from the same source if the playhouses really were as fractious and violent as might appear. Serious trouble was exceptional and tended to be the result of personal antagonism or political unrest.[54] A more regular disturbance was the kind it has always been possible to square with the idea of a sophisticated, civil function: Sir Charles Sedley, for example, nattering cleverly to a fellow spectator, his critique of the play more interesting than the play itself (discussed below, p. 167).[55]

As well as the attention to the timing of scenes that so often defeated D'Urfey, in Pepys we see an emergent critical vocabulary that later in the period would start to find more formal expression in publications such as *The Gentleman's Magazine*. Authenticity – a mark of the writer's authority – came into view as a critical concept. One of the landmark works of dramatic criticism to date from the period, Gerard Langbaine's 1691 *An Account of the English Dramatick Poets*, vilified playwrights for plagiarism, a habit condemned more than twenty years earlier by a discerning playgoer, Elizabeth Pepys.[56] Dramatic collaboration and borrowing were falling out of fashion rapidly; audiences and critics had begun to value the sole creator, and the trend could only be accelerated by the publication of play texts.

Plays in publication

Restoration plays usually began life in print as memorials of performance, published in the large pocket-size format known as the quarto within months of the premiere or to accompany revivals. The convention was to print the names of the actors next to their roles, as though to signify that casting patterns remained an important part of the play's meaning. Even readers who had not seen the play on stage might make deductions based on their knowledge of performers' customary stage profiles. Stage directions, scenic notes, prologues and epilogues and – in the case of more spectacular shows – elaborate descriptions of technical effects further underlined the role of play quartos as a record of a prior, and implicitly more important, event. Given the unpredictability of performance, of course, they also provided the playwright with the chance to set the record straight.

They did so through increasingly sophisticated introductory material. It was usual to dedicate a play in print to a noble patron, although friends, writers, and even booksellers might also be recognized. The 'epistle dedicatory' was used to describe the influence the dedicatee had exerted in the play's favour, to pay tribute to a patron's hospitality or even to suggest that the hero of the play had been modelled on the addressee. Typically, it might earn the playwright up to £10 (rather more than the bookseller would typically have paid for the script in the first place); the advantage for the bookseller was that aristocratic endorsements helped sell books.

Dedications were often complemented by a different kind of preface, sometimes called just that, sometimes an 'epistle to the reader', as though acknowledging that the play had passed from one kind of audience to another. Dryden used this form to give free rein to his comprehensive knowledge of English and European dramatic traditions, and helped form them in the process. Others pursued more local concerns. Having basked in the glory of the Duke of York's favour during the dedication of *Don Carlos*, Otway begins in an autobiographical mode like that of Laurence Sterne for his preface; he meanders around his own melancholy with reflections on the poor return a fellow gets on a preface ('[I]t will hardly keep us in *Ale* and *Cheese*'), on his poor Italian, and on his surprise at having finally cornered his muse. '[L]ike a bashful young Lover,' he describes how he fumbled his way to a 'dramatic birth'. He then settles into the more conventional business of reflecting on the reception of the play and disparaging its critics. The open-ended form of the preface gave playwrights licence to be as profound or as trivial as their capacities determined, but, above all, to draw attention to their interpretative authority in a way unmatched since the first reading.

A small number of play publications took this process to a new level. Booksellers who wanted to make a statement about the abiding importance of plays and playwrights published them in folio, the large, coffee-table format that carried with it an air of completeness and the bulk of a modern encyclopaedia. Jonson's 1616 *Works*, the 1623 first folio of Shakespeare and the 1647 folio of Beaumont and Fletcher's plays had introduced readers to the idea that texts born in the transient, indigent world of theatre might make their way into respectable libraries, and the trend continued with folio collections of the works of, among others, Davenant, Killigrew, Dryden and Congreve. For Davenant, a folio memorialized not performance but the life of the recently dead author, sharing the purpose as well as the weight of a tombstone.

Revivals

A theatre that thrived on short initial runs also depended on revivals, both of 'old' (i.e. pre-war) and more recent plays. The formula for long-term commercial success on the Restoration Stage lay not in the acknowledged masterpieces of the period, which still receive revivals today, but in two plays that kept the Duke's Company coffers full for many seasons. They are by very different writers. Sir Samuel Tuke, Gray's Inn student and civil war veteran, wrote no other play beside *The Adventures of Five Hours*, but this Spanish-inspired mixture of heroic drama and low comedy appears to have been performed more often between its premiere in 1663 and the end of the century

than any other Restoration play. The play has the structure of a
romantic comedy, with two serious-minded aristocratic couples desperate for consummation and a plethora of comic servants, misrecog-
nitions, reversals of fortune and other twists designed to keep an
audience guessing about how the ultimate resolution is to be achieved –
as though Julian Fellowes had fallen in with Ray Cooney. *The Adventures* exploited the full range of tragic and comic talent in the Duke's
Company and made, Evelyn heard, up to £5,000 in its first season,
substantially more than the annual production budget.[57] Tuke made
much of its moral purity – Pepys, who hinted that he preferred the
play to *Othello*, marvelled that there was not 'one word of ribaldry' in
it – and it is possible to trace its appeal to a broader kind of innocence:
typically for 1660s drama, the promotion of a world of fictively
unblemished motivation that compensated audiences for the anxieties
of war and the fear of domestic corruption and indecision.[58] *The
Adventures of Five Hours* was still being performed in 1705. Nostalgia
for lost innocence died hard.

Equal popularity was achieved on the basis of a simpler formula by
Dryden's *Sir Martin Mar-All, or, Feign'd Innocence*, fashioned out of
a Molière translation by the Duke of Newcastle. Pepys saw the second
performance in August 1667 and went home with a headache from
laughing too much. Although he attributed his reaction to the play's
'very good wit' rather than 'fooling', *Sir Martin* treats its dim-witted,
self-defeating eponymous hero in the idiom of farce. Looking for a
sure-fire way to boost company finances after the building of the
Dorset Garden Theatre in 1671, the Duke's Company turned again
to a play that had consistently been in the repertory for four years and
would continue to be revived into the 1690s. While *The Adventures of
Five Hours* released its audiences into an idyllic world in which
honour-driven behaviour wins out, *Sir Martin* offered something more
like a satire of aristocratic presumption. Tuke's innocence appealed to
fantasies about the success of the Restoration; Dryden's to fears of its
failure. The central performance had much to do with the effect. James
Nokes, former shopkeeper and a *farceur* in the mould of Norman
Wisdom or Rowan Atkinson, was given the task of impersonating a
member of the minor aristocracy so convinced of his own abilities
that his world collapses around him: the historic destiny of the Stuart
family seen through the contorted body language of Mr Bean. Along
the way, he is the subject of jokes that have died as surely as the play's

life in the theatre. 'I am sure I pass in all companies for a virtuoso,' he claims, only to receive the retort: 'Virtuoso? What's that? Is not virtue enough without virtue oh so?'[59]

Politics intervened in decisions about revivals. From the outset it had been usual for Restoration theatre companies to programme older plays that chimed with the terrors of the past. *Hamlet*, the supreme play about avenging a dead king, was acclaimed in 1661; *Macbeth*, the foremost treatment of regicide, was programmed on Bonfire Night at least from 1664 onwards. Other Renaissance dramatists also spoke to the times. In 1661 Pepys was taken aback by the anti-puritanism of Ben Jonson's *Bartholomew Fair* and wondered whether in the circumstances it was politic, since there had been puritan support for the Restoration.[60] Philip Massinger's *The Bondman*, on the other hand, the tale of a secret prince who heroically reclaims his inheritance, was a celebratory success in the same year.[61]

This life cycle of the Restoration play entailed a process of adaptation and revival against a variety of political and aesthetic contingencies, some of which are illustrated in the following three case studies. Where adaptation is concerned, there is no more conspicuous instance than Nahum Tate's version of *King Lear*.

Adapting to politics: Nahum Tate's *The History of King Lear* (1681)

However familiar the idea of adapting Shakespeare for the modern stage and screen, Tate's *King Lear* retains the capacity to upset. Instead of expiring in the forlorn hope that his dead daughter may still be breathing, Tate's Lear anoints Edgar and Cordelia as the next king and queen, then contemplates a serene retirement for himself, Kent and Gloster (as Tate spelled him) that suffuses the spirit of Shakespeare's play with a draught of *Last of the Summer Wine*:

> Thou, *Kent* and I, retired to some cool cell
> Will gently pass our short reserves of time
> In calm reflections on our fortunes past,
> Cheered with relation of the prosperous reign
> Of this celestial pair...[62]

Other changes signal a similar surrender to sentiment. Tate engineers an Act III reunion between the young lovers, Edgar and Cordelia, that might belong to *bel canto* opera. 'O Cordelia!' he cries. 'Ha! Thou knowst my Name,' she replies. 'As you did once know Edgar's,' he says, before her inevitable, swooning 'Edgar!'.[63] Tate is less forgiving as well. When Edmund, emphatically codified as 'Bastard' in the first printed text, faces his half-brother in single combat, he knows from the outset that it is Edgar, allowing him a moment of diehard libertinism that makes most Restoration rakes seem positively foppish:

Ha! My brother!
This is the only combatant that I could fear;
For in my breast, guilt duels on his side,
But, conscience, what have I to do with thee?
Awe thou thy dull legitimate slaves, but I
Was born a libertine, and so I keep me.[64]

Shakespeare's Edmund has his moment of redemption trying to avert the murder of Cordelia; denied that opportunity, Tate's Bastard dies confirmed in the arrogance of his 'daring Soul'.[65]

It is easier to deride Tate's changes – his occasional stylistic infelicities and his moral simplifications – than to understand them. In some respects he was a sensitive adapter, treasuring what he called the 'jewels' of Lear's poetry in particular. So what motivated him? What effect did his interventions have on the popularity of the play in the theatre and its fortunes in print?

Politics loomed large over the Dorset Garden premiere, which took place between November 1680 and March 1681. This was, after all, the Duke of York's playhouse. The parliamentary winter had been dominated by attempts to pass an Exclusion Bill that would have denied the Catholic duke his inheritance upon Charles II's death. Promoting the bill, the Whig faction favoured the claims of the Protestant Duke of Monmouth, the king's illegitimate son. Tate allowed audiences every opportunity to savour the evils of the bastard Edmund. Dispensing with Shakespeare's hushed prologue, in which Kent and Gloucester wonder whether Albany or Cornwall is to be more favoured in Lear's bequest (itself an unseemly reminder of how national politics were beset by rumour and secrecy), Tate placed the chief villain centre stage from the outset: 'Thou nature art my Goddess,' begins his play. Whereas Etherege and many other playwrights had breezily associated libertine values with those of the Stuart court, Tate sought to pin them on its half-connected son. The usefulness of the term 'libertine' is questionable when it covers so many different kinds of masculinity, from the wantonly aberrant to the partly reformed (Etherege's Dorimant, the next example, seems bent on ceasing to be one if he can find the right woman, which he duly does). But for Restoration playwrights it was a useful weapon whenever it was politic to argue that someone motivated by natural instincts was either opposed to or blessed with divine authority.

Tate's Edmund wants more than Gloucestershire, and warms in Lear's older daughters not just to 'majestic beauty' but to the cold tyranny that loads 'drudging peasants' with fresh taxes. The familiar erotic language of the libertine is voiced in order to discredit its imperial inclinations: 'sick of expectation', Tate's Edmund 'pant[s] for the possession'.[66] With his dying breath he conveniently doubts his own parenthood, but uses the moment as an excuse to float the most damnable idea he has yet concocted, and the one that matches him to Monmouth: that his real father was a king. Legitimacy of birth and succession are everything, and so, in an uncanny premonition of what was to happen in 1688, the princess assumes the throne with her husband. It is characteristic of the competitive nature of Restoration Theatre that a more emollient version of this message was presented at Drury Lane in March 1681 when the King's Company, by then on its last legs, performed Charles Saunders's *Tamerlane the Great*. Monmouth had been the dedicatee of a history of Tamerlane in 1679 that celebrated his 'noble mind, courage, fame and victories', but Saunders's play politely distanced itself from such comparisons by invoking God's providence and achieving narrative resolution through the marriage of Tamerlane's son to Bajazeth's daughter (as in Rowe's Tamerlane play of 1702, it had become customary to think of the hero as an indigenous Protestant and Bajazeth as a tyrannical and foreign papist).[67]

Tate seized the historical moment for his *Lear* adaptation; the Duke's Company had been performing Shakespeare's version without demur since the early 1660s. Incendiary topicality and front-rank casting (Betterton played Lear and Elizabeth Barry Cordelia) did not lead to overwhelming success. John Downes, always alert to box-office business, mentioned it only as an afterthought to the company's performances of Shakespeare's original, while *The London Stage* lists only five performances between 1681 and 1700, two of those taking place at court during the winter of 1687–8, when pressure on James II was growing. Reminding him of his victory over Monmouth was, perhaps,

loyal consolation.[68] Shakespeare's *Lear* had never been as popular
with Restoration audiences as *Hamlet*, *Macbeth* or *Othello*, and on
the evidence available Tate's adaptation did not do a great deal to
change their preference. The fact that it saw off the original until David
Garrick's 1756 performance does not mean that its 'lasting popularity'
originated in the Restoration period.[69] Published editions tell an interesting story. The first, in 1681, followed the premiere closely. It was a
timely stroke by Richard Bentley to reissue it in 1689, after James had
been ousted: now the ending seemed more than ever premonitory of
William and Mary's accession. Further editions followed in 1699 and
1712, but it was not until the 1720s and 1730s that interest in the play
really took flight. By 1745, the date of the tenth London edition and
the final defeat of the Stuart dynasty in the shape of Bonnie Prince
Charlie, the bastard Edmund had acquired a strong resemblance to the
very family from which Tate had been at pains to distinguish him. The
life cycle of this play had within little more than half a century inverted
its politics.

Revival without adaptation: Sir George Etherege's *The Man of Mode* (1676)

Etherege's final comedy of three, *The Man of Mode*, remained stub-
bornly true to its original ideological hue, and suffered for it. The play
might be described as a quintessential Restoration comedy: elegant,
libertine hero (a 'good' libertine to set against Tate's wicked one) meets
his match in a witty heroine; locks horns with a foppish clothes horse
of a rival fresh from Paris (so memorable a character that the play was
often referred to as *Sir Fopling*); cruises the fashionable meeting places
of London, dispensing crushing put-downs to servants and former
mistresses; and is ultimately rewarded with the hand – and the estate –
of the alpha female Harriet Woodville, whose family name promises a
harmonious union of town and country. Plot, so far as it exists at all
in this notoriously meandering play, is secondary to wit and character.
But, then, *The Man of Mode* did not need a clever plot to succeed;
it simply played out the dreams of the royal dynasty that so loved it.
Like Charles II himself, Dorimant seeks to shuffle off the past in order
to achieve his ultimate settlement; striving to prove his ability to prevail
over French competition, he asserts himself as the real man of mode,
the ultimate Englishman.

In the following exchange from Act II, Dorimant articulates the classic libertine position he is really intent on abandoning. Etherege hoped we would share his joke in naming Dorimant's angry ex-mistress 'Mrs Loveit', as though her sex drive were more acute than his. The idea that it was women's sexuality that was dangerously out of control was common in the seventeenth century, and here it is used to suggest that the hero is, in the very act of showing off the attributes of a libertine, applying his mind to higher things. What we actually hear from Mrs Loveit is not libido but an outdated moralism that has failed to notice how the revolutions of history have undermined it.

LOVEIT: Is this the constancy you vowed?

DORIMANT: Constancy at my years? 'Tis not a virtue in season; you might as well expect the fruit the autumn ripens in the spring.

LOVEIT: Monstrous principle!

DORIMANT: Youth has a long journey to go, madam. Should I have set up my rest at the first inn I lodged at, I should never have arrived at the happiness I now enjoy.

LOVEIT: Dissembler, damned dissembler!

DORIMANT: I am so, I confess; good nature and good manners corrupt me. I am honest in my inclinations, and would not, were it not to avoid offence, make a lady a little advanced in years believe I think her young...and seem as fond of a thing I am weary of, as when I doted on it in earnest.

LOVEIT: False man.

DORIMANT: True woman.

LOVEIT: Now you begin to show yourself!

DORIMANT: Love gilds us over, and makes us show fine things to one another for a time, but soon the gold wears off, and then again the native brass appears.

LOVEIT: Think on your oaths, your vows and protestations, perjured man.

DORIMANT: I made them when I was in love.

LOVEIT: And therefore ought they not to bind? Oh impious!

DORIMANT: What we swear at such a time may be a certain proof of a present passion, but to say truth, in love there is no security to be given for the future.

LOVEIT: Horrid and ungrateful, begone, and never see me more.[70]

The dialogue pits one kind of language against another. Loveit is a stuck record, a series of routine exclamations of outrage. Dorimant commands a range of metaphors in a cool exhibition of Restoration wit. He defeats her through poised appeal to principles of nature that find a counterpart in the philosophy of Thomas Hobbes and the poetry of John Wilmot, Earl of Rochester, who asked for release from his mistress on the basis that all his past life was his no more. 'Then talk not of inconstancy,' concludes Rochester in terms so Dorimantish that it is easy to see why he was thought a model for Etherege's hero,

> False hearts, and broken vows;
> If I by miracle can be
> This livelong minute true to thee
> 'Tis all that heaven allows.[71]

The English Civil War and the Restoration had entailed a wholesale switching of allegiance, so 'vows', the formal instruments of that process, were emptied out in the lurch from one regime to another. At the end of *The Man of Mode*, Dorimant attempts to restore integrity to the language of love, only to be undermined. 'The first time I saw you,' he swears to Harriet, 'you left me with the pangs of love upon me, and this day my soul has quite given up her liberty.' What he makes of her crushing reply is up to the actor, for she silences him: 'This is more dismal than the country!'

Was it Dorimant's freedom or his quest for restraint that appealed more to early audiences? Several years on from the March 1676 premiere, the dramatist and critic John Dennis remarked that 'all the world was charmed with Dorimant'.[72] Men admired him, women fell for him – the duality of the 'gaze' associated with cinematic heroes[73] (it is easy to train that gaze only on the new breed of female actresses). John Downes, the Duke's Company prompter who spent his retirement writing his memoirs, remembered it being so 'well clothed and well acted' that it 'got a great deal of money'.[74] Nine years on from the premiere it was still going strong in the theatre: the Earl of Middleton wrote to Etherege that the play had been performed 'with the usual applause', and there had even been an amateur performance in Brussels.[75] Revived at court in the aftermath of Popish Plot hysteria at the Dorset Garden Theatre, and again the autumn following James II's accession, the play perhaps offered to audiences a comforting feeling that English charm would always win out over French extravagance, and to the Stuart monarchy a sense that its abiding dream of redemption from the past remained within reach.[76]

As well as the charm of Dorimant, Dennis lighted on the topicality of the play. 'It was generally believed to be an agreeable representation of the persons of condition of both sexes, both in court and town,' he observed, going on to compare the gossip Medley with Sir Fleetwood Shepherd and Dorimant himself with the Earl of Rochester.[77] Other plays had exploited the audience's interest in the misdeeds of high society, sometimes with bruising consequences for actors, who might find themselves cornered in an alleyway by hired thugs. Etherege was diplomatic enough, as his later court appointments confirmed, to draw on *Hello!* magazine rapture without upsetting anyone, or placing his performers in a position in which they might do it for him. It helped that he was part of the world he celebrated. Only three months after the March premiere, he and Rochester picked a fight with seventeenth-century London's answer to the police, the London Watch.

It must always have seemed unlikely that the portly, pockmarked, forty-year-old and eminently respectable Thomas Betterton could persuade anyone that he was imitating the Earl of Rochester, for all his legendary skill. Rochester was a still diaphanous twenty-nine at the premiere, while Betterton's oldest acquaintance on the stage, Edward Kynaston (among the last of the drag actors and thus the subject of the film *Stage Beauty*), had been beaten up for impersonating Sir Charles Sedley in the Duke of Newcastle's play *The Heiress*.[78] Betterton was, in any case, cautiously deferential when it came to dealings with the nobility. What he brought to the part of Dorimant was something more important than mimicry. In a play that fell out of fashion because it seemed to the next generation so saturated with the values of a corrupt dynasty, Betterton embodied a quality that Joseph Roach has described as 'symbolic royalty'.[79]

Dennis's defence of *The Man of Mode* responded to a widespread backlash against the play by, among others, Sir Richard Steele, who found it 'a perfect contradiction to good manners, good sense, and common honesty'.[80] By the early eighteenth century the man Dorimant was a Stuart thug smothered by the reformed Whiggish heart-warmers who populated Steele's own (now largely forgotten) plays; by implication, those 'pangs' of love he feels for Harriet were mere hypocrisy. The plays of William Wycherley enjoyed similarly mixed fortunes. *The Country Wife* opened in January 1675 and was still in the repertory in May 1676; reprints in 1683, 1688 and 1695 imply revivals by the United Company and its successors. A revival of *The*

Plain Dealer in December 1685 was accompanied by perhaps the single most generous act of patronage extended to any writer in the period, when James II paid off the playwright's debts and gave him a pension of £200 a year.[81] Aphra Behn's *The Rover Part 1*, a comedy usually associated with a 'Yorkist' or pro-James perspective, preceded *The Man of Mode* in being performed at court after the Dorset Garden disturbances, and also featured among the autumn court performances of 1685. It had even been performed in the theatre when Charles II was on his deathbed in January of that year – a last reminder of the romance of Cavalier exile. Yet it made the transition to the values of the post-Stuart regime more successfully than the plays of Etherege and Wycherley, if still precariously: only William Mountfort's lead performance, which 'wash[ed] off the guilt from vice', persuaded Queen Mary to withhold her 'disapprobation'. A further revival followed in the 1690s, when *The Man of Mode* had fallen into disrepute.[82] Like its author, frozen out for his service to the disgraced tyrant James II, *The Man of Mode* died the death reserved for political exiles.

Although politics played a significant part in Restoration revivals and adaptations, changing aesthetic and technical contexts also helped determine what appeared on the stage, and when. Dryden, Howard and Purcell's extravagant dramatic opera, *The Indian Queen*, is a classic case.

John Dryden, Sir Robert Howard, Henry Purcell and *The Indian Queen* (1664 and 1695)

The Indian Queen began in 1664 as a heroic play co-authored by Dryden, a professional writer, and his aristocratic brother-in-law, Sir Robert Howard. Today it is largely known as a full-scale dramatic opera with music written by Henry Purcell thirty years later. The plot – and the scenic ambition – might be that of a Hollywood epic, with grandeur and anachronism warring for supremacy; this was a landmark on the journey that led to *The Conquest of Granada*. Montezuma, the dangerously capable outsider who foreshadows Almanzor, helps the Incas defeat the Aztecs and in return asks for the hand of the Inca princess Orazia. Refused, he changes sides, duelling with his love rival, Acaces, while fighting off the attentions of the Aztec queen Zempoalla. Eventually he marries Orazia.

From the outset, the staging was what people noticed above all else. John Evelyn recalled that it was 'so beautiful with rich scenes, as the like had never been seen here as happily (except rarely anywhere else) on a mercenary theatre'.[83] In other words, this was the moment when commercial playhouses approximated to the grandeur of the court masques that had flourished before the civil war. We can appreciate Evelyn's excitement from reading the stage directions for the start of Act V: '*The Scene opens, and discovers the Temple of the Sun all of Gold, and four Priests in habits of white and red Feathers attending by a bloody Altar.*' There was costuming to match. An anonymous play, *The Feast*, suggests that *The Indian Queen* was so awash with 'speckled plumes' that audiences flocked to see it.[84] A 'warlike Dance' of Indians in Act III and £40 worth of silk for the band alone, courtesy of Charles II himself, enhanced the thrill.[85] (Some of the effect is captured in a picture of Anne Bracegirdle as Semernia in Behn's *The Widow Ranter*, shown in Figure 2.1).

Songs, choral set pieces and interludes by Purcell made the 1695 revival an even richer concoction, and the new 'dramatic opera' became staple entertainment for visiting ambassadors and aristocrats.[86] Yet its ostentatious cultural value – now it surpassed in multimedia glory anything that had been achieved by the court masque – was achieved under very different conditions of patronage. Conceived before the split that took the veteran Thomas Betterton and his friends back to Lincoln's Inn Fields, this latest *Indian Queen* was revived by Christopher Rich as a reminder that the higher forms of theatre could be performed only by the company with the best material resources at its disposal; it was mounted at Dorset Garden, which Betterton had sweated to bring into being. Betterton's response was the low-tech, high-wit comedy *Love for Love*, which Congreve had withdrawn from Rich's grasp. Dryden and Howard's play had taken a strange journey. Their finely tuned celebration of love and honour in an exotic setting, enriched by Purcell's incomparable music, had become a weapon in a vicious theatrical war.

English dramatists of the early 1660s were conscious of competing calls on their attention. In 1662 Roger Boyle, Earl of Orrery, cited the king's preference for French classical tragedy as a reason for writing rhymed heroic plays; dedicating *The Rival Ladies* to the same writer two years later, Dryden observed that the convention was as much English as French, 'not so much a new Way amongst us, as an old Way

MRS BRACEGIRDLE AS "THE INDIAN QUEEN"

Figure 2.1 Restoration exoticism: Anne Bracegirdle as Semernia in Behn's *The Widow Ranter* (1696)

new Reviv'd'.[87] Dryden was perhaps eager to naturalize what to some people seemed part of a cultural conspiracy. English companies had reason to fear competition from the French actors who were frequently brought to the capital, while nervousness that French culture might tend towards French politics was widespread. The shadow of French absolutism was as dark as that of English regicide.

If Pepys thought the style of *The Indian Queen* excessively francophone he did not say so (French music he openly disliked), but he cared little for it nevertheless; '[T]he play good, but spoiled with the rhyme, which breaks the sense,' was his verdict on the performance that took place on 1 February 1664. Is that the problem with the following passage, in which Montezuma claims the Inca's daughter as his prize for defeating the Aztecs?

> I beg not empires, those my sword can gain;
> But for my past and future service too,
> What I have done, and what I mean to do,
> For this of Mexico which I have won,
> And kingdoms I will conquer, yet unknown,
> I only ask from fair Orazia's eyes
> To reap the fruits of all my victories.[88]

Dryden and Howard's clarity and rhetorical control here mean that the rhymes do not 'break the sense'; on the contrary, the passage helps the actor build momentum towards the final couplet, when Montezuma states the price of his loyalty. Discreet masculine and feminine rhymes quicken rather than impede the pulse. The problem, arguably, is with echoes of sense rather than sound. Montezuma's insistence on paraphrasing the already simple terms 'past and future' over the subsequent three lines may be intended to signal rumbling indignation, but they have the effect of dissipating dramatic energy in an archly observed display of the art of caesura. 'What I have done, and what I mean to do' may be a perfect demonstration of how to achieve classical balance with limpid language (a very French effect), but also as banal a gloss on 'past and future' as could be devised.

Montezuma's talk of the kingdoms he will conquer, of the empires he intends to gain without the Inca's help, is a reminder that in watching *The Indian Queen* and its sister extravaganzas the Restoration audience was faced with cultural questions that went beyond a hope that rhyme would not 'break' sense. These exotic, heroic dramas of rebellion, usurpation and restoration were therapy to people shaken by the experience of civil war and regicide. Turning to real places across the seas, they helped remind everyone of tensions with Catholic France: the 'bloody Altar' and attendant priests of *The Indian Queen* warned of the alleged savagery of popery, the representation of sultans and emirs were code for what excessive monarchical power might mean. But the seeds of actual empire were prominent and the consciousness of other cultures real. A significant proportion of Restoration Drama considers the problems of early colonial power; and a significant portion of the resources of the Restoration Theatre went into both glamourizing and interrogating them.

Dryden and Howard's play, with or without Purcell's music, has not been the subject of much recent criticism, but the attention it has received has polarized according to whether style or content should

prevail. Its 'pseudo-classicism', to use Allardyce Nicoll's term, critics
have tended to attribute to French influence, which, in Jean I.
Marsden's withering verdict, encouraged Dryden and Howard to
foster 'preposterous conclusions, belief in ideals and overall lack of
cynicism'.[89] French style was not ideologically neutral, since, however
little cynicism it betrayed, it could hardly conceal an anxiety that
France was, politically and culturally, a superior force deserving of
imitation. Yet in many ways *The Indian Queen* is an attempt to
refurbish heroic tragedy for the English stage. Robert D. Hume notes
its 'forward motion, psychology less freighted with the *précieuse*, and
less sophistic disputation'; in comparison with the more frankly
Francophile plays of the Earl of Orrey, spectacular successes of the
early 1660s, it is, for all its 'heroic elevation' and 'dead serious[ness]',
a model of narrative *élan*.[90]

The question of whether the play owes more to French or English
style has been overtaken by recent statements of what might appear
to be the obvious: that, since it is about Central America, its interest
might be defined in terms of the *translatio imperii*, the westward
movement of empire. Many Restoration plays that explore this theme
treat of the relationship between Christian and pagan, colonizer and
colonized. The most familiar example, Thomas Southerne's 1695 adaptation of Aphra Behn's novella *Oroonoko*, even shows what happens
when the colonized fight back. Amid this neglected body of work, *The
Indian Queen* stands as Mel Gibson's *Apocalypto* does in relation
to John Glen's ill-fated *Christopher Columbus*, representing pagan
society just before the arrival of the Western conquerors. In its
1664 dramatic form, that representation must have seemed more
ambiguous than it did in 1695, when a new musical prologue showed
an Indian boy and girl waking, as J. Douglas Canfield puts it, 'from an
idyllic sleep'. The sight of their new conquerors reassures them, since
the mission is not conquest but forgiveness. 'Forgive for what?' asks
Canfield. 'Obviously, for being pagans.'[91] This overlooks an important
point about how the text developed. The new prologue reflects
the need to find an English justification for empire. In its original form
the play implied that the Spanish invasion would be purely military,
since Mesoamerican and Iberian culture were already, in Dryden and
Howard's first version, remarkably alike.

It is patently risky to neglect the textual history of Restoration plays;
so is it to overlook the relationship between text and music in these

extravagant Restoration creations. Ever since the form of dramatic opera took root, critics have suggested that it is somehow inimical to true drama, and it is true that the large sums managers committed to this extravagant new form, conscious of competition from the music concerts that began to spring up in the afternoons, often produced results that were literally patchy.[92] Songs and choral set pieces, such as prologues and epilogues, could be assigned to existing plays without much regard for their relevance: thus, losing the masque between Fame and Envy that accompanies Zempoalla's entry in Act II would not cause the plot to grind to a halt. Yet it does serve to indicate that, while the queen's magnificence is also her doom, she remains a formidable adversary for Montezuma. 'Great minds against themselves conspire,' goes the penultimate chorus of Purcell's *Dido and Aeneas*, and the music for Zempoalla's triumphant entry strikes the same note to supply a complexity – even cynicism – that critics have found lacking in the play. Similarly, the Act III addition in which the queen's conjuror, Ismeron, appeals to the God of Dreams allows listeners to intuit a comparison with the tragic Dido that passes the reader by.[93] Purcell's musical language enriches the drama rather than diluting it. In the creation of the sumptuous theatrical event, there were, therefore, only co-authors. The life cycle of the Restoration play served to produce new grounds for authority not just through lone playwrights but in both medium and artistic process.

Endnotes

1 For a study of interregnum drama, see Dale R. Randall, *Winter Fruit: English Drama 1642–1660* (Lexington: University of Kentucky Press, 1995).

2 A figure given by Allan Richard Botica, 'Audience, playhouse and play in Restoration theatre, 1660–1710', unpublished DPhil thesis (University of Oxford, 1985).

3 *The Diary of Samuel Pepys*, 6 January 1668.

4 Ibid., 22 October 1662.

5 Downes, *Roscius Anglicanus*, 96–7.

6 See Gilli Bush-Bailey, *Treading the Bawds* (Manchester University Press, 2007).

7 For the licence, see LC 5/154, p. 35, dated 14 December 1704; in *Register*, vol. I, 388 (no. 1793).

8 Philip Stubbes lamented the public theatres in his *Anatomie of Abuses* (London, 1583). In 1980 Mary Whitehouse attempted to bring a case

against director Michael Bogdanov for staging a (failed) male rape in Howard Brenton's *The Romans in Britain* at the National Theatre.

9 British Library Additional Manuscripts collection [hereafter BL Add. MS] 22,609, fols. 85–90; reprinted in *Register*, no. 1685.

10 See Thomas Jordan, 'Prologue, to introduce the first Woman that came to act on the Stage, in the tragedy called the Moor of Venice', in his *A Royal Arbour of Loyal Poesie* (London, 1664), cited in LS1 22. John Harold Wilson, *All the King's Ladies* (University of Chicago Press, 1959), 6–8, discusses the likely identity of this first English actress. Anne Marshall is the current favourite. See Elizabeth Howe, *The First English Actresses* (Cambridge University Press, 1992), 24.

11 *Peter Hall's Diaries*, ed. John Goodwin (London: Hamish Hamilton, 1983), 311.

12 For an uncompromising account of the way professional actresses were visually exploited, see Jean I. Marsden, 'Rape, voyeurism and the Restoration stage', in Katherine M. Quinsey, ed., *Broken Boundaries: Women and Feminism in Restoration Drama* (Lexington: University Press of Kentucky, 1994), 185–200.

13 An essay by Deborah C. Payne explores this duality: 'Reified object or emergent professional? Retheorizing the Restoration actress', in J. Douglas Canfield and Deborah C. Payne, eds., *Cultural Readings of Restoration and Eighteenth-Century English Theater* (Athens: University of Georgia Press, 1995), 13–38. For chronology and the rape scene, see Derek Hughes, 'Rape on the Restoration stage', *The Eighteenth Century: Theory and Interpretation* **46** (2005), 225–36, esp. 227. For the female audience, see my study *The Ladies: Female Patronage of Restoration Drama, 1660–1700* (Oxford: Clarendon Press, 1989).

14 Virginia Scott, *Women on the Stage in Early Modern France 1540–1750* (Cambridge University Press, 2010)

15 Patent issued under the Great Seal to Thomas Killigrew, 25 April 1662, Public Records Office C66/3013, no. 20; reproduced in *Register*, no. 131 [hereafter items from the Public Records Office are given as 'PRO', followed by the reference number].

16 For actresses' pay, see Howe, *The First English Actresses*, 27.

17 Peter Thomson, *Shakespeare's Theatre*, 2nd edn (London: Routledge, 1992), 113.

18 Simon Schama, *Rembrandt's Eyes* (Harmondsworth: Penguin Books, 2000).

19 *The Diary of John Evelyn*, 17 November 1644.

20 Paul Griffiths, 'Lost tradition,' *The Times*, 9 February 1984, 10.

21 Blow's *Venus and Adonis* is thought to have been performed at court, Purcell's *Dido and Aeneas* possibly at Josias Priest's school for girls.

22 Letter from Edward Bedingfield to the Countess of Rutland, reprinted in LS1 334. On admission and process generally, see LS1, lxx–lxxiv.

23 Colley Cibber, *An Apology for the Life of Mr Colley Cibber* (London, 1740), 61–6.

24 John Dryden, 'Preface', *The Tempest, or, The Enchanted Island* (London, 1670).

25 Paulina Kewes, *Authorship and Appropriation: Writing for the Stage in England, 1660–1710* (Oxford: Clarendon Press, 1998).

26 See LS1, lxvii–lxx.

27 See LS1, 153–4, 161–2.

28 See LS1, lxxv–lxxviii.

29 Downes, *Roscius Anglicanus*, 51–2.

30 John Le Neve, *The Lives and Characters of the Most Illustrious Persons British and Foreign* (London, 1713), 534–5.

31 See William J. Burling, *Summer Theatre in London, 1661–1800* (Madison, NJ: Fairleigh Dickinson University Press, 2000).

32 Downes, *Roscius Anglicanus*, 84.

33 Tiffany Stern, *Rehearsal from Shakespeare to Sheridan* (Oxford University Press, 2000), 140.

34 LS1, 308–9.

35 See, for example, LC 5/139, p. 125, a warrant of 31 August 1668 for plays acted by the Duke's Company; reproduced in Allardyce Nicoll, *A History of Restoration Drama 1660–1700*, 4th edn (Cambridge University Press, 1950), 308. The schedule indicates the use of theatre to support Christmas festivities, with a concentration of plays in December and the New Year.

36 See my *Thomas Betterton: The Greatest Actor of the Restoration Stage* (Cambridge University Press, 2010), 124–30. The plays performed were Shadwell's *The Sullen Lovers*, from Molière's *Les Facheux*; John Caryll's *Sir Salomon Single*, from Molière's *L'Ecole des Femmes* and *L'Ecole des Maris*; and Matthew Medbourne's version of *Tartuffe*, in which the hypocritical priest becomes a scheming, licentious puritan, so turning Molière's play into Catholic propaganda.

37 LC 5/12, p. 212; reproduced in LS1, 151–2.

38 *The Diary of Samuel Pepys*, 6 January 1663, 29 September 1662; Downes, *Roscius Anglicanus*, 54.

39 The plays are Gildon's *Love's Victim* (1701), Settle's *Distress'd Innocence* (1691), Dennis's *Liberty Asserted* (1704) and Dryden's *Troilus and Cressida* (1679). Betterton acted in each of them. For Otway, see anon., 'A Satyr Against Poetry', in Vincent de Voiture, *Familiar Letters of Love, Gallantry, and Several Occasions*, 2 vols. (London, 1718), vol. I, 92.

40 Summarized by Thomson, *Shakespeare's Theatre*, 86.

41 Ibid., 68.

42 Ibid.

43 Stern, *Rehearsal*, 147, 170–2.

44 For Cibber, see his *An Apology*, 168; for Betterton, see Charles Gildon's *The Life of Mr Thomas Betterton, the Late Eminent Tragedian* (London, 1719), 15.

45 Cibber claimed that he was once given a part between 11:00 and 12:00 in the morning and was word perfect for a rehearsal later in the day; see *An Apology*, 115.

46 Aphra Behn, 'Preface', *The Dutch Lover* (London, 1673); *The Diary of Samuel Pepys*, 4 September 1667.

47 Gildon, *The Life of Mr Thomas Betterton*, 37.

48 Cited by Stern, *Rehearsal*, 183–4.

49 Shakespeare, ed. Harold Jenkins, *Hamlet* (London: Methuen, 1982), III.ii.35, 9; George Farquhar, *The Recruiting Officer* (London, 1706), 24 (II.iii.215–18); anecdote cited by Stern, *Rehearsal*, 184; for Powell, see *The Spectator*, I, 171.

50 LS1, clvii.

51 Thomas D'Urfey, 'Preface', *The Banditti* (London, 1686), a3b.

52 George Granville, 'Preface', *Heroick Love* (London, 1698), A2; for its success, see Downes, *Roscius Anglicanus*, 93.

53 See Stern, *Rehearsal*, 189–90.

54 For a rather pessimistic view of the audience, see, for example, chapter 4 of Mark S. Dawson's fine study, *Gentility and the Comic Theatre of Late Stuart London* (Cambridge University Press, 2005).

55 *The Diary of Samuel Pepys*, 18 February 1667.

56 Ibid., 20 June 1668.

57 *The Diary of John Evelyn*, 8 January 1663.

58 For the premiere, see LS1, 61; for Pepys, see *The Diary of Samuel Pepys*, 8 January 1663; the 1671 edition of the play contains epilogue reflections by Tuke on his 'innocent piece'. For 'lunatic nobility', see Hume, *The Development of English Drama*, 75.

59 John Dryden, *Sir Martin Mar-All* (London, 1668), 24.

60 *The Diary of Samuel Pepys*, 8 June, 7 September 1661.

61 Among many entries, see *The Diary of Samuel Pepys*, 1 March 1661.

62 Nahum Tate, *The History of King Lear* (London, 1681), 67 (V.vi.148–52), in Sandra Clark, ed., *Shakespeare Made Fit: Restoration Adaptations of Shakespeare* (London: Dent, 1997).

63 Tate, *The History of King Lear*, 35 (III.iv.57–60).

64 Ibid., 59 (V.v.14–19).

65 Ibid., 60 (V.v.60).

66 Ibid., 25–6 (III.ii.5–25).
67 De Sayncton, *The History of Tamerlan the Great*, trans. D'Assigny (London, 1679).
68 Downes, *Roscius Anglicanus*, 59, explains that in its early years the Duke's Company acted '*The Tragedy of King Lear*, as Mr. *Shakespear* Wrote it; before it was alter'd by Mr. *Tate*'. LS1, 358, 362, lists court performances on 9 May 1687 and 20 February 1688.
69 Clark, *Shakespeare Made Fit*, lxvii.
70 George Etherege, *The Man of Mode, or, Sir Fopling Flutter* (London, 1676), 28 (II.ii.218–53).
71 John Wilmot, Earl of Rochester, 'Song', in *Rochester: Complete Poems and Plays*, ed. Paddy Lyons (London: Dent, 1993).
72 John Dennis, *In Defence of Sir Fopling Flutter* (London, 1722), 18.
73 Laura Mulvey, 'Visual pleasure and narrative cinema', *Screen* 16 (1975), 6–18.
74 Downes, *Roscius Anglicanus*, 77.
75 The Earl of Middleton to Etherege, 7 December 1685, in LS1, 244; for Brussels, where the Duke of York was staying for his safety during the Popish Plot crisis, see letter from Princess Anne to Frances Apsley, 3 October 1679, in LS1, 282.
76 For court performances in February 1680, after an anti-Jamesian riot at Dorset Garden, and November 1685, see LS1, 284, 344.
77 Dennis, *In Defence of Sir Fopling Flutter*, 18.
78 See *The Diary of Samuel Pepys*, 1 February 1669. Kynaston had been Betterton's fellow apprentice working for the bookseller and theatre manager John Rhodes, and there is some evidence of an old family connection between them.
79 Joseph Roach, *Cities of the Dead: Circum-Atlantic Performance* (New York: Columbia University Press, 1996), 75.
80 Sir Richard Steele, *The Spectator*, no. 65
81 For performances of *The Country Wife*, see LS1, 227, 244, 322, 368, 440; for *The Plain Dealer* and James's patronage, see LS1, 344. The pension was promised for the duration of James's reign, which, unfortunately for Wycherley, turned out to be short.
82 Cibber, *An Apology*, 128. For this and earlier performances, see LS1, 256, 284, 391, 467.
83 *The Diary of John Evelyn*, 5 February 1664.
84 For *The Feast*, see LS1, xciii.
85 Warrant to the Master of the Great Wardrobe (LC 5/138, f.15) to provide Thomas Killigrew with silk 'to cloath the Musick [i.e. the orchestra] for the play called the Indian Queen': *Register*, no. 268.
86 See, for example, LS1, 461, 476.

87 For Orrery, see his letter of 23 January 1662; for Dryden, see his 'Epistle Dedicatory', *The Rival Ladies* (London, 1664).

88 Sir Robert Howard (with John Dryden), *The Indian Queen,* in *Five New Plays* (London, 1692), 115.

89 Nicoll, *A History of Restoration Drama*, 88; Jean I. Marsden, 'Tragedy and varieties of serious drama', in Susan J. Owen, ed., *A Companion to Restoration Drama* (Oxford: Blackwell, 2001), 228–42, 232.

90 Hume, *The Development of English Drama*, 242.

91 J. Douglas Canfield, *Heroes and States: On the Ideology of Restoration Tragedy* (Lexington: University Press of Kentucky, 2000), 24. See also Bridget Orr's invaluable study, *Empire on the English Stage, 1660–1714* (Cambridge University Press, 2001).

92 For a more detailed introduction and a survey of concerts, see LS1, cviii–cxxi.

93 Curtis Price, sleeve note to Henry Purcell, *The Indian Queen,* cond. Alfred Deller (Paris: Harmonia Mundi, 1976).

3 | *Playwrights*

Authority is, for certain, hardly the first attribute that springs to mind for most Restoration dramatists. Of the 600 or so known plays and entertainments written between the Restoration of Charles II and the death of Queen Anne, only a small proportion are known today by more than a handful of specialists. The same is inevitably true of the people who wrote them. Approximately 200 playwrights were active, however briefly, in the period from 1660 to 1714, but the names of fewer than thirty enjoy any sort of currency today. One-tenth of the known plays of the period are anonymous. Substantially more are by authors with only a single, invariably doomed attempt to their names. They might be doctors or critics, actors or impresarios, hacks or aristocrats. Even clergymen tried – and failed. The Reverend Joseph Arrowsmith's sole play, *The Reformation*, staged by the Duke's Company in 1672 with a heavyweight cast, 'quickly made its Exit'.[1]

Arrowsmith's play was less significant than what its existence tells us about Restoration Theatre, which fostered the contributions of large numbers of amateur playwrights with little chance of enjoying more than three hours' exposure. Necessary and disposable, they were creatures of the prevailing appetite for novelty. Pepys relates how a Navy Office colleague, Silas Taylor, caught the bug. Antiquary, naval storekeeper, musician and captain, Taylor tried his hand with a play prophetically subtitled and hoped to persuade the Duke's Company to take it. Henry Harris, by then joint manager, said he would judge it by the first act, a reasonable response that Pepys and Taylor thought rather mean. Taylor huffily took the play to the King's Company and told Pepys, with the bravado of the failed writer, that 'it will be acted there, though...they are not yet agreed upon it'. That night Pepys asked his wife, Elizabeth, to start reading the play to him as they sat in the garden – the last that has been heard of *The Serenade, or, Disappointment*.[2] Even the loyal Pepys did not finish it.

If there is little pattern to the backgrounds and future careers of these hopeful, frustrated souls, the same may be said of the dramatists whose work represents the core achievement of Restoration Drama, except that most of them attended university and descended on London as outsiders with a keen sense of opportunity that would often dwindle tragically.[3] Aphra Behn (1640?–1689) came to playwriting from a past of colonial residence, espionage and poverty, to the latter of which she returned; but John Crowne (1641–1712), son of an MP, was educated at Harvard and died well pensioned in an apartment on Great Russell Street. John Dryden (1631–1700) was a Cambridge graduate who had been reared in puritan Northamptonshire; he would marry into the minor aristocracy and convert to Catholicism, only to lose out when James II fled the country. George Etherege (1636–1692) had spent up to nine years working with or studying law before he fell in with the fast set and began to write; the family of William Congreve (1670–1729) had moved from Yorkshire to Ireland before their most famous son fled to London to study law, for no more than a few months before writing took over. Ten years earlier Thomas Southerne (1660–1746) had beaten the same path. Nahum Tate (1652–1715) also grew up in Ireland and went to university there as the son of Protestant clergy (his brother was called Faithful). Congreve's contemporary at Trinity College Dublin, George Farquhar (1677–1707), started as an actor and, unlike Congreve, died in abject poverty. Nathaniel Lee (1652?–1692), another Cambridge graduate, also started out as an actor but ended even more miserably than Farquhar: released from the lunatic asylum known as Bedlam in 1688, he was found literally dead drunk in the street four years later. Thomas Otway (1652–1685), apparently cut out of his Sussex clergyman father's will, failed to complete his Oxford degree and had to be supported with unprecedented generosity by the Duke's Company. Thomas Shadwell (1641–1692) also grew up in the shadow of loss, claiming to have received 'the Birth and Education without the Fortune of a Gentleman' after his family of Norfolk gentry had lost their money during the civil war. By contrast, the family of Sir John Vanbrugh (1664–1726) had grown rich in the sugar trade; they bought him an army commission and paid for a training in architecture, which bore spectacular fruit at Blenheim Palace and Castle Howard. The last scene of all belongs to William Wycherley (1641–1715), son of country gentry (his father had been High Steward to the Marquess of Winchester), whose success in charming his Stuart patrons spectacularly failed to outlast their dynasty. The fear and reality of debt never left him.

Playwrights, then, were party to the general feeling among theatre people that their livelihoods were precarious, for all the differences in social class that separated them. Yet in their difference they also brought reassurance. To actors, many of whom were Londoners born and bred and from solid trade backgrounds, these migrant playwrights brought the sophistication of university learning combined with the feeling that the metropolis was the only worthwhile place to be. Just as actors might dread having to work beyond the two licensed companies in what the order papers tended to describe as 'Town Halls Moat Halls Guildhalls, School Houses or other convenient places' (surely a euphemism) in Maidstone, Norwich or a dozen other provincial locales, so playwrights reinforced London's cultural supremacy with their disparagement of country cousins from Shropshire to Hampshire.[4] They were partly covering their own tracks – a preoccupation doubly enforced by the accelerating prestige of the city and the trauma of civil war.

Translators and adaptors: Wycherley and *The Country Wife* (1675)

As theatre managers depended on revivals, so playwrights turned frequently to existing plays for ideas. Ancient Rome, Renaissance England, seventeenth-century Spain and contemporary France provided a wealth of material across all dramatic genres; contemporary England too. The dividing line between native and foreign borrowing and between translation and adaptation is often very hard to draw, but anxiety about where it lay is obvious.

The playwriting career of William Wycherley shows how. His first comedy, *Love in a Wood* (1671), looks back to James Shirley's *The Changes, or, Love in a Maze* (1632) and to the mixed plot of Etherege's first play, *The Comical Revenge, or, Love in a Tub* (1664), borrowing its conventional love and honour plot from Pedro Calderón's 1632 *Mañanas de Abril y Mayo* (in English, *April and May Mornings*). Calderón's *El Maestro de Danzar* was the starting point for Wycherley's second play, *The Gentleman Dancing Master* (1672), which is nevertheless more notable for its references to *Romeo and Juliet*, then in the repertory of the Duke's Company. By the time Wycherley wrote *The Country Wife*, first performed in January 1675, his eye had been caught by the prodigious output of Molière, whose *L'Ecole des Femmes* (1662) had been a landmark success in Paris. That play gave Wycherley the idea of the reformed rake Pinchwife, who discovers the dangers of his would-be bride's innocence. But that is only half the story. Not only did Wycherley introduce the 'love and honour' pairing of Alithea and Harcourt familiar from his previous plays, adding to them the idiotically self-cuckolding Sparkish; in place of Molière's honourable young suitor Horace he devised a figure suggested by the Roman dramatist Terence's *Eunuchus*. The predatory, depraved rake Horner pretends that his bravura sexual history has caused him to have an operation that makes him no threat to any woman's (or any husband's) honour. Horner is a nightmarish incarnation of Pinchwife's own past: a satiric nod, perhaps, at the impossibility of the Stuart dynasty reforming itself at a time of widespread disillusionment with Charles's regime. In this sense it is the antithesis of Etherege's *The Man of Mode*, written a year later, whose rakish hero successfully sloughs off his past. Satire was the prime objective of Wycherley's final play, *The Plain Dealer* (1676). Like *The Country Wife*, this play appears to be an adaptation of a single Molière play (in this case *Le Misanthrope*, whose hero, Alceste, is a comic Coriolanus who cannot bear to live in polite society) but in fact turns out to be a palimpsest of other French plays, novels and real-life observation. Its satire tapped into the conscience of the last Stuart monarch. Seeing the play at court in December 1685, James II, ashamed of his late brother's excesses, ordered Wycherley's release from the Fleet prison.[5]

If Wycherley took freely from many different sources, he also adapted individual scenes with a close eye on the original. Disguising any openly satirical intent, such passages also give a valuable insight into his working methods and the texture of his writing. Compare this passage from the 1971 Richard Wilbur translation of Act II Scene 5 of *L'Ecole des Femmes* – a rendering faithful in its ingenuity – with Wycherley's free rendition in *The Country Wife*. Here, Molière's Arnolphe is interrogating Agnès about her recent meeting with her young admirer, Horace.

ARNOLPHE: Besides these compliments, these sweet addresses,
 Were there not also kisses, and caresses?
AGNÈS: Oh, yes! He took my hands, and kissed and kissed
 Them both, as if he never would desist.

ARNOLPHE: And did he not take – something else as well?
   Agh!
AGNÈS: Well, he –
ARNOLPHE: Yes?
AGNÈS: Took –
ARNOLPHE: What?
AGNÈS: I dare not tell.
   I fear that you'll be furious with me.
ARNOLPHE: No.
AGNÈS: Yes.
ARNOLPHE: No, no.
AGNÈS: Then promise not to be.
ARNOLPHE: I promise.
AGNÈS: He took my – oh, you'll have a fit.
ARNOLPHE: No.
AGNÈS: Yes.
ARNOLPHE: No, no. The devil! Out with it!
   What did he take from you?
AGNÈS: He took –
ARNOLPHE: *(aside)* God save me!
AGNÈS: He took the pretty ribbon that you gave me.
 Indeed he begged so that I couldn't resist.
ARNOLPHE: *(taking a deep breath)* Forget the ribbon.
 Tell me: once he'd kissed
 Your hands, what else did he do, as you recall?
AGNÈS: Does one do other things?
ARNOLPHE: No, not at all...[6]

Molière makes virtuosic use of rhyme, its effect aptly captured in Richard Wilbur's translation. He makes us hear its rhythm at the start of the exchange, with Arnolphe and Agnès exchanging self-contained couplets, before stretching it out between the speakers with musical precision so that, by the end, each completes the other's speech. Arnolphe's exasperation and Agnès's fear build like a counterpoint within the tight formal structure of the dialogue, creating and releasing tension. Structured according to the *Commedia dell'Arte* convention of the *lazzo*, in which highly skilled performers repeat a physical routine for comic effect, it treats human psychology as an elegant, symmetrical prison from which there is no escape. In Agnès's innocence, Arnolphe has met not his ideal but his nemesis.

Wycherley's version of the scene turns the husband into a morbid obsessive and his wife into a woman who turns out to understand male psychology better than he could have suspected. *Commedia* is transformed into the satirical comedy of manners as Pinchwife requires Margery to revisit the primal act of disobedience yet again, like a detective combing a crime scene. There is the added complication that Pinchwife has insisted that Margery appear in public dressed as a young man, to deflect Horner's attention.

PINCHWIFE: Come, tell me, I say.

MARGERY: Lord, haven't I told it an hundred times over?

PINCHWIFE: (*aside*) I would try if, in the repetition of the ungrateful tale, I could find her altering it in the least circumstance, for if her story be false, she is so too. – Come, how was it, baggage?

MARGERY: Lord, what pleasure you take to hear it, sure!

PINCHWIFE: No, you take more in telling it, I find; but speak, how was it?

MARGERY: He carried me up into the house next to the Exchange.

PINCHWIFE: So, and you two were only in the room.

MARGERY: Yes, for he sent away a youth that was there, for some dried fruit and China oranges.

PINCHWIFE: Did he so? Damn him for it – and for –

MARGERY: But presently came up the gentlewoman of the house.

PINCHWIFE: O, 'twas well she did; but what did he do whilst the fruit came?

MARGERY: He kissed me an hundred times and told me he fancied he kissed my fine sister, meaning me, you know, whom he said he loved with all his soul and bid me be sure to tell her so and to desire her to be at her window by eleven of the clock this morning and he would walk under it at that time.

PINCHWIFE: (*aside*) And he was as good as his word, very punctual – a pox reward him for't.

MARGERY: Well, and he said if you were not within, he would come up to her, meaning me, you know, bud, still.

PINCHWIFE: (*aside*) So – he knew her certainly; but for this confession, I am obliged to her simplicity. – But what, you stood very still when he kissed you?

MARGERY: Yes, I warrant you; would you have had me discovered myself?

PINCHWIFE: But you told me he did some beastliness to you, as you called it; what was it?

MARGERY: Why, he put –

PINCHWIFE: What?

MARGERY: Why, he put the tip of his tongue between my lips and so mousled me – and I said, I'd bite it.

PINCHWIFE: An eternal canker seize it, for a dog!

MARGERY: Nay, you need not be so angry with him neither, for to say truth, he has the sweetest breath I ever knew.[7]

Wycherley's scene assumes a different performance style: he expects a pair of soloists rather than a duet. The explicit cues, adroitly absorbed into the psychological dynamic of interrogation, point to the culture of actors' 'parts' whereby performers focus first on their own roles and only secondarily on those around them. From that culture Wycherley fashions an appealing but disturbing solipsism in his characters. Pinchwife's attention is split between this instance of Margery's narrative and all its predecessors, Margery's between absorption in the scene of pleasure she is recollecting and her growing resentment of her husband. Whereas Molière looked back to the older form of drama that was *Commedia*, Wycherley looked forward to the leisurely psychological sophistication of the novel. Like other dramatists of the period, he found new textures in contemporary French romances and memoirs and learned from them a multi-layered, inward approach to characterization that contrasts vividly with the orchestrated, farce-like physicality of Molière.

But Wycherley learned a deeper lesson from his sources. Molière was the pre-eminent dramatist of male folly: his protagonists dream of a control they can never exercise. The complexity of *The Country Wife* – and much of its critical controversy – is founded on its exploration of male weakness in the context of what looks like a conventional 'libertine' plot. In what sense does the scheming Horner succeed? Even sexually, he turns out to be easily exhausted. The play's most notorious scene features a number of women visiting him off-stage to buy what is euphemistically called 'china'. Before long he has to make the shamefaced admission that he has run out. Lady Fidget and her friends may be voracious ('What, do you think if he had any left, I would not have had it too?' she asks), but they are hardly passive victims in a play in which almost every character is an object of satire, with the possible exception of the country wife herself, who discovers in all innocence the pleasures of sex.

It remains routine for critics of adaptations such as *The Country Wife* to suggest that they are merely coarsened versions of the original texts. Both technically and morally, there is a sense in which the scene from *The Country Wife* is less 'pure' than its counterpart in *L'Ecole des Femmes*: Margery Pinchwife embodies the doubleness of the Restoration actress – a gorgeous airhead who knows her pleasures but turns out to have a sharp line in talking back – and there is no attempt to reproduce the giddy virtuosity of Molière's rhymes. Absorbing the

French master meant keeping him at bay, and, politically, that was just what was at stake in the business of translation and adaptation.

Calderón and Corneille were educated by Jesuits; Racine was a fiercely radical Catholic; Molière was the darling of the French court. What did it mean to adapt these icons of the great European enemy for the English stage? What implications did it have for politics and for conceptions of the playwright's function? Paulina Kewes's narrative of increasing authorial prestige poses one answer. Borrowing from French and Spanish playwrights was necessary for as long as France, with the Stuarts in its pocket, was regarded as the superior cultural and military power; as England asserted itself through the campaigns of William III, however, French models were discarded by a process of cultural exorcism. So, the rash of borrowing from Continental sources we find in the 1660s and 1670s was an act of anxious homage ahead of the time when new models of Englishness could assert themselves. This is only partly true, however, and not only because French culture was more deeply engrained in English stage practice than could comfortably be admitted. At any time between 1660 and 1714, when John Ozell published his translation of the complete works of Molière, it was likely that playwrights would express uncomplicated admiration for the French playwright's achievement. Where such homage seems anxious, it was determined by local fears about commercial success or recent political events. Wycherley paraded his dependence on French sources while his contemporary Shadwell tended to disguise them, laying claim to a more fundamental Englishness based on the works of Ben Jonson.[8]

Playwrights and censorship

A more immediate political challenge was posed by the threat of censorship. Numerous Restoration plays were suppressed because they seemed to encourage undesirable political views, with censorship inevitably becoming more intense in times of national emergency. Playwrights saw an opportunity in events such as the Popish Plot crisis to exploit, and in some cases stoke, public anxiety; theatre companies, their box-office takings hit, took greater risks with repertory that in fatter times they might have overlooked or toned down. As the example of Nathaniel Lee's *Lucius Junius Brutus* has shown, the strategy could backfire. In the same month the King's Company tried its hand with a story that had always spelled danger. The fall of the doomed and decadent King Richard II, controversial enough in Shakespeare's day to attract first censorship and then the championship of would-be usurpers, became newly topical in Nahum Tate's version. After the first version failed to gain a licence, Tate thought to throw the Lord Chamberlain's office off his trail by simply changing the setting and all the names, so producing *The Sicilian Usurper*. He underestimated their intelligence, and the King's Playhouse was shut for ten days. On the last day of the closure Charles II was reported to be on the verge of doing the same to the Duke's.[9]

If Tate showed a kind of heroic stupidity in his dealings with the censor, the example of Dryden's *The Spanish Fryar* shows how hard it was for playwrights to immunize their work against the march of events and the sporadic attention of the censor. The play attracted 'all the world' for its premiere in November 1680 – the height of the Exclusion Crisis – and was still going strong four years later, but in December 1686 it was banned by order of James II.[10] Three years on, after James's deposition, it was performed again but proved so embarrassing for James's daughter, now Queen Mary, that she had to take refuge behind her fan.[11] In the longer term Dryden paid for his attempt to pacify both ends of the political spectrum with a double plot. On the one hand, he seems to take a stand against usurping conspirators via an Oedipal narrative: thinking himself a mere low-born soldier, but in love with the usurper's daughter Queen Leonora, Torrismond discovers that he is really the son of the murdered king, declaring in a moment of melodramatic recognition worthy of *East Lynne* or *Star Wars* that

> The usurper of my throne, my house's ruin,
> The murderer of my father, is my wife![12]

But, then, Restoration politics was rather melodramatic: married to her father's usurper, Mary might well have reached for her fan in 1689. Lest the audience of Popish Plot London failed to grasp the point in 1680, Torrismond concludes the play with a couplet that might have had the entire Stuart family (barring one illegitimate son) rising from its seats to cheer:

> But let the bold conspirator beware
> For heaven makes princes its peculiar care.[13]

The reason why the play was not hounded by Whigs in 1680 was precisely what led to its prohibition in 1686. The second plot concerns the comic, venal Catholic priest of the play's title, Father Dominic, a creation partly drawn from Dryden's deep love of Chaucer ('I always loved the female saints,' he drools), but an easy target when tragic, principled priests were being condemned to death on the word of Titus Oates. For James, it proved too much.[14] Given the Jamesian bias of the main plot it might be inferred that the play was banned in 1686 not because of its politics but because it was thought to be in desperately poor taste: a trivialization of martyrdom that, like Chris Morris's 2009 film *Four Lions* (Islamic jihad meets *Dad's Army*), was greeted with hilarity by some audiences and disgust by others. In the 1660s the tragicomic play style that combined serious and comic plots had been the perfect vehicle for regulating the emotional ambiguity of a Restoration built upon regicide. By the 1680s such regulation had back-pedalled into fragmentation, the double plot an index of divisions that resisted healing.

The experiences of Lee, Tate and Dryden show how high politics supplied a motive for censorship. Lower-level allusion and perceptions of moral failings played just as important a role, and here too actors took a significant share of pain for the transgressions of writers. In April 1667 Edward Howard's *The Change of Crowns* featured a bumptious provincial, played by John Lacy, who laments the corruption of the court: not an ideal subject when, in Pepys's words, the 'King and Queen, the Duke of York and Duchess...and all the Court' had made a block booking. Expecting to see the 'great' and 'serious' play again the day afterwards, Pepys was, predictably, disappointed. But it wasn't Edward Howard who had incurred the king's wrath. '[A]ngry at the liberty taken by Lacy's part to abuse him to his face', Charles II closed the theatre and imprisoned the actor; ownership of parts, the foundation of an actor's professional identity, also carried risks. It was not the end of the story. Released from gaol, Lacy met Howard at the theatre and the two men had an ugly spat, with Lacy being saved from being 'run through' only because he was 'too mean a fellow to fight with'. Then Howard complained to the king, who apparently skated over the playwright's responsibility: '[T]he whole house is silenced,' wrote Pepys, 'and the gentry seem to rejoice much at it, the house being become too insolent.'[15] Across the normally collaborative enterprise of playwriting, in which writers and actors worked together to produce performable scripts, might be etched the dividing line of social class.

The loyal playwright: Thomas Otway and *Don Carlos* (1676)

Playwrights were never more political than when the threat of the censor lay miles off – in other words, when a powerful patron was so charmed by a play's attentions that bounty followed. Politically, this was often a theatre not of dissent but assent. Among the many Faustian bargains so struck, no writer in the period made better box office of loyal sentiments than Thomas Otway, whose epistles to his patrons almost matched his ardour for the woman who played most of his leading roles, Elizabeth Barry. His 1675 dedication of *Alcibiades* to the Earl of Middlesex reads:

[U]nder your umbrage only I would court protection, to whom heaven has given a soul, whose endowments are as much above flattery, as itself abhors it; and which are as impossible to be described, as I am unable to comprehend them. But as poorest pilgrims, when they visit shrines, will make some presents where they kneel: so I have here brought mine...[16]

The mention – indeed, the metaphorical enactment – of the Catholic rite of pilgrimage demonstrates Otway's intense loyalty to the Duke's Company, for which all his plays were written. His next play marked the first high point of his commitment to the Duke's cause and proved one of the biggest successes of the period. *Don Carlos*, which premiered in June 1676, was perfectly timed to coincide with James's public renunciation of the Anglican faith: the moment when, most vulnerable to satire, he most needed support. Otway's choice of subject was hardly an obvious one; in fact, he turned material that was downright dangerous into pure political gold. What better way – or what worse – of celebrating the next Catholic King of England than by putting on stage the last one?

He found his plot in a French novel.[17] Philip II of Spain, formerly married to Mary I of England, is rendered as a tyrant who had promised the radiant Elizabeth to his son Carlos only to marry her himself. Distracting the young prince from this Oedipal nightmare are his pursuit by the scheming Princess Eboli and his determination to join the rebellion against Spanish rule in Flanders. A Whiggish writer could have taken the same material and turned it into a bitter anti-Catholic polemic: audiences could all too easily have associated Philip with the Duke of York and Carlos with the Duke of Monmouth. As it was, Otway clearly managed to persuade James himself – for he was the play's dedicatee – that it was *his* situation that was best represented by the ardent, disappointed Carlos. 'I was born high, and will not fall less great,' exclaims the hero, 'Since triumphs crowned my birth, I'll have my fate'[18] (no triumphs crowned Monmouth's birth, for obvious reasons). Consistently, Otway suggests that Philip is a kind of Charles II, a ruler who breaks up meetings for a bout of sex – 'Now winged with rapture let us fly, my sweet,' he cries at the end of the first scene – and Carlos representative of the destitution that exile would bring for James and for his Church:

> [H]alf my miseries thou can'st not know:
> Make myself happy! Bid the damned do so;
> Who in sad flames, must be for ever tossed,
> Yet still in view of the loved heaven they've lost.[19]

These analogies made it important for Otway to engineer a conclusion less bleak than the source, which showed Carlos dying a Roman bathtub death and his father succumbing to ulcers and lice. He decided to give them time for a reconciliation before Carlos dies in Elizabeth's arms and Philip 'runs off raving'.

Thomas Betterton, who commissioned the piece and played Philip, thought its substantial commercial success outstripped its quality.[20] The initial run of ten performances was startling indeed and earned, according to John Downes, 'more money than any preceding modern tragedy'.[21] Betterton would have known as well as anyone that Otway had dolloped onto his French source lashings of Shakespeare. Carlos is a pastiche Hamlet, haunting his father's wedding like a dark cloud when all else appears to be sunshine; the scheming Don John parodies Monmouth in his politics and Shakespeare's bastard Edmund in his language; when he becomes jealous of his son, Philip is an off-the-peg Othello. The credibility of the piece lay partly in references to other performances as well as older texts. But it is possible too that Betterton simply underestimated the play's potential for being read as though it were anything but a tribute to the duke, who had allowed the playwright to kiss his hand 'in token of [his] permission to make a dedication'.[22] He might well wonder how a play so professedly loyal to such a controversial figure could succeed as it did. Perhaps the answer lay in the profoundly ambiguous effect of Otway's baroque extravagance. When the curtain went up on the first act, and the audience saw the Spanish court in all its gleaming splendour, it was a frightening glimpse of their own future, a dystopia that lay a mere king's death away. When the play was reprinted in 1695 readers could scoff at Otway's professions of loyalty while finding fresh entertainment, or bitter regret, in the idea of a Catholic king running off raving.

Writing as a woman: Aphra Behn's *The Luckey Chance* (1686)

Sources and politics have been a long-standing point of focus for studies of Aphra Behn – more so than for the other women playwrights who made it to the Restoration Stage, such as Mary Pix, Susanna Centlivre, Katherine Phillips and Mary de la Riviere Manley. Allegations of undue borrowing haunted early criticism of Behn's work. If they provided cover for male anxiety about her role as a female writer, they also underestimated the speed with which she picked up how to turn current events into drama, how to construct trickster plots in the style of Thomas Middleton and John Marston or how to use Molière to leaven satire with psychology; or simply how to look at the comic style of her contemporaries on the London stage and give it an ingenious, sideways slant. Her rakish heroes are generally less appealing and successful than those of Etherege and Wycherley. Yet they sometimes embody a world view that Otway, fellow stalwart of the Duke's Company, would have found congenial.

Behn's biography suggests an ambiguous allegiance to the Stuart dynasty. She was on good terms with people who would become its bitter critics, such as Rochester and the Duke of Buckingham, and had an affair with a man called John Hoyle who was suspected of outright republicanism. The group of plays critics sometimes refer to as her 'Tory comedies' – both parts of *The Rover*, *The Roundheads* and *The City Heiress* – certainly express support for a Yorkist ideology during the five years (1677 to 1682) when it was needed most. But they do so in an unusual way. As Robert D. Markley has put it, the plays evoke

a golden age that paradoxically can be represented only in the refracted images of her heroes' exile and dispossession.[23]

They are, like Rochester's satires, a lament for lost royalist unity but with a strong infusion of hope that King James II, of all people, might somehow restore it – an exercise in doomed wishful thinking if ever there was one. But wishful thinking is precisely the business of *The Luckey Chance*, a play that has frustrated source hunters and was the first that Behn wrote after a silence of nearly four years following *The False Count* in 1682.

Since *The Luckey Chance* was first performed in April 1686, it is reasonable to infer that Behn was encouraged to write it by the accession of King James II the previous year. Repertory at that time looked back. Records of public and court performances show a succession of plays that had been popular in the 1660s, such as Shakespeare's *Hamlet* and *Othello*, Fletcher's *The Humorous Lieutenant*, Webster's *The Duchess of Malfi* and Dryden's *An Evening's Love*.[24] A play such as Behn's, which deals with the attempts of the impoverished Gayman – symbolically christened 'Charles' – to prize Julia from the gross clutches of her moneybags husband, the splendidly named Sir Cautious Fulbank, sits comfortably in such familiar territory, as does the parallel subplot in which a more conventionally appealing Belmour contrives to get the better of Sir Feeble Fainwood's attempts to marry Laetitia. Even the casting would cause minds to drift back to an age that seemed golden both for theatre people and Stuart ideologues, with Betterton (now stout and fifty) as Gayman and, in case anyone felt inclined to credit his character with sympathetic intelligence, James Nokes as Sir Cautious. It was unusual for Betterton to play a Behn hero rather than their square-jawed foils, so here perhaps was a statement that the excitement of early Restoration stardom was to be consciously revived.

The rake's attractions had diminished as his girth had grown, however; Gayman is unattractively obsolete in a way Belmour is not. Consider this scene, at the start of Act II. Gayman is at his miserable lodging, 'his old campaign coat tied about him; very melancholy'. He begins with an old Cavalier lament on his exile from love and fortune but, when his servant, Rag, suggests he might pay court to his landlady instead, he soon moves to the kind of ranting misogyny Behn was quick to identify in rakes and bankers alike, having first established that, for an aristocratic mindset, moral and financial bankruptcy are near relations.

GAYMAN: Curse on my birth! Curse on my faithless fortune!
  Curse on my stars, and cursed be all – but love!
  That dear, that charming sin, though it has pulled
  Innumerable mischiefs on my head,
  I have not, nor I cannot find repentance for.
  No – let me die despised, unbraided, poor;

Let fortune, friends, and all abandon me,
But let me hold thee, thou soft smiling god
Close to my heart while life continues there,
Till the last pantings of my vital blood.
May the last spark of life and fire be love's!
Enter Rag
How now, Rag, what's o'clock?

RAG: My belly can inform you better than my tongue.

GAYMAN: Why, you gormandising vermin you, what have you done with the threepence I gave you a fortnight ago?

RAG: Alas, sir, that's all gone, long since.

GAYMAN: You gutling rascal, you are enough to breed famine in a land. I have known some industrious footmen, that have not only gotten their own livings, but a pretty livelihood for their masters too.

RAG: Aye, till they came to the gallows, sir.

GAYMAN: Very well, sirrah, they died in an honourable calling. But hark'ee, Rag: I have business, very earnest business abroad this evening. Now, were you a rascal of docity [i.e. quick on the uptake], you would invent a way to get home my last suit that was laid in lavender, with the appurtenances thereunto belonging, as periwig, cravat, and so forth.

RAG: Faith, master, I must deal in the black art, then, for no human means will do't; and now I talk of the black art, master, try your power once more with my landlady.

GAYMAN: Oh! Name her not, the thought of it turns my stomach. A sight of her is a vomit, but he's a bold hero that dares venture on her for a kiss, and beyond that, sure, is hell itself.

Gayman's last clause is a startling comic reminiscence of Lear's mad denunciation of women as 'Centaurs' from the waist down: '[T]here's hell, there's darkness, / There is the sulphurous pit.' But he has no corresponding wish for civet to sweeten his imagination.[25] His disgust for less attractive prospects than Julia is a narcissistic endorsement of his own (supposed) appeal. The scene drives a further wedge between Gayman and the ideal of the glamorous Cavalier. His old campaign coat is a dead relic, useless for civil success; he must put on the costume of the man about town if he is to get his way with Julia. If the old coat is a symbol of an unrewarded authenticity, his 'last suit' renders his libertine persona as precisely that: a role, and moreover one for which he seems entirely dependent on a servant's intervention. In Jules Wright's 1984 revival of the play at the Lyric Hammersmith, Alan Rickman caught this note of languid arrogance perfectly.

So, in what sense did this remain a play loyal to the interests of the newly crowned Catholic King James? Gayman's soliloquy is key, its blank verse nobility contrasting with the earthy prose of the exchange with Rag (such extremes of style have always been the lingua franca of the rakish class, whether at White's coffee house in the 1660s or the Bullingdon Club in the 1990s). Like Behn's 1676 tragedy *Abdelazer* and the earlier poems of Robert Southwell and Richard Crashaw, the poetry creates a violently erotic metaphor for the ardours of Catholic devotion. Gayman's 'last spark of life and fire' brings to the Restoration rake the body language of Bernini's orgasmic *Ecstasy of St Teresa*. Having taken his vow of hermit-like poverty, Gayman can devote all his thoughts to worshipping the 'soft, smiling god' that stays '[c]lose to [his] heart' whatever the weather. It is possible to read such language ironically, of course, but more true to the disturbingly double impact of Behn's plays to see them, in Markley's words, as manifestations of

radical Royalism...idealizations of desire...inclinations to cut rather than untie the Gordian knot of political and sexual repression, self-policing morality, and bourgeois materialism.[26]

Markley's words indicate a truly individual formula for any writer, but especially a woman: so radically conservative as to represent a threat to normal assumptions about what is right and normal behaviour.

The contradictions in Behn's work are complemented by those she identified in the business of writing as a woman. Frequently the prefatory material to her plays laments the hypocrisy of critics more offended by her sexual frankness than that of many of her male contemporaries. In the preface to *The Luckey Chance*, her indignation turns into a striking and complex manifesto:

All I ask, is the privilege for my masculine part the poet in me (if any such you will allow me) to tread in those successful paths my predecessors have so long thrived in, to take those measures that both the ancient and modern writers have set me, and by which they pleased the world so well. If I must not, because of my sex, have this freedom, but that you will usurp all to yourselves, I lay down my quill, and you shall hear no more of me – no, not so much as to make comparisons, because I will be kinder to my brothers of the pen than they have been to a defenceless woman – for I am not content to write for a third day only. I value fame as much as if I had been born a hero.

The very existence of the woman playwright is presented as being in the gift of a male cartel. Behn wishes to join, to show the 'masculine part' that is her writing self; by political implication, that would be her natural right, since the alternative is for men to 'usurp' the business of writing 'all to [them]selves' (the term allies such carping men to the defeated Monmouth and confirms Behn in her radical loyalty to James). She is not afraid to play the vulnerability card, but the paradoxical effect of doing so is to suggest that it is precisely because she is a woman – literally without the 'masculine part' – that she should be allowed to write, since it is always ungallant to attack a defenceless woman. It has been argued that this proposes 'a radical split between her work and her private self', since the public self, as for many powerful women since, is compelled to present itself as masculine.[27] Leaving aside the fact that Behn's statement of her own position is repeatedly mirrored in that of her heroines, her language of the 'masculine part' seems as much private as public: 'the poet in me' would be silenced, not obliterated, by male censorship; it is as much a part of her private self as the 'defenceless woman', and therein lies the real boldness of her statement. There is no radical split, but a radical, essential hybridity of self.

Behn's desire for 'fame' points to a hope – forlorn for centuries until her revival in modern university syllabuses – that readers would be kinder to her than audiences and even actors. From *The Dutch Lover* (1673) onwards, the suspicion lingered that those rehearsing her work went about it in a slapdash way because they thought it would fail. Against such odds, Behn regularly reached the third, or author's benefit, day, but was clearly spurred on by the less material rewards of publication. Defying her critics to stop her writing for the theatre, she mounts the more daring boast that she is intruding not just into the world of theatre but into world literature. Valuing 'fame' as much as any 'hero', she offers to walk in the footsteps of 'ancient' writers with the confidence of a John Milton: a hand overplayed, perhaps, but endorsed by her very ability to say so at all in print.

Playwrights in theory

Such a resounding claim voiced Behn's satisfaction in having survived so long as a writer. When she published *The Dutch Lover* she distanced herself from those who thought of drama as a 'grand affair of

human life', preferring instead a more immediate, commercial justification: 'I studied only to make this as entertaining as I could.'[28] It was
the index of a suspicion that 'discours[ing] formally about the rules' of
drama was a pastime for dull, university-educated men programmed to
prefer the past to the present, an imposition of 'politic grave fool[s]'
upon 'monarch wit'.[29] Her language implies that the Stuart regime
gave licence to a creativity stifled by the pedantry of critics tarred with
the brush of puritan gravity. With experience came greater willingness
to engage with the civic purpose of drama, and her critical language in
the later 1670s starts to show the influence of Dryden's essays. In the
prologue to one of her last plays, *The Emperor in the Moon* (1687),
there is even a potted history of Restoration Drama that attempts to
define Behn's own niche amid a downward spiral from 'heroes' and
'gods' through satire and 'humbler comedy' that finally 'dwindl[ed]
down to farce'. The collapse of taste is, ultimately, a collapse of
allegiance to Stuart magnificence. Lacking the technical assurance
of Dryden, Behn's verse mimicry nonetheless captures the slow erosion
of faith in the heroism of drama and politics alike:

> Some dying love-sick queen each night you enjoyed,
> And with magnificence, at last were cloyed.

A cognate but more elusive form of politics preoccupied Dryden and
others who rightly applied a politic gravity to the business of considering
the conditions for success in dramatic writing. How French had English
dramatic writing become? Were French models of drama in fact more
English than people supposed? How should an English dramatic tradition be defined, and who were its best exemplars? Some of the busiest
playwrights of the age – Dryden, Shadwell, Crowne and D'Urfey – wrote
extensively about the relationship between their work and existing
bodies of dramatic theory, whether English, French or ancient Greek;
others now known largely for their criticism, such as Thomas Rymer
and John Dennis, tried their hand – with limited success – at putting
theory into practice. Rymer's flatulent neoclassical tragedy of 1678,
Edgar, or, The English Monarch, probably did not even match the
achievement of Joseph Arrowsmith's *The Reformation* in reaching the
stage for a single performance; its publication bordered on vanity.

Partly because of its marvellously assured four-way dialogue,
Dryden's *An Essay of Dramatick Poesie* is often taken as the paradigmatic work of Restoration dramatic criticism. But if it succeeds in

capturing a panorama of competing views on the virtues of French versus English, ancient versus modern practice, its form is nearly unique and its conclusions part of a much wider dialogue that evolved well beyond the moment of the late 1660s and the Dutch War, when *entente cordiale* was necessarily flavoursome. Some of the least temperate dialogue took place within the closed circle of Dryden's own family. His brother-in-law, Sir Robert Howard, is Crites to Dryden's Neander in the *Essay*, and their disagreements over rhyming couplets, Aristotelian unities and the merits of older drama spilled out in a series of publications. Underneath rumbled a more fundamental concern that will be familiar in a poststructuralist world. Perhaps with one eye on the background of his parvenu brother-in-law and measuring him by the standards of those who populated the boxes, Howard thought Dryden arrogant in assuming that the author should prescribe rules at all. It was for the audience to decide, even when it came to something as apparently clear-cut as dramatic genre: '[I]n the difference of tragedy and comedy...there can be no determination but by the taste.'[30]

More pointed still was Dryden's sparring with Thomas Shadwell over the merits of Ben Jonson's plays, prompted by the *Essay* and then continued over a series of prefaces by both. Jonson's comedy of humours endowed Restoration dramatists with a legacy that is apparent simply from their lists of *dramatis personae*. From Horner and Dorimant to Addle and Witwoud, the name helps determine the fate of hundreds of characters. Dryden championed a quality of wit or 'sharpness of conceit' that presumed the more supple, mobile interaction not only of Fletcher's and Shakespeare's plays but in the conversation of the most refined sort of people; this was perhaps his best rebuke to his brother-in-law Howard. In the epilogue to the second part of *The Conquest of Granada*, Dryden marked a high point of confidence that the dark past of civic strife, the cloying legacy of humours that doomed people to repeat their mistakes, had finally been shed. If he was answering and to some extent bending to Howard, he also had in mind Shadwell's more democratic but darker assessment of the purpose of comedy, which was to expose the 'cheats, villainies, and troublesome follies in the common conversation of the world'.[31] Here is Dryden's epilogue:

> They, who have best succeeded on the stage,
> Have still conformed their genius to their age.
> This Jonson did mechanic humour show,
> When men were dull, and conversation low.

Then comedy was faultless, but 'twas coarse:
Cobb's tankard was a jest, and Otter's horse.
And, as their comedy, their love was mean;
Except, by chance, in some one laboured scene,
Which must atone for an ill-written play,
They rose, but at their height could seldom stay.
Fame was then cheap, and the first comer sped;
And they have kept it since, by being dead.
But, were they now to write, when critics weigh
Each line, and every word, throughout a play,
None of them, no, not Jonson in his height,
Could pass without allowing grains for weight.
Think it not envy, that these truths are told;
Our poet's not malicious, though he's bold.
'Tis not to brand them, that their faults are shown.
But, by their errors, to excuse his own.
If love and humour now are higher raised,
'Tis not the poet, but the age is praised.
Wit's now arrived to a more high degree;
Our native language more refined and free.
Our ladies and our men now speak more wit
In conversation, than those poets writ.
Then, one of these is consequently true;
That what this poet writes comes short of you,
And imitates you ill (which most he fears),
Or else his writing is not worse than theirs.
Yet, though you judge (as sure the critics will),
That some before him writ with greater skill,
In this one praise he has their fame surpassed,
To please an age more gallant than the last.

Restoration prologues and epilogues can be described as a species of stand-up comedy in which the performer, half in and half out of character, jokes with different sections of the audience to plead on the company's or the play's behalf. Dryden's epilogue demands and gives nourishment to performance, from the innuendo of 'They rose, but at their height could seldom stay' (a line that would have suited equally, but resounded differently in, the voices of Michael Mohun and Nell Gwyn, either of whom may have spoken it) to the halting stress in 'Except, by chance, in some one laboured scene', which makes the line plod along as dully as the scene it describes. Yet its performativity is inseparable from its ingenuity and consistency as criticism. The actor is not the author but speaks the author's words, so that the performance of the epilogue is an act of advocacy bent on sustaining a tone of reasonable defence: 'Our poet's not malicious, though he's bold.' Made both visible and distant by the actor, the author seeks ultimate refuge in precisely the body identified by Sir Robert Howard: the gallant, refined and witty audience. Dryden's critical argument is therefore not simply explained but enacted by the performer.

Not everyone was convinced, and Dryden resorted to a 'Defence of the Epilogue', better known as *An Essay on the Dramatic Poetry of the Last Age*. Here, he finds a number of plays by Shakespeare and Fletcher to be 'grounded on impossibilities' or 'meanly written', and devotes pages to identifying imperfections in Jonson's style. Tradition casts him as the first person to bemoan 'the preposition in the end of the sentence' as a 'common fault' of Jonson's, although it is less commonly pointed out that he admits to having 'lately observed [the same fault] in my own writings'. But it was less infelicity than indulgence that concerned him. The 'Defence' reserves its sternest language for those who spend their time 'perpetually playing with... words', in particular clergymen, 'the first corrupters of eloquence, and the last reformed from vicious oratory'. Dryden the critic is squarely the spokesman for cultural moderation, the hope that reason and clarity will put paid to the extreme linguistic obfuscation of radicals of all colours. Ending on the same note as the epilogue he defends, he identifies the way ahead for drama as an imitation of a society taking the first steps away from the burden of the past through what the epilogue calls 'a native language more refined and free':

To conclude all, let us render to our predecessors what is their due, without confining ourselves to a servile imitation of all they writ; and without assuming to ourselves the title of better poets, let us ascribe to the gallantry and civility of our age the advantage which we have above them and, to our knowledge of the customs and manners of it, the happiness we have to please beyond them.

This echoes the authoritative plea of Bishop Thomas Sprat, whose 1667 *History of the Royal Society* called for a limpid language free from the excesses of wartime obscurantism.

If Dryden's 'Defence' seems on close inspection less an arrogant claim to superiority than a desperate plea for his country to move on, his intentions were widely suspected. In 1673 a group of unidentified writers used the so-called 'Rota' pamphlets to ransack Dryden's work for political hypocrisy, terminal prepositions and other lapses. Like today's social network sites, cheap print provided anyone who could read and write with the chance to pit his or her wits against established authorities under cover of anonymity. 'Burlesque criticism' flourished, sometimes as an open expression of hostility but occasionally, as in today's culture of trolling, through praise by an imaginary and overtly sycophantic reader. Authors might create their own avatars in the persons of actors to expound a critical argument, but in Dryden's case they were likely to find others less friendly massing around them.

A playwright who found such sustenance in the 'gallantry and civility' of the present was unlikely to be impressed by criticism that found in the audience and context for contemporary drama everything that was wrong about the English stage. Such was the view of Thomas Rymer, whose *Tragedies of the Last Age* (1677) and *A Short View of Tragedy* entered – and sought to end through scathing disparagement that borrows the language of burlesque criticism – the long-standing debate about the virtues of Shakespeare and Fletcher. *Othello* he ridiculed as '*The Tragedy of the Handkerchief*', a kind of soap opera that coaxed an illusion of seriousness from domestic trivia. Neither Dryden nor the new generation of critics represented by Charles Gildon and John Dennis were impressed, partly because of Rymer's insistence that gallantry and civility were no basis for healthy cultural life. Anticipating Jeremy Collier in the 1690s, but without the impact or legal force of Collier's arguments, Rymer argued that drama had been reduced to sordid entertainment, separated from the politico-religious roots that had nourished not only the work of Sophocles and Euripides but that of Corneille and Racine. The only answer, he proposed, was more government regulation.

Posterity has been unkind to Rymer, partly because of his own failure as a playwright. But his trenchant thinking belongs to a tradition of English criticism that includes L. C. Knights's celebrated *Scrutiny* denunciation of Restoration Drama as 'trivial, gross and dull', and builds its aversion on not dissimilar cultural anxieties: a fear of the monstrously accelerating modern metropolis, with its deracination of rural populations and practices, and of the self-conscious play that comes of urban living.[32] No group of people embraced the latter phenomenon more enthusiastically than the organizations that represent the antithesis of the value system propounded by Collier and Rymer: the theatre companies.

Endnotes

1 Downes, *Roscius Anglicanus*, 71. The former prompter blamed the play's immorality (the eponymous scene was 'the Reverse to the Laws of Morality and Virtue'), but the text does not corroborate his claim. Three of the leading actors in the company took major roles: Henry Harris, Cave Underhill and Mary Betterton. The play was a satiric riposte to Dryden's *Marriage à la Mode*, which had been staged by the King's Company six months beforehand.

2 *The Diary of Samuel Pepys*, 7 May 1669.

3 For further details of playwright biographies, see Paula R. Backscheider, *Dictionary of Literary Biography*, vol. LXXX, *Restoration and Eighteenth-Century Dramatists* (Detroit: Gale Research, 1989).

4 Licence to John Rhodes to form a theatre company, dated 2 January 1664: LC 5/138, p. 387; in *Register*, no. 265.

5 LS1, 344.

6 Molière, *The School for Wives*, translated by Richard Wilbur, in *Molière: Five Plays* (London: Methuen, 1981), 59–60.

7 William Wycherley, *The Country Wife* (London, 1675), 58–9 (IV.ii.1–49).

8 I develop this line of argument in '"Ranked among the best": translation and cultural agency in Restoration translations of French drama', *Modern Language Review* 108 (2013), 396–415.

9 Newdigate *Newsletter* of 29 January 1681, in LS1, 294.

10 Hatton correspondence, cited in LS1, 292.

11 For the popularity of the play, see Letter of Anne Montague, 1 November 1680, in LS1, 292. For James's prohibition, LS1, 354. For Mary's embarrassment, LS1, 371: Daniel Finch wrote that 'unhappy expressions [in the play]...put her in some disorder, and forc'd her to hold up her fan, and often look behind her and call for her palatine and hood, and anything she could next think of...'.

12 John Dryden, *The Spanish Fryar* (London, 1681), 63.

13 Ibid., 83.

14 Ibid., 23. For the trials of priests at the time, see Kenyon, *The Popish Plot*, 150–201.

15 *The Diary of Samuel Pepys*, 15, 16, 20 April 1667. For other references to the same incident, see LS1, 106–7.

16 Thomas Otway, 'To the Right Honourable Charles Earl of Middlesex', *Alcibiades* (London, 1675), np.

17 Charles Vischard, Abbé de Saint Réal, trans. H. J., *Don Carlos, or, An Historical Relation of the Unfortunate Life and Tragical Death of That Prince of Spain* (London, 1674).

18 Thomas Otway, *Don Carlos* (London, 1676), 33; in J. C. Ghosh, ed., *The Works of Thomas Otway*, 2 vols. (Oxford: Clarendon Press, 1932), vol. I, IV.18–19.

19 Ibid., 17 (II.321–5).

20 Letter from Barton Booth to Aaron Hill, 19 June 1732; in *A Collection of Letters, Never Printed Before* (London, 1751), 82.

21 Downes, *Roscius Anglicanus*, 76.

22 Thomas Otway, 'To His Royal Highness the Duke', *Don Carlos*, sig. A2.

23 Robert Markley, '"Be impudent, be saucy, forward, bold, touzing, and leud": the politics of masculine sexuality and feminine desire in Behn's Tory comedies', in Canfield and Payne, *Cultural Readings*, 114–40, 137.

24 LS1, 345–9.

25 William Shakespeare, *King Lear*, ed. Kenneth Muir (London: Methuen, 1952), IV.vi.123–30.

26 Markley, '"Be impudent"', 137.

27 See, for example, Kate Aughterson's *Aphra Behn: The Comedies* (Basingstoke: Palgrave, 2003), 229–30.

28 Aphra Behn, 'Epistle to the Reader', *The Dutch Lover* (London, 1673), np.

29 Aphra Behn, 'Epilogue', *The Rover* (London, 1677), np.

30 Robert Howard, 'Epistle', *The Great Favourite, or, The Duke of Lerma* (London, 1668), np.

31 Thomas Shadwell, 'Preface', *The Humorists* (London, 1671), np.

32 L. C. Knights, 'Restoration comedy: the reality and the myth', *Scrutiny*, September 1937, 122–43.

4 | *Companies*

Icons of metropolitan life, Restoration theatre companies were also (metaphorically) that more reassuring phenomenon, the family. They could certainly be as hospitable or as quarrelsome. In August 1673 the actor Philip Cademan had to play out a sword fight with foils in a revival of Davenant's *The Man's the Master*. His adversary, Henry Harris, accidentally caught him, piercing 'near the eye, which so maimed both the hand and his speech, that he [could] make little use of either'. Cademan was Lady Davenant's son from a former marriage, and the company's response was generous: '[F]or which mischance,' continues Downes, 'he has received a pension ever since 1673, being 35 years ago.'[1] It was no mean sum: thirty shillings a week (about four times what a skilled craftsman earned), and only the intervention of the lawyer-manager Christopher Rich in the 1690s frog-marched Cademan back into the playhouse to earn his keep by selling tickets.[2] The contrasting treatment of the injured actor in 1673 and 1695 said everything about the values of the old company and its new manager. No wonder Betterton complained that Rich dealt with his actors 'not as we were the King's and Queen's servants but [Rich's] slaves'.[3]

The language of feudal indulgence masked the capacity of royal servants to behave like spoiled children. Ten years before accidentally maiming Cademan, Harris had gone on strike for more money and better roles, and got his way.[4] The year before that he and Betterton (of all people) had been fined for assaulting the Master of the Revels' messenger, who had demanded payment. Their indiscretions pale by comparison with the antics of the King's Company actors during the 1670s, when senior actors made a habit of absence and theft, and even subcontracted their roles without telling management. When the Duke's Company visited Oxford in 1670 it needed protection from unruly citizens; four years later it was the citizens who needed protection, the King's Company 'going about the town breaking of windows and committing many other unpardonable rudenesses'.[5] Restoration theatre companies might look inwards for charity and mutual reliance, but once out on the town they could match any hooligan mob.

The idea that they were 'the King's and Queen's servants' carried more weight in 1660 than in 1695. With political and social control in mind, Charles II authorized only two patent companies in 1660, although separate licences were eventually given to George Jolly and John Rhodes, with a special dispensation granted to a troupe maintained by Charles's illegitimate son, the Duke of Monmouth. Not having one of the two royal patents meant no access to a London base, though Rhodes was given an occasional booking at court to offset the ambiguous delights of provincial touring. Theatre historians sometimes cite the 1660 patents as a sign of the privilege given to London over the regions, but the arrangement was arguably the biggest boost to provincial performance that could be devised short of banning theatre in the capital. Experienced practitioners were pushed out to do their best for the people of Norwich, Maidstone and other less fashionable locales. Thomas St Serfe, a one-failure wonder as a playwright, ended up in Edinburgh.

The fringe companies had a flat structure, with a single, experienced theatre man at the helm (John Rhodes had been a wardrobe keeper to the King's Men in the 1620s) and a small company of performers recruited for their adaptability. By contrast, the patent companies were hierarchical, with sufficient resources to permit a degree of specialization. The patent holder was also a major shareholder in a company in which senior actors held shares too, as long as they were male. The patentee therefore exercised overall control, though it was common to sell shares or use them as loan collateral whenever cash needed to be raised.

Davenant excelled at personnel management, repertory choices and technological innovation, but the long-term health of the Duke's Company was also down to his careful share dealing. When he sold, he largely did so cleanly and to people who were willing to stay at arm's length; his only serious mistake, perhaps, was in underestimating Harris's ambitions when the company was formed, but that proved to be a problem that could be resolved without detriment to the company, whatever it cost Davenant in dignity. Coming into management in 1668, Betterton and Harris observed the same principles. Although they had to borrow to finance the building of the Dorset Garden Theatre in 1671, they chose their creditors well. There was always the risk of drawing into company management people who, like Christopher Rich, had a keen interest in the theatre, but only as a commercial enterprise. Even without such interference, debt management was a reality for many actors, not least Harris, who was sued for money half a dozen times, once by his own wife.[6] The impoverished rakes of Restoration Comedy who repel their creditors with such *élan* paraded an actor's mentality as much as a down-at-heel aristocrat's.

Theatre manager case study: Sir William Davenant and the Duke's Company

For Davenant, his grant of patent was a lifetime's ambition. He had obtained the promise from Charles I in 1639, but war had intervened. This meant that in 1660 he had the strongest possible card to play in negotiating with Charles II, who in granting Davenant his patent would only be fulfilling his late father's wishes. A successful playwright and Poet Laureate before the war, Davenant had all the credentials for running a theatre. Even his modest, orderly upbringing helped. He was the son of an Oxford vintner who owned the Crown Inn there. John Davenant was a pillar of the community: mayor of Oxford at his death in 1621, he was said to have been 'a very grave and discreet citizen' who nonetheless admired 'plays and playmakers'. His will suggests a father who was anxious to provide for his children. William he earmarked for an apprenticeship with 'some good merchant or other tradesman'; another son, Robert, became a fellow of St John's, while his brother Nicholas practised law.[7] For all the excitement of an alleged affair between Davenant's mother and the famous playwright who allegedly passed through from time to time en route to Stratford or London, the family was, like the Duke's Company, an orderly, well-run unit that understood its obligations.

The roots of Davenant's success as a manager are clear from his activities in the 1630s. He wrote comedies, dramas and masques both for the court and for the Middle Temple, the latter for the sons of the Elector Palatine. His published texts boast a wide range of prefatory contributions by fellow poets and courtiers; he was a relentless networker. When, on 27 June 1639, he was granted the title of 'Governor of the King and Queen's Company, acting at the Cockpit in Drury Lane', he had earned his position by graft and diplomatic acuity. Already his thoughts had turned to a new building: three months earlier he had been given permission to 'erect a playhouse' in Fleet Street, a scheme that fell foul of war. He had laid the seeds for the activity he was to pursue once the storm had passed. Even in the unpromising circumstances of the 1650s he would be pushing at his connections to mount plays. In 1656 the Cromwellian government, which had thrown him in prison five years beforehand, was persuaded to allow a new kind of 'entertainment' at Rutland House: the dramatic opera that would later become *The Siege of Rhodes*. The success of Davenant, a born entrepreneur, lay in the way he straddled court and commerce: in the industry he applied to patronal networks as well as the business nous he brought to running a company. Only by professionalizing the task of cultivating connections was he able to gain experience of theatre management during the 1650s, a project that glided smoothly over Davenant's former political loyalties.

The Siege of Rhodes became a significant popular success in the early 1660s; Pepys saw it four times and had to restrain himself from making it five.[8] Its novel scenery helped (an example is shown as Figure 4.1), but it was one of those pieces that, like Davenant himself, moved

Figure 4.1 Prospect of the city of Rhodes: a scenic sketch for Davenant's *The Siege of Rhodes*

conveniently with the times. In 1656 its tale of righteous Christian knights besieged by the Ottomans struck a chord for a government anxious to create its own post-royalist mythology; it could be represented, at least, as a kind of republican masque. By 1661 Sultan Solyman seemed more like Cromwell, turning a mordant eye on the excesses of the (nominally) Christian court:

> Ebbing out wealth by ways as strange
> As it flowed in by avarice.[9]

Although Davenant deserves credit as a modernizing manager, setting new standards of company discipline and committing money and energy to new stage technology, he also had an unrivalled instinct for making the past speak to the present. In his hands, old repertory came up shining and contemporary, partly because he was careful to enliven it with new actors.

In 1660 he and Killigrew had a limited number of performers to choose from. There were survivors from the pre-war years; there were those who had begun to act on the fringes of legality in 1659; and there were others who were completely new to the trade. With his lengthy pedigree, Davenant might have bid for the older generation; instead, he formed a company of newer blood, including several actors who had been apprenticed to John Rhodes. They were more pliable, less entrenched in old ways, but also willing to take on the mantle of tradition. When Davenant's leading actor, the young Thomas Betterton, learned the parts of Hamlet and Henry VIII he spoke a theatrical language that had been shaped in the days of the King's Men, when Shakespeare himself was the house dramatist. 'The part of the King was so right and justly done by Mr Betterton,' wrote Downes of *Henry VIII*, 'he being instructed in it by Sir William, who had it from Old Mr Lowen, that had his Instructions from Mr Shakespeare himself.'[10] Not all Downes's thumbnail histories can be relied on, but in this case the link is entirely credible. *Hamlet* and Massinger's *The Bondman* became, along with *The Siege of Rhodes*, signature successes for the young Duke's Company. The Danish prince, a man in black amid universal rejoicing, reminded everyone that Restoration festivity was stalked by the ghost of a dead father. Massinger's Marullo is a loyalist who emerges from disguise to assert his right to restoration: like Nahum Tate's Edgar or Charles Stuart himself, he is a prince in hiding who inherits his birthright.

It was this play that led Pepys, who saw it seven times, to proclaim Betterton 'the best actor in the world'.[11]

Company tradition was reinforced by the presence of memorabilia. The Chandos portrait of Shakespeare, which has the best claim to be a likeness of the playwright, was owned by Davenant until his death in 1668, when Betterton acquired it, and he appears to have kept it at least until 1704; some time after that he sold it for forty guineas. One authority speculates that the poor condition of the painting's surface might be the effect of its being kept on public display at the Duke's Theatre, where people (perhaps actors and playwrights hoping for inspiration) might lay hands on it.[12]

Davenant left his own bequest: not an object, but a methodology, and one that his successors implemented with considerable success. He knew that, whatever the appeal of the past, what excited audiences was the hybrid form he had invented before the Restoration period even began. Appointed to run the Duke's Company by Davenant's widow, Mary, Betterton and Harris continued with the policy of innovation through scenic and musical extravagance. Yet even here the new breed of dramatic opera succeeded best when it was blended with something traditionally English; it struggled to make the same impact when the impulse was to imitate the cultural manners of France. As Downes put it, Thomas Shadwell's 1675 *Psyche*, an imitation of the Molière/Lully ballet, 'proved very beneficial to the company; yet the *Tempest* [in Shadwell and Locke's musical adaptation] got them more money'.[13] Anxiety about the alleged superiority of French forms was played out, and to some extent quelled, at the box office.

Theatre manager case study: Thomas Killigrew and the King's Company

Davenant's rival, Thomas Killigrew, came from a different background and was, though not necessarily for that reason, less successful. His father was a minor aristocrat and a major entrepreneur – the ideal family pedigree, in theory, for a life in Restoration Theatre. But somehow Killigrew never lived up to his father's reputation for keeping commercial plates spinning. As a child he is said to have gone to the Red Bull Theatre to 'be a devil upon the stage, and so get to see [the] play', and the handwriting and spelling he committed to the family

Bible certainly do not suggest strong application to study.[14] Where Davenant Senior provided for his son with an apprenticeship, Robert Killigrew left his son 100 acres in Lincolnshire and a remote manor house in Cornwall – assets that had more symbolic than practical value. Like Davenant, Killigrew wrote plays during the 1630s, only less industriously: Davenant worked hard at different genres and connections while Killigrew graciously accepted Latin tributes.[15] Surrendering the King's Company patent in 1677, Killigrew handed over control to a son, Charles, who had gone to court to obtain it. Charles's inheritance turned out to be a rabble of disgruntled actors who felt they had been cheated for years by management. The contrast with the Duke's Company is clear. In 1668 the Davenant family ensured an orderly succession in which actor-managers predominated; for the Killigrews, 1677 nurtured the practice (which would grow to frightening proportions in the 1690s) of having theatre companies run by self-appointed money men.

Yet it is easy to deride Killigrew. He did, after all, oversee the emergence of major actors such as Lacy and Gwyn, the best work of Dryden and Wycherley and the building of the first Theatre Royal, Drury Lane, and, beyond all that, he maintained the longest association between a manager and a single company in the period. He started well enough, reaching an agreement with the truculent Master of the Revels, Henry Herbert, when Davenant and company felt more inclined to scrap, and moving quickly into a series of temporary venues in the autumn of 1660 (this was the season when a 'very pretty lady' next to Pepys, perhaps unused to the theatrical illusion, cried out 'to see Desdemona smothered').[16] In the Vere Street theatre he found a venue with better access and surroundings than Davenant's Lincoln's Inn Fields playhouse, and his core formula of recognized older plays performed by established older actors in front of very little scenery largely succeeded. When he built a new Theatre Royal in Bridges Street (1663) to accommodate more of the scenic display favoured by Davenant, it cost less than a third of the £9,000 spent by the Duke's Company on Dorset Garden in 1671. So far so good. But, if Killigrew could just about handle the capital and legal aspects of running a theatre, he was less adept when it came to the people he needed to work in it.

Alienating senior actors became something of a speciality. The initial share deal Killigrew offered was so generous that they attained majority control. The small print, however, said that all the actors' shares could be reclaimed by their manager, and that right he exercised as soon as 1663. Unsurprisingly, problems with company discipline festered well into the next decade, from minor infringements such as borrowing costumes for the occasional night out to filching the day's takings, fighting during rehearsals or just not turning up at all. Pepys heard that Killigrew even retained a prostitute to keep his younger actors happy. Sympathy may have been in short supply when he suffered what it is hard not to call bad luck. In 1664 one his leading actors, Walter Clun, was set upon and murdered after a performance of *The Alchemist* by someone Pepys darkly referred to as 'an Irish fellow' (contrast this with the astonishing luck that befell the Duke's Company actor William Smith, who committed murder in 1666 and got off).[17] Eight years later he lost another actor, Richard Bell, and an entire theatre to the fire that destroyed the Bridges Street playhouse, at the very time when Dorset Garden was starting to draw crowds.

Killigrew's initial repertory decisions might suggest a man of conservative instincts who did not possess the artistic vision or adventure of Davenant: he advocated good scripts and actors when audiences were being seduced by painted scenery and special effects – or so the argument goes. But he had his own distinctive appetite for risk. As early as 1663 he was investing in new scenery for old plays such as John Fletcher's *The Faithful Shepherdess* and spoke to Pepys of his plans for 'Italians' and 'operas', mounting an elaborate *Psyche* five years before the Duke's Company.[18] He had the sense, if not the money, at least to follow Davenant's example. The (presumably) titillating innovation of an all-female cast he tried more than once, with modest success.[19] Most conspicuously, as a man who had spent long hours exchanging quips with the king, he sanctioned the kind of outspokenness that the more cautious Duke's Company tended to avoid. To the theatre historian intent on careful business management, the freedom with which John Lacy abused the king 'to his face' in *The Change of Crowns* was a commercial misjudgement; to Killigrew and anyone interested in the way theatre speaks back to power, it was an extraordinarily brave joke.

His boyish desire to be a little devil on the stage might have cost him his livelihood or even, in the threat of one aggrieved courtier, his nose, but it was his fractious relationships with actors and other shareholders – his son Charles included – that finally put an end to his sixteen-year managerial career.[20] When his senior actors went on strike in February 1676 his panicked response combined legal threats, false promises on pensions and yet more risky deals with creditors. The sorriest indication of his difficulties is that, when he ceded control of the King's Company to Charles in 1677, it was not even clear that the patent was his to surrender. Wrangling over entitlements, share ownership and toxic debts went on. Four years after taking over, Charles Killigrew was in court to prove that he was indeed the lawful patentee.[21]

Christopher Rich and the United Company

Seldom in English theatre history has a man been more subject to abuse. In 1782 David Erskine Baker, compiler of the *Biographia dramatica*, described 'a lawyer, whose name is often to be found in the future annals of the Theatre'. Just why, Baker proceeded to explain in withering detail:

This gentleman, who was not possessed of abilities calculated to make the stage flourish under his administration, soon contrived to engross the whole power into his own hands. By various instances of mismanagement, he alienated the affections of the principal performers from him, and by wanton oppressions provoked them to attempt their deliverance from the tyranny he exercised over them.[22]

This, largely, is the Christopher Rich portrayed by recent studies of Restoration theatre management, which, like Baker, take their cue from a number of Rich's contemporaries. In 1702 the author of *A Comparison Between the Two Stages* wrote of

an old snarling lawyer...a waspish, ignorant pettifogger in law and poetry; one who understands poetry no more than algebra.[23]

But another history gave a slightly more nuanced view of an operator who knew how to keep at least some of his actors onside:

Rich appears to have been a man of great cunning, and intimately acquainted with all the quirks of law; he was as sly a tyrant as was ever at the head of a theatre, for he gave the actors more liberty and fewer days' pay than any of his predecessors; he would laugh with them over a bottle and bite them in their bargains; he kept them poor, that they might not be able to rebel, and sometimes merry, that they might not think of it.[24]

If not a complex brute, then certainly a cunning and successful one: a Somerset boy who, contrary to the usual stereotypes of the Restoration Stage, out-thought his metropolitan associates.

Rich is an important figure not because he represented a paradigm shift from one form of management to another, as though the theatrical economy passed from an ethos of royal service to one of commercial gain: an inglorious revolution to match the officially glorious political one that was happening in the same period. That was how his enemies liked to represent him. He simply brought into stark definition a set of practices on which his predecessors – and, indeed, his bitterest rivals – had always depended, achieving power with tools they had created. He was his competitors' parody, not their antithesis. Davenant had raised cash by selling shares in the early 1660s; Killigrew had defrauded his actors of their shareholdings and paid the consequences; they both had to cope with disciplinary problems, and with varying degrees of aptitude and willingness among their performers. Betterton, Rich's principal antagonist, was a master at using share dealing for personal gain. Such practices required theatres to accept the risk that they might one day be taken over by men such as Rich.

That day dawned on 24 March 1688, when Rich acquired a share in the United Company from the hopeless Alexander Davenant, a scion of the famous dynasty who had inherited none of its managerial talent and got himself so far in debt that he eventually had to flee to the Canary Islands. Rich had been lending Davenant money with the company shares as collateral, and there is something reminiscent of Uriah Heep's dealings with Mr Wickfield in *David Copperfield* in the way he silently acquired control of the company. After a terrible denouement in 1693, when Rich and his business partner, Thomas Skipwith, revealed to the company their controlling share (like the end of *The Way of the World*, but with Fainall as the winner), the new regime flexed its muscles. Historic concessions and allowances disappeared; benefit performances were reduced; fines for indiscipline multiplied; and, worst of all for actors whose professional pride depended on their stage profiles, parts were reassigned.

Betterton grandly complained of being overlooked in favour of 'ignorant, insufficient fellows', and engineered a break from Rich's management, returning to the old Lincoln's Inn Fields playhouse in 1695.[25] If the days of William Davenant and Thomas Killigrew present contrasting models of theatre management, commercial success and production styles, the renewal of competition after 1695 saw different contrasts emerge. Betterton had one small, ill-equipped theatre at his disposal, Rich two good ones. Betterton ran his company with two fellow senior performers, Elizabeth Barry and Anne Bracegirdle (although the latter do not appear to have held shares), in the manner of a kindly patriarch; Rich maintained a tight grip on money and seems to have kept his performers in a state of fear. It was in Betterton's interest to think of Rich's priorities as lowbrow, and in Rich's to view Betterton's efforts as the twitches of a moribund lion, but in reality both were engaged in a rush to the middle ground of theatrical taste at a time when the theatre as a whole struggled to maintain an audience. Study of the seasons at Lincoln's Inn Fields and Rich's two houses, Dorset Garden and Drury Lane, shows convergence in repertory and box-office success from 1695 to 1705.

Rich's fifteen-year conflict with Betterton suggests a war of personalities, but it was merely part of a pattern for both men. Betterton had a history of antipathy towards people who attempted to restrict the autonomy of the theatres, while Rich went on to alienate his own business partners. In October 1706, with Betterton in semi-retirement, Rich secured the lease of the Queen's Theatre in Haymarket through his agent, Owen Swiney, so acquiring control of all three major London playhouses. But Swiney and Rich fell out, and in 1708 Rich's Drury Lane actors (Cibber among them) took Betterton's cue and plotted to rebel. By 1709 this had led to the closure of the Drury Lane Theatre and a pamphlet war against the actors, with the company treasurer – the fittingly named Zachary Baggs – publishing the amounts of money paid to the discontented actors, which is perhaps one of the few moments in theatre history when a theatrical entrepreneur has attempted to trade on popular prejudice against actors. The resulting legal battle saw Rich strip Drury Lane of all its props and costumes so that no one else could perform there – an act of vandalism that seemed to symbolize his approach to the stage. In a final irony, he died while building a new theatre in Lincoln's Inn Fields, where Betterton's career had first taken off in 1661.

In his 1922 entry for *The Dictionary of National Biography*, Joseph Knight seeks to balance the vitriol Rich inspired, citing accounts of his charity and personal modesty. It is characteristic of the press Rich has received that such balance comes with a heavy qualification. Against the vitriol, Knight concludes, 'may be placed the less trustworthy testimony of authors who dedicated to him plays he had produced, or was expected to produce', as though trustworthiness were somehow the prerogative of playwrights writing panegyrics to noble patrons.[26] It is perhaps more accurate to suggest that, by bringing into stark definition the financial imperatives on which theatre had depended since 1660, Rich became a scapegoat for theatre people – actors and historians alike – on whom a narrative of decline could conveniently be pinned.

Three case studies illustrate the ways in which the intensity of company life suffused the creation of drama in the period: managerial and personnel regime change could be as significant a subject for Restoration playwrights as the convolutions of high politics.

Managing debts: William Congreve and *Love for Love* (1695)

Congreve's third comedy celebrated new beginnings for the theatre of 1695 as much as for a society rid of the Stuarts, but it could do so only by returning to old crime scenes. It is stalked by the shadows of tyrants: by memories of Christopher Rich, whose oppression had forced Betterton's company to break away and dust down Sir William Davenant's old theatre in Lincoln's Inn Fields; but it also reflects a discredited ideology that dreamed of absolute power and found in theatrical libertinism a convenient, attractive and comic apology for its excesses. London liked the combination, and the play ran initially for thirteen days.

A bare description of the plot makes *Love for Love* sound like *The Man of Mode* or *The Luckey Chance*, stories of impoverished but attractive young men attaining sexual, intellectual and financial salvation in the shape of rich and clever young women. Add chirpy servants and male friends *au fait* with high society news, and the formula is complete. The hero's polite continence is one hallmark of *Love for Love*, but it is his family that really catch the eye. For all his charms, Valentine falls a little into the background thanks to the looming presence of his sailor brother, Ben, and his monstrously comic father, whose name oozes undesirable antiquity. Sir Sampson Legend is an old-style rampaging Carolean libertine who in a breath boasts of paying court to China and India, riding an elephant in Mongolia and cuckolding the king of Java: '[T]he present Majesty of *Bantam* is the Issue of these Loins,' he crows.[27] The emergent language of sentiment gave hope of human relations built on sympathy and affection, but Sir Sampson has other ideas:

I warrant my son thought nothing belonged to a father but forgiveness and affection; no authority, no correction, no arbitrary power; nothing to be done but for him to offend and me to pardon.

Their Act II confrontation, in which Sir Sampson accuses Valentine of having a 'Tyburn face', focuses debate on the tendency of tyrants to manipulate the laws of natural succession: Valentine's dilemma is that his father is offering to clear his debts in return for surrendering to sailor Ben his rightful inheritance. There is a ghost here of the fateful triangle between Charles II, his illegitimate son, Monmouth, and his brother and head of the Navy, later James II, but also a more general reflection on the blight of 'arbitrary power', its capacity to poison the hopes of the generation to come. Sir Sampson enters into a ploy to marry Valentine's quarry, Angelica, but is outdone by her legal sleight of hand. Like Mirabell in *The Way of the World*, she asserts rights through paperwork rather than swordplay, tearing up the bond that would mark Valentine's agreement to his father's demands. 'Oons, you're a Crocodile,' snarls Sampson to this wily Cleopatra, who has undone his empire with a couple of swift rips. Congreve himself had pulled off a similar ploy: the play, promised to Rich, was transferred to the rebels once it was clear they were on their way.

When Angelica turns to Valentine at the end of the play, and his friend Scandal begins to see the error of his own ways, there is a hopeful gesture to a new age:

ANGELICA: I have done dissembling now, Valentine, and if that coldness which I have always worn before you should turn to an extreme fondness, you must not suspect it.

VALENTINE: I'll prevent that suspicion – for I intend to dote on at that immoderate rate that your fondness shall never distinguish itself enough to be taken notice of. If ever you seem to love too much, it must be only when I can't love enough.

ANGELICA: Have a care of large promises; you know you are apt to run more in debt than you are able to pay.

VALENTINE: Therefore, I yield my body as your prisoner, and make your best on it.

SCANDAL: The music stays for you.

Dance

SCANDAL: Well, Madam, you have done exemplary justice, in punishing an inhuman father, and rewarding a faithful lover; but there is a third good work which I in particular must thank you for; I was an infidel to your sex, and you have converted me. For now I am convinced that all women are not like fortune, blind in bestowing favours either on those who do not merit, or do not want them.

ANGELICA: 'Tis an unreasonable accusation that you lay upon our sex: you tax us with injustice, only to cover your own want of merit. You would all have the reward of love, but few have the constancy to stay till it becomes your due. Men are generally hypocrites and infidels; they pretend to worship, but have neither zeal nor faith. How few, like Valentine, would persevere even unto martyrdom, and sacrifice their interest to their constancy! In admiring me, you misplace the novelty.

> The miracle today is that we find
> A lover true, not that a woman's kind.[28]

Over their love vows, replete with the language of sentimentality that dissolves individual identity into the other, hovers a warning about the precarious finances of the new company; but, in the recovered family home of Lincoln's Inn Fields, at least the actor's body is imprisoned willingly. With bad fathers, out goes buccaneering masculinity, to be replaced by the holy faith of the devoted lover. It has been claimed, controversially, that the religious language of Restoration Drama signifies a systematic Christian purpose.[29] Here, there is a satiric edge to Angelica's references to zeal, faith and martyrdom: whether at prayer or in bed, she seems to suggest, mankind is largely driven by money or desire. The true hero is the one who has thrown off Dorimant's cursed bequest.

Continuing the point, Anne Bracegirdle's Angelica stepped straight from her final couplet into a special epilogue for 'the opening of the New House'. The terms of occupation are reminiscent of Valentine's quest for Angelica's protection, and similarly tinged with the language of deprivation that came so readily to Restoration theatre people:

> Sure providence at first designed this place
> To be the player's refuge in distress;
> For still in every storm they all run hither,
> As to a shed that shields them from the weather.

If this 'shed' was a nonconformist chapel set against the gaudy cathedral of Dorset Garden, it did at least allow for the sort of reformation that returned the company, even in the midst of revolutions social and theatrical, to first principles, in a spirit of zeal and – no doubt – martyrdom.

A dying star: Dryden and *All for Love* (1678)

Love for Love marked one playwright's devotion to the cause of building a new company; *All for Love* is the point at which another finally gave up on an old one. By December 1677 Dryden had worked with the King's Company on eleven plays, including signature successes such as *The Conquest of Granada* and *An Evening's Love*. He had helped create major performances and double acts for Charles Hart, Nell Gwyn and others, as well as sticking with the company through lean times, writing three plays for them during the temporary occupation of Lincoln's Inn Fields that followed the loss of the Theatre Royal to fire in 1672. But the chronic indiscipline of the company during the 1670s took its toll, and, for the play that succeeded *All for Love* in March 1678, Dryden turned to the Duke's Company.

It is no coincidence that *All for Love*, Dryden's telling of the Antony and Cleopatra story, has one of the shorter cast lists among Restoration plays; he was, perhaps, drawing in King's Company resources to create the best chance of a disciplined performance. Whereas Shakespeare's play lists thirty-four named roles with miscellaneous officers, attendants and messengers, Dryden's reduces the roster to ten, plus servants and, tear-jerkingly, 'Antony's two little daughters'. Octavius, Enobarbus and Rome itself have melted into the Tiber in a tightly focused retelling that takes the action up in the latter stages of Shakespeare's Act III, after the battle of Actium and with Antony moping in a temple. The preface derides the formal niceties of contemporary French tragedy; Racine's masterpiece, *Phèdre*, had been published eight months earlier, and Dryden saves his most scathing comments for its depiction of Hippolytus, who has 'good manners with a vengeance'. Yet in many ways *All for Love* is very much a chamber, neoclassical distillation of the famous story, entirely set in Egypt and focused on the rival claims on Antony's attention of his wife Octavia and his lover Cleopatra.

The burden of the past, both ancient and recent, was heavy. Dryden compared his task to that of Penelope's suitors in the *Odyssey*, required to string the hero's bow in order to prove their worth: the subject 'has been treated by the greatest wits of our nation after Shakespeare'. By that he meant not only Samuel Daniel's *The Tragedy of Cleopatra*, revised in 1607, the year Shakespeare's version first appeared, but the play by Sir Charles Sedley that had been staged by the Duke's Company as recently as February 1677. Sedley's *Antony and Cleopatra*, later revised under the modishly sentimental title of

Beauty the Conqueror (1702), was Dryden's most obvious model and point of departure. It too is a pared-down, neoclassical play, deploying the same timescale as *All for Love*; it was to Sedley that Dryden owed the device of making Cleopatra's scheming court responsible for the false news of her death, so ennobling her in the final act. But he rejected Sedley's piously rigid couplets, which it is polite to say resemble the sort of thing Dryden and Howard were writing in the early 1660s. For her last words, Sedley's Cleopatra addresses the snake:

> Good asp, bite deep and deadly in my breast,
> And give me sudden and eternal rest.[30]

By contrast, Dryden tried to 'imitate the divine Shakespeare' in the fluidity, compression and metaphorical richness of his blank verse. His best biographer thinks he succeeds by excess: 'Dryden deliberately exceeds even Shakespeare's metaphorical density,' writes James A. Winn of the beautiful passage in which Cleopatra compares the asp to the key that will unlock her life.[31]

Modern productions of the play face the challenge of what might be described as an excess of telling over showing, however. It is a skilful actor who copes with passages such as this, in which Antony succumbs to familial pity and embraces his sweet little daughters:

> VENDITIUS: Was ever sight so moving! Emperor!
> DOLABELLA: Friend.
> OCTAVIA: Husband!
> BOTH CHILDREN: Father!
> ANTONY: I am vanquished: take me,
>   Octavia; take me, children, share me all.[32]

For once, the objection to such writing raised by F. R. Leavis seems an understatement: the 'emotion doesn't emerge from a given situation realized in its concrete particularity; it is stated, not presented or enacted', like an opera libretto awaiting music.[33] Arguably, however, Dryden reworks a problem he found in Shakespeare, in which the evocations of Antony's glory may appear to be out of kilter with the hell-bent man we see before us. Numerous passages in *All for Love* seek to interpret events that have happened elsewhere: Dryden's highly wrought, sometimes over-explicit language dramatizes the conceptual difficulty the characters have of agreeing about, or even grasping, the events going on around them.

If Dryden's rejection of Sedley's style only partly succeeded at best, the same might be said for his politics. Sedley's play sprang from the culture of disappointed libertinism: the 'greatest wits' who had surrounded and nourished Charles II in the 1660s fell out of favour in the 1670s, prompting a rash of barely coded satire from Rochester and others.[34] Sedley's Antony is a disenchanted reflection on Charles: moody, sensual, secretive and misled as much as by scheming advisers as heroic appetite. His Cleopatra is barely different, except that she does most of the scheming. In comparison to Almanzor in *The Conquest of Granada*, Dryden's Antony is doomed to fail, because (like Charles) he cannot reconcile the divided calls on his duty.

The doomed love of a heroic prince for a foreign woman was a popular subject in 1677, with suspicion of a Catholic succession mounting and the king besotted with his French mistress, Louise de Keroualle, Duchess of Portsmouth. Dryden's attempt to Anglicise Sedley's language was mirrored in his drive to recuperate heroic love for an English audience on political tenterhooks. Antony is drawn 'as favourably as Plutarch...would give me leave', and so is Cleopatra. Dryden reached after the poetry of dazzling immortality he found in Shakespeare. In Act III Antony even translates Enobarbus's great barge speech ('The barge she sat, like a burnished throne') into Restoration blank verse. The playwright also engineered one of those high-octane, head-tossing, teeth-flashing showdowns between disdainful women that were the staple of heroic tragedy. Tracking down Antony in Alexandria, Octavia collides, by the law of neoclassical compression, with Cleopatra. Dryden worried that the 'compassion [Octavia] moved to herself and her children was destructive to that which I reserved for Antony and Cleopatra', but the Act III scene in which the two rivals attempt to get the better of each other leaves the audience relishing Cleopatra's bitchy superiority:

OCTAVIA: I need not ask if you are Cleopatra:
   Your haughty carriage –
CLEOPATRA: Shows I am a queen:
   Nor need I ask you who you are.
OCTAVIA: A Roman;
   A name that makes, and can unmake, a queen.
CLEOPATRA: Your lord, the man who serves me, is a Roman.
OCTAVIA: He was a Roman, till he lost that name
   To be a slave in Egypt; but I come
   To free him thence.

CLEOPATRA: Peace, peace, my lover's Juno.
　When he grew weary of that household clog,
　He chose my easier bonds.
OCTAVIA: I wonder not
　Your bonds are easy:
　you have long been practised
　In that lascivious art. He's not the first
　For whom you spread your snares: let Caesar witness.
CLEOPATRA: I loved not Caesar: 'twas but gratitude
　I paid his love. The worst your malice can
　Is but to say the greatest of mankind
　Has been my slave. The next, but far above him
　In my esteem, is he whom law calls yours,
　But whom his love made mine.
OCTAVIA: I would view nearer
　That face which has so long usurped my right,
　To find the inevitable charms that catch
　Mankind so sure, that ruined my dear lord.
CLEOPATRA: Oh, you do well to search, for had you known
　But half these charms, you had not lost his heart.
OCTAVIA: Far be their knowledge from a Roman lady,
　Far from a modest wife. Shame of our sex,
　Dost thou not blush to own those black endearments
　That make sin pleasing?
CLEOPATRA: You may blush, who want 'em.
　If bounteous nature, if indulgent heaven
　Have given me charms to please the bravest man,
　Should I not thank them? Should I be ashamed,
　And not proud? I am, that he has loved me;
　And when I love not him, heaven change this face
　For one like that.
OCTAVIA: Thou lov'st him not so well.
CLEOPATRA: I love him better, and deserve him more.
OCTAVIA: You do not, you cannot: you have been his ruin.
　Who made him cheap at Rome, but Cleopatra?
　Who made him scorned abroad, but Cleopatra?
　At Actium who betrayed him? Cleopatra.
　Who made his children orphans, and poor me
　A wretched widow? Only Cleopatra.
CLEOPATRA: Yet she who loves him best is Cleopatra.[35]

　This stages a classic Restoration encounter between duty and desire, between social allegiance and Hobbesian nature, between divine and human law (also, in the imagination, between Queen Catherine and the Duchess of Portsmouth, however much Dryden sought to tone down Sedley's critique of the king). To what extent that encounter is resolved, and in whose favour, is a question that has preoccupied critics of the play. But the passage also gives an audience the chance to dwell on the contradictions of the Restoration actress. Octavia wants a closer look to find out what it is about this strange abomination that is so attractive to men, this 'shame of our sex' that 'makes sin pleasing'. She is met by 'if you've got it, flaunt it' defiance – 'bounteous nature' has been kind to her, and she's not about to disguise her good fortune. Yet Octavia herself is the sum of a performance, of the kind of dutiful enactment that kept theatre companies running at all. The misfortunes of the King's Company were not the fault of its actresses, who wore the 'household' clog while their male counterparts were busy filching the day's takings and trying to kill each other.

It was towards an actor that Dryden glanced in creating his Antony: Charles II the king, inevitably, but also Charles Hart the actor, a performer of kingly bearing who had shared Nell Gwyn and Lady Castlemaine with his royal patron. In a story whose protagonists invariably show an interest in their own fame, retellings often exploit the fame of actors, whether in the Richard Burton / Elizabeth Taylor blockbuster film *Cleopatra* or Peter Hall's magisterial 1987 National Theatre production of Shakespeare's play, with Anthony Hopkins and Judi Dench. Charles Hart was reaching the end of his career in 1677; records survive of only three more new roles after Antony. He had embodied Dryden's greatest heroic character, Almanzor in *The Conquest of Granada*, in 1671. Earlier in 1677 he had played another dying hero fought over by proud lovers in Lee's *The Rival Queens, or, The Death of Alexander the Great*. John Downes did not let his devotion to Betterton mask his admiration:

Towards the latter end of his acting, if he acted in any one of these but once in a fortnight, the house was filled as at a new play, especially Alexander, he acting with such grandeur and agreeable majesty, that one of the court was pleased to honour him with this commendation: that Hart might teach any king on earth how to comport himself.[36]

Reviving the role, Betterton asked a former colleague of Hart's for his 'key' or tone in a particular speech, and, whatever Dryden's desire to redeem Charles II from explicit comparison with Antony, the fact that Hart played the role made it more 'agreeabl[y] majestic' than was quite comfortable.[37] The moody, distracted Antony who hides away at the start of *All for Love* is both the king who frustrated Sedley and his clan and the actor who was prone to falling out with his fellows, not least Michael Mohun, who played Antony's exasperated adviser, Ventidius. In the Act V death scene, Dryden catches the key of Hart's own growing disillusionment with the theatre:

> I'm weary of my part.
> My torch is out, and the world stands before me
> Like a black desert at the approach of night.[38]

The meta-theatrical language Shakespeare routinely brings to such moments is here refined to take a glance at the particular actor and the gathering gloom of the auditorium into which he speaks: no longer the fashionable 'world' he had charmed, but a 'black desert'. Within three years Hart would be doing something that could not be more reminiscent of the monarch with whom he was so often compared: negotiating a secret treaty with the enemy to bring down his own company and see it absorbed by the Duke's. Truly weary of his part, what he wanted most was a good pension.

New recruits: Farquhar's *The Beaux' Stratagem* (1707)

If *All for Love* was a lament for a heroic actor at twilight, *The Beaux' Stratagem* (1707) provided a vehicle for a dashing young talent. Farquhar and his leading actor, Robert Wilks, were Irish migrants united by an instinct for opportunity. They had both acted at the Smock Alley Theatre in Dublin, where Farquhar's indifferent career had been cut short by his shock at wounding a fellow actor in a stage duel.[39] In London he created a series of roles for Wilks that exploited the latter's carefree charm: neutralizations of the rapacious 'Irish rogue' figure who had stalked the pamphlet literature of the civil war and shadowed the rakes of Restoration Comedy. Sir Harry Wildair in the play of that name and *The Constant Couple*, and Captain Plume in *The Recruiting Officer* (see below, pp. 179–80 and 222–8 respectively), were post-sentimental heroes who rehabilitated, at relatively safe distance, the type of the Restoration rake. The twin heroes of *The Beaux' Stratagem*, Aimwell and Archer (the latter written for Wilks), are conniving tricksters in a good cause, and, while they admit to having feelings, they do not indulge them.

The familiar theme of Restoration rakes preying on unworthy husbands and their frustrated wives acquires a new twist as the play dramatizes the impact of migrants on a closed community. Unlike many Restoration comedies, *The Beaux' Stratagem* is set outside London, in the decidedly provincial town of Lichfield. Aimwell and Archer's cultural double is present in the form of a gang of highwaymen who run their trade from the local inn: the stereotypical 'Irish' are in fact the indigenous English, and they need supplanting by the charming tricksters with the Irish lilt from London. Farquhar was as much a victim of the marauding stereotype as anyone; in the aftermath of 1688 his Protestant family had been burned out of their house by a Catholic mob, and his trickster heroes represent a plea for an Anglo-Irish *entente cordiale* based on shared hostility to thieves and housebreakers. Wilks's part, Archer, rehearses the conventional destiny of the Irishman by acting as Aimwell's servant before the denouement reveals that it is Aimwell who is the real English lord, announced as such by the exemplary modern Englishman, Sir Charles Freeman, 'the honestest fellow living'.[40] For all its optimism, the performance gestured towards avenues that remained closed to most Irishmen of opportunity.

The initial success of the play was down to a quality that remains evident to anyone who performs it today. Vibrantly attractive though the twin heroes are, this is a company piece in which a host of individual roles stand out. Farquhar's 1702 *Discourse upon Comedy* famously argued that the 'rules of English comedy do not lie in the compass of Aristotle and his followers, but in the pit, box and galleries', in an audience with a distinct 'complexion and temperament of the natural body as in the constitution of our body politic'.[41] The Irishman speaks confidently of his new identity in a way guaranteed to appeal to those suspicious of Continental fashion – Jonson and Middleton seem to be his *eminences grises* here, with *A Mad World My Masters* a particularly strong presence. His comedy of natural and national humours locates within the four walls of the playhouse not just parameters of taste but diversity of type, and not just in front of the curtain. Lady Bountiful dispenses herbal remedies to the local poor with the enthusiasm of a retired hippie; her daughter-in-law, Mrs Sullen, parodies her zeal with this recommendation for treating a sore leg:

You must lay your husband's leg upon a table, and with a chopping knife you must lay it open as broad as you can; then you must take out the bone, and beat the flesh soundly with a rolling pin; then take salt, pepper, cloves, mace and ginger, some sweet herbs, and season it very well; then roll it up like brawn, and put it into the oven for two hours.[42]

The crooked landlord, Boniface, bequeathed his name to others and became famous for his catchphrase 'As the saying is'. When the actor who created him, William Bullock, had a benefit performance in April 1707, the play was advertised as being 'For the benefit of Will Bullock, as the saying is'. Norris's idiot servant Scrub, for whom a string of unanswered questions constitutes a thrilling 'packet of news', would refer to himself as 'Scrub' in a prologue two years later. Actors, roles and catchphrases fused as tightly as Clive Dunn, Corporal Jones and 'Don't panic!'.[43]

If the play dwells optimistically on the lot of the expatriate Irishman, it reserves a darker mood for the fate of women uprooted from their native soil to marry uncongenial men. *The Beaux' Stratagem* may recall the boisterous trickster comedies of Middleton, but its real distinctiveness is in its sustained allusions to a source that failed to trouble most Restoration playwrights: John Milton's 1643 tract *The Doctrine and Discipline of Divorce*, which presented the most radical manifesto ever written for dealing with an unhappy marriage by arguing that incompatibility, not adultery, should be the prime grounds for divorce. Biographers have argued that Farquhar's interest in Milton was fuelled by his own anxious marriage to Margaret Pemell, a widow with children but, contrary to her own report, no money. If that is true, he spent a truly startling amount of time in *The Beaux' Stratagem* on the question of how it felt for a woman to be trapped in the loveless provinces – so much so that readers of the play could be forgiven for thinking that the play it most vividly calls to mind is not *A Mad World My Masters* but Anton Chekhov's *Three Sisters*.

Other dramatists, notably Southerne in *The Wives' Excuse* (1691), had attempted a sober look at the prospects of women oppressed by their husbands, but Southerne's Mrs Friendall (discussed below at p. 172–6) is faced with either imitating her husband's sexual freedom or just putting up with it and shutting up; the stalemate at the end of the play is arguably the result of the playwright's own struggle to detach himself from the social sphere he satirizes. Farquhar's Mrs Sullen enjoys the greater narrative impetus that comes of being an exiled urban sophisticate in a place where the entertainment is 'leaping of ditches. . .-clambering over styles. . .drinking fat ale, playing at whisk, and smoking tobacco with my husband'.[44] The better world to which she wants to escape is agonizingly real to her, and it is embodied in Archer. Speaking to her sister-in-law Dorinda, she adopts a familiar Hobbesian language of natural law and uses it to illustrate her own disadvantage:

MRS SULLEN: Patience! The cant of custom. Providence sends no evil without a remedy.
Should I lie groaning under a yoke I can shake off, I were accessory to my ruin, and my patience were no better than self-murder.
DORINDA: But how can you shake off the yoke? Your divisions don't come within the reach of the law for a divorce.
MRS SULLEN: Law! What law can search into the remote abyss of nature? What evidence can prove the unaccountable disaffections of wedlock? Can a jury sum up the endless aversions that are rooted in our souls, or can a bench give judgment upon antipathies?
DORINDA: They never pretended, sister; they never meddle but in cases of uncleanness.
MRS SULLEN: Uncleanness! O sister! Casual violation is but a transient injury, and may possibly be repaired, but can radical hatreds be ever reconciled? No, no, sister, nature is the first lawgiver, and when she has set tempers opposite, not all the golden links of wedlock nor iron manacles of law can keep 'em fast.

> Wedlock we own ordained by Heaven's decree,
> But such as Heaven ordained it first to be –
> Concurring tempers in the man and wife
> As mutual helps to draw the load of life.
> View all the works of Providence above:
> The stars with harmony and concord move.
> View all the works of Providence below:
> The fire, the water, earth, and air, we know,
> All in one plant agree to make it grow.
> Must man, the chiefest work of art divine,
> Be doomed in endless discord to repine?
> No, we injure Heaven by that surmise:
> Omnipotence is just, were man but wise.[45]

Awkwardly by the usual laws of dramaturgy, the scene continues into the next act, in which Mrs Sullen reflects on the injustice of her position in a country now ruled by a woman, Queen Anne:

Were I born an humble Turk, where women have no soul nor property, there I must sit contented. But in England, a country whose women are its glory, must women be abused? Where women rule, must women be enslaved? Nay, cheated into slavery, mocked by a promise of comfortable society into a wilderness of solitude! I dare not keep the thought about me.[46]

We are used to hearing of the supremacy of nature over law from characters such as Dorimant and Horner, but Mrs Sullen lends it a new resonance that casts nature not only as irresistible but unfathomable, a 'remote abyss' of 'unaccountable disaffections'. Finding argument in Milton, Farquhar also took snatches of his grand poetry of space and emotion. Mrs Sullen rejects the prissy, pseudo-puritan language of 'uncleanness' to describe adultery, proposing with Milton that it is remediable, unlike 'radical hatreds'. But there are no devils in her universe: the world has been designed according to warped deist principles, a work of endless concord upset less by man than by men.

The result is a character of genuine imaginative power, in the sense that Farquhar focused in Mrs Sullen a whole range of personal and cultural preoccupations and transformed them through a process of what might almost be called (as John Keats described a similar quality in Shakespeare) negative capability. Farquhar is a frustrating subject for biography – no letters or personal testimonies survive – but, with Otway, he is the period's most intriguingly biographical playwright, if not straightforwardly so. *The Recruiting Officer* derives from personal experience of the army, but *The Beaux' Stratagem* imaginatively inverts every piece of biographical data thrown at it. Farquhar's interest in Milton might be traced to his own marriage to a woman who turned out to be impoverished, yet in Mrs Sullen's lament he highlights the wife's indignation at being 'cheated into slavery'. He escaped Dublin to pursue the bright lights of a stage career in London, and Mrs Sullen crystallizes all the dread and confusion of exile from the cultural centre. Perhaps the darkest truth she embodied for Farquhar is represented by Lichfield, which, with its robber gangs, leaping of ditches and 'dozen bottles of usquebaugh' (Irish whiskey), condenses all the stereotypes of the place he and his leading actor and fellow Irishman Wilks had, at least geographically, left behind.

Endnotes

1 Downes, *Roscius Anglicanus*, 66–7.
2 See Cademan's plea, LC 7/3, fols. 26–7; in *Register*, no. 1521.
3 'The petition of the players', LC 7/3, fols. 2–4; in *Register*, no. 1483.
4 *The Diary of Samuel Pepys*, 22 July, 24 October 1663.
5 For the assault on Edward Thomas, see Middlesex Sessions books, III.322, in *Register*, no. 144; for Oxford, order in the Oxford City Council Book, 29 June 1670 (*Register*, no.,564), and BL Add. MS 28,929, fol. Iv (*Register*, no. 859).
6 LC 5/190, fol. 134; in *Register*, no. 956.
7 For details, see Mary Edmond, *Rare Sir William Davenant* (Manchester University Press, 1996), 9–27.
8 *The Diary of Samuel Pepys*, 21 May 1667.
9 Davenant, *The Siege of Rhodes: The First and Second Part* (London, 1663), 12.
10 Downes, *Roscius Anglicanus*, 55.
11 *The Diary of Samuel Pepys*, 4 November 1661.
12 On this history of the portrait up to Betterton's death, see my *Thomas Betterton*, 173–81. For a broader account, see Tarnya Cooper, *Searching for Shakespeare* (London: National Portrait Gallery, 2006), 51–5.
13 Downes, *Roscius Anglicanus*, 75.
14 *The Diary of Samuel Pepys*, 30 October 1662; Philip H. Highfill Jr, Kalvin A. Burnim and Edward A. Langhans, eds., *A Biographical Dictionary of Actors, Actresses, Musicians, Dancers, Managers and Stage Personnel in London, 1660–1800*, 16 vols. (Carbondale: Southern Illinois University Press, 1973), vol. IX, 9.
15 See the 1641 edition of Killigrew's *The Parson's Wedding* and *Claricilla*.
16 *The Diary of Samuel Pepys*, 11 October 1660.
17 For Clun, see *The Diary of Samuel Pepys*, 3 August 1664; for Smith, 14 November 1666.
18 *The Diary of Samuel* Pepys, 12 February 1667. For Heywood's *Psyche*, see LS1 162.
19 *The Diary of Samuel* Pepys, 11 October 1664.
20 Sir William Coventry, cited in *The Diary of Samuel* Pepys, 6 March 1669.
21 C7/331/29, *Register*, no. 1126.
22 David Erskine Baker, *Biographia dramatica*, 2 vols. (London, 1782), vol. II, xxvii.
23 Anon., *A Comparison Between the Two Stages* (London, 1702), 15.
24 John Genest, *Some Account of the English Stage*, 10 vols. (Bath, 1832).
25 From 'The Petition of the Players'; reprinted as Appendix A of Judith M. Milhous, *Thomas Betterton and the Management of Lincoln's Inn Fields 1695–1708* (Carbondale: Southern Illinois University Press, 1979).

26 Joseph Knight, 'Christopher Rich', in Sidney Lee, ed., *The Dictionary of National Biography*, 22 vols. (Oxford University Press, 1917), vol. V, 996.

27 William Congreve, *Love for Love* (London, 1695), 22 (II.i.198–202).

28 Ibid., 91–2 (V.i.708–29).

29 For example, Aubrey Williams, *An Approach to Congreve* (New Haven, CT: Yale University Press, 1979).

30 Charles Sedley, *Antony and Cleopatra* (London, 1677), 61.

31 James A. Winn, *John Dryden and His World* (New Haven, CT: Yale University Press, 1987), 301.

32 John Dryden, *All for Love* (London, 1678), 41 (III.i.361–4).

33 F. R. Leavis, *The Living Principle: 'English' as a Discipline of Thought* (London: Chatto & Windus, 1977), 153.

34 See Jeremy Webster, *Performing Libertinism in Charles II's Court: Politics, Drama, Sexuality* (New York: Palgrave, 2005).

35 Dryden, *All for Love*, 42–4 (III.i.416–55).

36 Downes, *Roscius Anglicanus*, 41.

37 For Betterton and Hart, see Thomas Davies, *Dramatic Miscellanies*, 3 vols. (London, 1784), vol. III, 271–2.

38 Dryden, *All for Love*, 71 (V.i.286–8).

39 W. R. Chetwood, *A General History of the Stage* (London, 1749), 149.

40 George Farquhar, *The Beaux' Stratagem* (London, 1707), 68 (V.iv.139).

41 George Farquhar, 'A Discourse Upon Comedy', in *Love and Business: In a Collection of Occasionary Verse* (London, 1702), 143.

42 Farquhar, *The Beaux' Stratagem*, 40 (IV.i.20–30).

43 Ibid., III.i. For Norris, see Philip Roberts, 'Vanbrugh's lost play: the prologue', *Restoration and Eighteenth-Century Theatre Research* 12 (1973), 57–8.

44 Farquhar, *The Beaux' Stratagem*, 11 (II.i.37–44).

45 Ibid., 38–9 (III.iii.477–512).

46 Ibid., 39 (IV.i.1–9).

5 | Actors

Margery Pinchwife's translation to the capital and its playhouses was no less bedazzled than Farquhar's. Reflecting on her first experience of the theatre, she tells her sister-in-law, Alithea,

I was a-weary of the play, but I liked hugeously the actors; they are the goodliest, properest men, sister![1]

Her innocence is to mistake performance for text; fetching up in the wrong academic department, she prefers the show to the play. If this is another reminder that the 'gaze' of recent theory was by no means directed only at actresses, it also highlights the fraught symbiosis of playwrights and performers. Actors were integral to the process of writing, but their business was to steal the show – a habit in which audiences were thoroughly complicit. Actors' 'lines' or customary stage profiles determined to a significant a playwright's understanding of what roles could and could not be written for a particular play, while their personal qualities and history might form an important part of the overall effect of performance – a sign system that would become commonplace in the eighteenth-century theatre as much as in the celebrity culture of commercial cinema today.[2] Good actors could rescue a poor play and bad ones spoil a masterpiece. 'Lord, what prejudice it wrought in me against [Macbeth],' lamented Pepys, to see John Young deputize for Thomas Betterton.[3]

Actors in society

What does that say about the social status of Restoration actors? It depends which ones, and who's talking. Robert Gould published this rabid denunciation of the profession, making it sound less 'goodliest' or 'properest' than oldest:

A pack of idle, pimping, sponging slaves
A miscellany of rogues, fools and knaves;
A nest of lechers, worse than Sodom bore,

117

And justly merit to be punished more:
Diseased, in debt, and every moment dunned;
By all good Christians loathed, and their own kindred shunned.[4]

But Gould had been disappointed in an attempt to have a play staged, and he saved his worst for the manager who had turned him down. Betterton was, he alleged, like an oriental despot who kept a harem of actresses for his own pleasure, the innocent explanation of which is that since 1660 it had been customary for younger actresses to board with the company manager. Gould's diatribe was not unique, with the new generation of actresses attracting venom that sometimes did not get as far as words. In 1665 Rebecca Marshall of the King's Company twice complained of being stalked and abused, on one occasion by a thug who 'clapped a turd upon her face and hair'.[5] Spurned admirers rather than angry puritans were responsible, but they would have found common cause in the assertion of Jeremy Collier that actors were 'sirens' who 'devoured' the 'unwary'.[6] Their real threat, he claimed, just as Philip Stubbes had more than a hundred years earlier, was in encouraging people to confuse 'behaviour' (the performance of gentility) with 'virtue' (the real thing).[7] So, it is sometimes argued, the attention given to performers' occasionally colourful private lives became a way of reinstating the difference. When Moll Davis flashed the £700 ring that being the king's lover had earned her, Pepys was moved to call her, in an uncanny premonition of twenty-first century celebrity culture, a 'jade'. Why? Because, in words by Deborah C. Payne that could equally apply to other Jades since, she represented the 'nouveau aristocrats of an emergent visual culture that rewards a captivating performance more than the reorganization of the British navy'.[8] 'Poor Pepys, lucky actress,' concludes Payne – but no one ever 'clapped a turd– on Pepys's face.

Against this, it is easy to underestimate, first, the tributes to the professional and artistic skill of actors and, second, their visibility beyond the theatres. Pepys may have thought Moll Davis a 'jade' but he admired her performances, as he did those of other actresses, and could even see how the company exploited her: once she gave a jig at the end of the play 'only to please the company to see her dance in boy's clothes'.[9] Friendship with Henry Harris, and observations about Harris's colleague Thomas Betterton, suggest the respectable civil servant Pepys hardly peered down his nose at men who sat at the coffee house with Dryden 'and all the wits of the town', enjoying 'very witty and pleasant discourse' – at least, not until Harris took him to a pub near the New Exchange for an evening of dirty talk with the infamous Harry Killigrew, who had been banished from court for suggesting that Lady Castlemaine, then the king's mistress, liked to masturbate.[10] Pepys even had Harris round for dinner, admiring his 'curious and understanding' mind and 'fine conversation'. Whatever his exploits at the Blue Balls, this was a man to be emulated, not despised.

Pepys did not get to know Betterton but admired his performances and reports of his 'studious and humble' attitude, which as early as 1662 had led to him becoming 'rich already with what he gets and saves' – an observation made without apparent resentment.[11] Betterton's connections further undermined Gould's claim that actors were social pariahs. He appears to have been on good terms with John Tillotson, Fellow of the Royal Society and from 1694 Archbishop of Canterbury; he assisted at court with the preparation of entertainments such as John Crowne's *Calisto* in 1675, and helped a Member of Parliament with his amateur theatricals by staying with him during the summer.[12] He corresponded with Thomas Thynne, Viscount Weymouth, about their respective art collections.[13] In the sole letter of his that survives we learn from his somewhat ponderous hand that he kept a country house near Reading in addition to lodgings in Covent Garden; the sale of his private collection in August 1710 aimed to dispose of approximately 600 books and seventy paintings.[14] Most striking of all for the lubricious harem keeper denounced by Gould, he remained married to the same woman for nearly forty-seven years. The bourgeois respectability proclaimed by *The Life of Mr Thomas Betterton* months after his death was not the fabrication of someone keen to promote the status of acting but an accurate statement of where Betterton's studious humility had got him.

Aristocrats had no difficulty consorting with actors, however much Collier and his readers might complain about them. Harris could drink with the Earl of Dorset and any number of actresses shared the king's bed; Betterton could claim friendship with Henry St John, 1st Earl of Bolingbroke. Perhaps there was less of a perceptible threat, as there was for middle-class spectators, from the confusion of 'behaviour' and 'virtue' lamented by Collier. Moll Davis's ring was aggravating to someone on Pepys's earnings, but hardly to an earl. Nevertheless, actors did sometimes overstep the mark in the eyes of their patrons, and suffered for it with beatings or imprisonment.[15]

Ritual condemnations of the profession such as Gould's probably rubbed off on some of the performers themselves, and the Restoration Stage echoed to the sound of actors leaving it. With varying degrees of success Hester Davenport, Nell Gwyn and Moll Davis used their professional profiles in precisely the way applauded by Deborah C. Payne: for the advancement that came of associating with the aristocracy. Senior actors including Charles Hart and Michael Mohun sought tidy pension deals when the patent companies united in 1681–2, while Betterton himself might well have retired early but for the loss of his savings in a merchant shipping disaster in 1692.[16] Comparison of six performances a week with life at the country house presumably sharpened the temptation.

Actors and their backgrounds

Actors' backgrounds illustrate how far they had travelled to be in such a position, but they were not quite as humble as Gould claimed. Memories of loss, rather than low social standing per se, hung over many of them. Some actresses were illegitimate while others, such as Betterton's wife Mary Saunderson, appear to have been orphaned. Elizabeth Barry is believed to have been the daughter of a Royalist barrister who had lost his fortune after the civil war; anecdotal evidence attributes her training for the stage to an affair with the Earl of Rochester. Anne Bracegirdle was probably an orphan who grew up with the Bettertons, the stage a part of her life from infancy. When Pepys decided to engage Winifred Gosnell as a maid for his wife in 1662 he found her 'pretty handsome' and admired her singing, while fearing she had been 'bred up with too great liberty for my family', which would lead to 'great inconveniences of expenses'; clearly, her upbringing had not exactly been deprived. A few days into her new employment, Gosnell took her looks and voice to the Duke's Company, relieving Pepys of the risk that she might drain his finances.[17]

The picture for male actors is slightly different. Betterton's father, Matthew, had styled himself a gentleman but worked as a junior cook for Charles I before the court at Whitehall broke up in the winter of 1641–2. In 1660 a significant clutch of King's Company actors could claim not only to have acted for the king in exile (and, indeed, for his father in power) but to have fought in battle for the royal cause. Michael Mohun was referred to as 'Major Mohun' throughout his stage career. Their Duke's Company counterparts presented a different picture again: they were tradesmen who had weathered the interregnum by keeping their heads down and doing business. Thomas Lillieston, Betterton's first Claudius, was a Holborn weaver, while Cave Underhill was from a family of cloth workers. James Nokes, the company clown, had run a knick-knack shop in Cornhill with his brother Robert. A small group of actors had been apprentices with John Rhodes of the Draper's Company, whose past in the King's Men made him a theatrical entrepreneur as well as a bookseller. Betterton himself had worked as Rhodes's boy in bookselling, and there is some evidence that he continued with his own business even when his acting career began to take off.[18]

In so far as the Duke's Company set the standard for professional theatre practice in the period, its success cannot simply be attributed to the firm direction given by Sir William Davenant. The social backgrounds of the Duke's Company's actors in 1660 show why the company was the most organized, efficient and entrepreneurial of its time: their multi-tasking, DIY attitude was well suited to the fast-changing conditions of the restored theatre. Whatever pleasure they took in being servants to royalty, they were that very English phenomenon: a company of shopkeepers.

Actors and performances

Although actors had 'lines', or types of roles for which they were suited, versatility was at a premium in companies set up to perform what the patent documents tended to describe as 'tragedies, comedies, plays, operas, music, scenes and all other entertainments'.[19] Elizabeth Barry, the age's paradigmatic tragic heroine, who (like Betterton) brought 'an enchanting harmony' to the most extreme passions, took major roles in comedies by Behn, Southerne and others, although her casting as the scheming Marwood in *The Way of the World* and the angry ex, Loveit, in *The Man of Mode* (at least in revivals) indicates the way her 'elevated dignity' and 'violence of passion' helped weave a tapestry richer than the term 'comedy of manners' might imply.[20] In the female roles created by Otway, she developed as a performer uniquely able to embody impossible dilemmas. Anne Bracegirdle was noted for her skill in witty comedy, to the extent that Congreve wrote Millamant for her in *The Way of the World*; but she also played roles

that demanded tragic vulnerability, such as Desdemona in *Othello* and
Lady Anne in *Richard III*, and those that played – with varying degrees
of complexity – on her reputation for innocence, such as Isabella in
Measure for Measure and Mrs Sightly in Southerne's *The Wives'
Excuse*. As it did for most performers, playing foreigners – whether
French, Spanish, Greek, African or South American – came with the
territory. Bracegirdle sang well too, with a 'potent and magnetic
charm', and featured in extravagant musical entertainments such as
Peter Motteux's *The Loves of Mars and Venus*, in which her casting as
Venus was surely, in view of her spotless reputation, an outright
joke.[21] A conspicuous exception to the law of adaptability was
Nell Gwyn, who flourished in comic repartee but could not do tragic
grandeur: 'Nell's ill speaking of a great part made me mad,' wrote
Pepys of her performance in Dryden's *Indian Queen* sequel, *The
Indian Emperour*.[22]

In addition to his fine conversation, Henry Harris also sang with
considerable grace – so well, in fact, that, when Pepys's former maid
Gosnell slipped a tone or two during Davenant's *The Rivals*, he had
the skill to 'go out of tune to agree with her'.[23] He was an extremely
versatile performer whose career embraced heroes and villains, philosophers and cardinals, romantic leads and dull foils, the mad and
the trenchantly sane. More than Betterton, he possessed the conventional attributes of the leading man, and John Downes's tribute to his
performance of Cardinal Wolsey in *Henry VIII* suggests a difference
of approach. 'State, port and mien' were the qualities he brought to
the role, as opposed to the painstaking study that had led Betterton
to absorb 'instructions' from Davenant.[24] Although he had trained
as a painter, Harris was what might now be called a 'natural', and
conscious of it. After the strike that had seen him return to the Duke's
Company on improved terms, he was described by Pepys as 'ayery',
and it was his social ease and capacity for fine discourse that earned
him the role of the gossip Medley in Etherege's *The Man of Mode* and
the parallel doom of yet again playing second fiddle to Betterton
as Dorimant. Like others before him, Harris fell short of lifelong
commitment to the stage; after his ten-year stint as co-manager of the
Duke's Company he disappeared at the very moment when the duke
himself assumed the greatest controversy, and promptly lost his court
positions when his former patron was crowned as King James II. The
heat of working for the country's most controversial Catholic was

something the diplomatic Betterton could stand; Harris, it appears, could not, and his case illustrates how actors were directly at the mercy of the state. To be a royal servant came with privileges, but also responsibilities.

Bisket, Buffoon, Cocklebrain, Credulous, Doodle, Dunce, Foppering, Ninny, Noddy, Puny: alone, the list of roles assigned to James Nokes tells us what sort of actor he was, even though it includes a number of surprises such as Cornwall in *King Lear* (imagine Norman Wisdom putting out Gloucester's eyes) and the Nurse in *Romeo and Juliet* (actresses did not immediately replace drag actors for senior or comic female roles).[25] His Polonius must have been a vivid foil to Betterton's awestruck, solemn Hamlet. Nokes made a career of the physical accidents and contortions associated with the new genre of farce, his brain miles behind the audience's and his body doggedly refusing to keep up. Downes describes how, during a court performance, he contrived to resemble 'a Drest up Ape', putting 'the King and Court to an Excessive Laughter'.[26] With physical clowning went verbal dexterity; a visitor to his dressing room thought he overheard him reciting lines from a play, only to discover that he was chatting away to a colleague.[27]

It is hard to imagine Thomas Betterton having time or inclination to chat, although, as with Nokes, it was easy to confuse the actor with the role. In the view of one satirist he carried his 'stiff comportment' and 'formal' manner straight from the stage into the coffee house, so making his own statement about the dignity of his profession amid the world at large. A French visitor recalled him, pointedly, as 'agreeable in serious Conversation'.[28] But Betterton's professional skill embraced almost every kind of performance, sober or not. Estimates of his total repertory vary between 183 and 264 roles.[29] Up to a half were in comedy, ranging from glamorous wits to resentful schemers and concluding with men well past their prime, such as Falstaff and Heartwell, the hero of Congreve's *The Old Bachelour*, a 'battered debauchee [surprisingly] come into the trammels of order and decency: he neither languishes nor burns, but frets for love'. Alienated temporarily from his renowned 'order and decency', the actor strove towards it, finding a distinctively moderating note for the passion of a character too old to languish or burn, but still capable of fretting.[30] Betterton preferred such complex modulations to the gross physical comedy of Nokes. He generally steered clear of farce, either standing on the dignity amply

Figure 5.1 Thomas Betterton, by Godfrey Kneller

suggested by Godfrey Kneller's portrait (Figure 5.1) or mistrusting the ability of his outsize feet to do his bidding.[31]

Posterity associated him with the 'oratorical' or 'teapot' school of acting – one hand in the waistcoat, the other gesturing – but Colley Cibber, who worked with him, evokes a subdued complexity of style. This is how Cibber describes Betterton's performance of the moment in *Hamlet* when the Ghost first appears to the Prince, a moment often spoiled in Cibber's recollection by lesser actors more anxious for effect:

You have seen a Hamlet perhaps, who, on the first appearance of his father's Spirit, has thrown himself into all the straining vociferation requisite to express rage and fury, and the house has thundered with applause... [T]he late Mr Addison, while I sat by him to see this scene acted, made the same observation, asking me, with some surprise, if I thought Hamlet should be in so violent a passion with the Ghost, which, though it might have astonished, it had not provoked him? – for you may observe that in this beautiful speech the passion never rises beyond an almost breathless astonishment, or an impatience, limited by filial reverence, to enquire into the suspected wrongs that may have raised him from his peaceful tomb and a desire to know what a spirit so seemingly distressed might wish or enjoin a sorrowful son to execute towards his future quiet in the grave. This was the light into which Betterton threw this scene; which he opened with a pause of mute amazement, then rising slowly to a solemn, trembling voice, he made the Ghost equally terrible to the spectator as to himself, and in the descriptive part of the natural emotions which the ghastly vision gave him, the boldness of his expostulation was still governed by decency, manly, but not braving, his voice never rising into that seeming outrage or wild defiance of what he naturally revered. But alas! to preserve this medium, between mouthing and meaning too little, to keep the attention more pleasingly awake by a tempered spirit than by mere vehemence of voice, is of all the master-strokes of an actor the most difficult to reach. In this none have yet equalled Betterton.[32]

Studies of Restoration acting by scholars such as Joseph Roach and Dene Barnett focus on the antique sign systems – vocal, gestural and kinetic – that would make any recreation of such period style seem absurdly inflated to any modern audience. Betterton's library catalogue includes a copy of the handbook of seventeenth-century gestural language, John Bulwer's 1644 *Chirologia, or, The Natural Language of the Hand*, which prescribes how thoughts and passions were to be communicated by orators and, by inference, actors. Acting styles, like the social behaviour they are modelled on, update themselves with every generation, to the extent that old acting can easily look like bad acting simply because it does not conform to recognizable behaviour. Seeking to explain these differences, the study of performance codes is clearly of immense value in helping us understand what actors *looked* like, but not necessarily what they or their audiences *felt* about the experience, and that is the value of writing such as Cibber's.

Conventionally, actors of the period identified the 'passion' of a particular speech and sought to express it through a range of established vocal and gestural devices. 'Her action is always just and produced naturally by the sentiments of the part,' writes Cibber of Elizabeth Barry.[33] Yet the originating 'passion' might not be self-evident: in *Hamlet*, the actor must choose between 'rage and fury', 'breathless astonishment' and 'impatience', the latter 'limited by filial reverence'. It took an inquiring mind to consult the text, to ask the questions it poses, at the level of both the individual speech and the wider relationship between characters that supplies its context: it is not

'Angels and ministers of grace defend us' that tells us Hamlet is a 'sorrowful son'. As with Congreve's Heartwell, for every emotion there is a counterpoise. 'Boldness' is 'governed by decency', 'impatience' by 'filial reverence'; the actor must be 'manly' in a 'tempered' way. In texts that encumbered the performer with fewer choices, 'false fire and extravagancies' were moderated into 'flowing numbers'. Barry too possessed this quality, bringing an 'enchanting harmony' to the most 'impetuous and terrible' scenes. Study of historical performance codes may struggle with such complexity of intention and effect.

Cibber's is, perhaps, is the first definition of what it means to be a *classical* actor in the richest sense of that term: not just a player of Shakespeare but a performer able to deploy reason and feeling in equal balance; to make textual inquiry the starting point rather than jumping straight to dazzling the audience; to construe an interpretation or 'reading' that can satisfy a critical connoisseur such as 'the late Mr Addison'. In arriving at this definition, Cibber prescribes a manner that seems very English and very eighteenth-century. Betterton's avoidance of rant, his middle way between 'mouthing and meaning too little', represents an ideal of social as well as theatrical performance.

The man who bequeathed subsequent generations a critical reading of Prince Hamlet was himself a critical reader. One emblem of those qualities that provides a series of clues to Betterton's approach to his craft is the sale catalogue of his books and pictures published in 1710 by the bookseller Jacob Hooke and grandly entitled *Pinacotheca Bettertonaeana*. As well as translations of Greek and Latin histories, Betterton owned Le Vayer's *Animadversions on the Greek and Latin Historians* (1671). He acquired literary and dramatic criticism: René Rapin's *Reflections on Aristotle* (1674), Thomas Pope Blount's *Remarks upon Poetry* (1694), Rymer's *Tragedies of the last age* (1678), Dennis's *The Advancement and Reformation of Modern Poetry* (1701), François Hédelin's *Whole Art of the Stage* (1684). He collected Hobbes and Locke, Thomas Browne and Francis Bacon, Niccolò Machiavelli and Michel de Montaigne; his run of books by Robert Boyle suggests an active interest in the new science that is only slightly tempered by an allegiance to astrology. A relentlessly busy practitioner, he was also a learned one, collecting books that took a longer view of the instruments of his profession, such as Géraud de Cordemoy's *Philosophical Discourse of Speech* (1668). His stage impersonations of eastern despots were conceivably informed by reading about them in books such as William Seaman's translation of Saddedin's *Life of Sultan Orchan* (1652), and he owned paintings of some of the historical personages he acted, as well as prints that may supply clues for how performances were costumed.[34] Most of all, he seems to have been interested in reliving through reading the experience of civil war in which he had grown up.[35]

If the examples of Betterton and Barry point to the development of acting as a craft that enabled the performer to astound an audience beyond the limitations suggested by physique or instant attractiveness, other actors traded on natural charisma. Where Betterton laboured under 'instructions' as Henry VIII, Harris brought 'port and mien' to Wolsey. Where Barry was 'gracefully majestic', Anne Bracegirdle 'threw out such a glow of health and cheerfulness that…few spectators that were not past it, could behold her without desire'.[36] Male playwrights such as Congreve and Nicholas Rowe were 'not past it' any more than male spectators, seeming to 'plead their own passions and make their private court to her in fictitious characters'. There must have been dozens, perhaps hundreds, of other such conversations between playwrights and actors that are now unheard: an intriguing but largely unexplored annex to the rise of the dramatic author.

Double acts

Many of those conversations necessarily took place between the contrasting identities and stage profiles of the actors themselves: as it continues to be, acting was a relational art in which partnership was key to the effect. Sexual frisson played its role. Betterton played Macbeth opposite his wife, Mary Saunderson, as Laurence Olivier did to Vivien Leigh; Charles Hart and Nell Gwyn were the period's most engaging witty couple, an item on stage slightly more permanently than off it. Just as often, performances exploited either knowingly or not the tensions that arose between egos. The twin stars of the King's Company, Charles Hart and Michael Mohun, existed in a state of semi-permanent hostility, which gave charge to their performances of great antiphonal double acts such as Othello and Iago.[37] The more orderly Duke's Company had found itself in such territory when Henry Harris went on strike in 1663.[38] The duke himself intervened, and Harris got a pay rise, but in his comeback show his manager, Davenant, exacted a subtle revenge, casting him as the doomed Wolsey in

Shakespeare and Fletcher's *Henry VIII* against the king (played by Betterton, of course), whose authority was bound to prevail.[39]

Rival masculinities are central to what we think of the Restoration repertory, and what unites the twin heroes of tragedy and comedy can seem more significant than what distinguishes them, as *The Way of the World* and *The Country Wife* abundantly show. Theatre naturally distinguishes identities that reading may confuse – no other Restoration leading man looked at all like Betterton – but the recurrence of the rival male motif gave dramatists and audiences the opportunity to reflect on the psychological and political disturbance that came of putting one actor up against another. A prime example is found in one of the very few Restoration tragedies that has a modern production history.

Thomas Otway and *Venice Preserv'd* (1682)

As *Don Carlos* shows, Otway bathed in the language and characterization of Shakespeare, and in *Venice Preserv'd* his pairing of the tough cynic Pierre and the more vulnerable Jaffeir owes much to Cassius and Brutus in *Julius Caesar*. Otway's play speaks to modern audiences partly because it is a star vehicle for contrasting actors: in Peter Brook's 1953 production, John Gielgud (Jaffeir) and Paul Scofield (Pierre); in 1984, Ian McKellen and Michael Pennington in Peter Gill's grandly rhetorical version at the National Theatre. There, the play stood up to casting against type, with the more cerebral Pennington as the emotive Jaffeir and McKellen exploring in Pierre the reserved, soldierly brusqueness that would make him a peerless Iago for the Royal Shakespeare Company six years later. As in many Restoration tragedies, brotherly love in *Venice Preserv'd* hinges not just on a cause but on a woman. Jaffeir's Belvidera was one product of Otway's obsession with Elizabeth Barry, and the wounded passions of the role have been reanimated by generations of fine actresses since then, from Sarah Siddons to Jane Lapotaire in Gill's production. In 1682 Otway's play was remarkable partly for what seems to be its bold denunciation of Whig politicians; nowadays its distinction is in psychological complexity, not least in the way Jaffeir yearns to find in Pierre a substitute for Belvidera, using the language of a playwright tormented by his love for a woman who was also a series of performances:

Oh Pierre, wert thou but she,
How I could pull thee down into my heart,
Gaze on thee till my eye-strings cracked with love,
Till all my sinews with its fire extended,
Fixed me upon the rack of ardent longing;
Then swelling, sighing, raging to be blest,
Come like a panting turtle [i.e. dove] to thy breast,
On thy soft bosom, hovering, bill and play,
Confess the cause why last I fled away;
    Own 'twas a fault, but swear to give it o'er,
    And never follow false ambition more.[40]

Struggling to escape from the double that is Pierre, Jaffeir imagines him as his wife, knowing the transformation to be impossible but wishing it all the same.

If *Venice Preserv'd* borrows from Shakespeare, it also shows a debt to French classical tragedy. Otway had written a very playable version of Racine's *Berenice* in 1675, and the outline of his greatest play suggests how much he had learned (perhaps fatally) from the French preference for handing irresolvable crises to a small number of characters.[41] Like Othello, the impoverished Jaffeir has married a Venetian lady, Belvidera, against the wishes of her father, a senator called Pruili – a motive for Jaffeir to listen to his friend Pierre's anti-government tirades. But Pierre has his own private quarrel. His mistress, Aquilina, is being paid by another senator, Antonio, for kinky sex, in which the senator pretends to be a bull, then a dog, before being whipped (the Duke of York's bitterest political enemy, the Earl of Shaftesbury, is often thought to be the model). Otway's dialogue here, although usually played for laughs, is more graphically debased than almost anything else in English drama, and it would not be out of place in Sarah Kane: 'Spit in my Face,' Antonio begs, '. . .now, now, spit.'[42] Producing the public cause, private quarrels also undermine it. As in *Julius Caesar*, the plotters assemble, and a rum lot they are, led by a dubious Frenchman called Renault. Jaffeir, a new arrival to the conspiracy, they do not trust, and require of him a pledge. He gives them for safe keeping something 'worth more than all the World can pay for', his wife (so, arguably, spitting in *her* face). Renault abuses his trust and attempts to rape Belvidera, whereupon Jaffeir informs on his co-conspirators, but on the somewhat naïve condition that the Senate spares their lives. They don't, of course, so Jaffeir turns on

Figure 5.2 David Garrick and Susannah Cibber, by Johan Zoffany

Belvidera, threatening to kill her in the moment immortalized by Johan Zoffany's great painting of David Garrick and Susannah Cibber (Figure 5.2): she has, he believes, robbed him of manly virtue (if only Pierre *had* somehow combined the roles of brother and wife!). She sues for the conspirators' pardon, but too late. Visiting Pierre on the scaffold, he agrees to spare him the dishonour of hanging and stabs him. Less complex heroes might retire to a peaceful domestic existence, but Jaffeir makes it clear where his allegiance lies and kills himself sooner than return to the arms of Belvidera, who runs mad and dies.

The double act enjoyed by twentieth-century performers was created by the intriguing partnership of Betterton as Jaffeir and, as Pierre, the man who was about to become his fellow manager of the United Company, William Smith. Casting gave to the performance a singular political colour: mounted during the last days of the Duke's Company, the play looked back at the high tide of the Popish Plot through a prism of performance convention. Betterton's previous co-manager and acting foil, Harris, had disappeared from the scene in 1678. Smith had enjoyed the Duke of York's favour long before his performance as Don Carlos and his creation of the series of lovable

Yorkist heroes written for him by Aphra Behn. In 1666 the duke had saved him from the gallows, and more than twenty years later Smith would declare his gratitude in the most perilous terms, attaching himself to the Jacobite cause after the accession of William III. Cibber reports that, after an altercation between Smith and an unnamed courtier, the duke saw to it that it was the courtier who was rebuked.[43] So, in *Venice Preserv'd*, here is Smith, the heir apparent of the company and diehard ducal loyalist, playing a man with a deep grudge against a character who resembled the duke's worst enemy in what was, after all, the parliamentary body of the Venetian Senate.

Other political plays of the previous two years (Tate's *The Sicilian Usurper* of 1681, Lee's *Lucius Junius Brutus* in 1680) had foundered upon censorship. Otway evaded official attention by balancing opposing sides in the interests of loyal endorsement (arguably another Shakespearean attribute): he shows us conspirators doomed to fail because of their own weakness or corruption, and a conspiracy legitimated because it is precisely not like the Popish Plot; the attack is on parliamentary rather than royal privilege. The loyal actor playing the chief conspirator, but in a cause of the greatest loyalty: the double significance of Smith's casting crystallizes perfectly the ambiguity that critics have found in a play that constantly exalts and then undermines its heroes' motives.

Ambiguity is not a word that instantly comes to mind when reading some of the rhetorical and dramatic peaks of Otway's writing, as in the scene pictured by Zoffany. Jaffeir finds out from Belvidera that the conspirators are not, after all, to be saved; in Zoffany, Garrick's raised dagger has an iconic force that anticipates the prelude to the shower sequence in Hitchcock's *Psycho*, but the scene is in fact a prolonged phallic tease in which the audience is led to wonder whether Jaffeir will summon the resolve to get his weapon out at all:

JAFFEIR: What means this dreadful story?
    Death, and tomorrow? Broken limbs and bowels?
    Insulted o'er by a vile butchering villain?
    By all my fears I shall start out to madness,
    With barely guessing, if the truth's hid longer.
BELVIDERA: The faithless senators, 'tis they've decreed it:
    They say according to our friend's request,
    They shall have death, and not ignoble bondage:
    Declare their promised mercy all as forfeited;

False to their oaths, and deaf to intercession;
    Warrants are passed for public death tomorrow.
JAFFEIR: Death! Doomed to die! Condemned unheard! Unpleaded!
BELVIDERA: Nay, cruellest racks and torments are preparing,
    To force confessions from their dying pangs;
    Oh do not look so terribly upon me,
    How your lips shake, and all your face disordered!
    What means my love?
JAFFEIR: Leave me. I charge thee leave me – strong temptations
    Wake in my heart.
BELVIDERA: For what?
JAFFEIR: No more, but leave me.
BELVIDERA: Why?
JAFFEIR: Oh! By Heaven I love thee with that fondness
    I would not have thee stay a moment longer,
    Near these cursed hands: are they not cold upon thee? (*Pulls the dagger*
        half out of his bosom and puts it back again)
BELVIDERA: No, everlasting comfort's in thy arms,
    To lean thus on thy breast is softer ease
    Than downy pillows decked with leaves of roses.
JAFFEIR: Alas, thou thinkest not of the thorns 'tis filled with,
    Fly e're they gall thee: there's a lurking serpent
    Ready to leap and sting thee to thy heart...
    ...hark thee, traitress, thou hast done this;
    Thanks to thy tears and false persuading love. (*Fumbling for his dagger*)
    How her eyes speak speak! Oh thou bewitching creature!
    Madness cannot hurt thee: come, thou little trembler,
    Creep, even into my heart, and there lie safe;
    'Tis they own citadel – ha! – yet stand off,
    Heaven must have Justice, and my broken vows
    Will sink me else beneath its reaching mercy;
    I'll wink and then 'tis done. (*Draws the dagger, offers to stab her*)[44]

A dozen lines later he '*offers to stab her again*'; she kneels, then '*leaps upon his neck and kisses him*', before the melodramatic climax in which he '*throws away the dagger and embraces her*'. The psychopathy of Alfred Hitchcock's interest in the mutilation of vulnerable blondes has been the subject of recent studies and films, and this manifestation of Otway's obsession with Elizabeth Barry seems a no less complex phenomenon. Yet it is written *for* its performers, not against them: Belvidera reads Jaffeir's face as an audience would ('Oh do not look so...'), and the dagger business gives the actors a physical structure on which to build the emotional crisis. For all its violent rhetoric and Shakespearean flashes (compare the rapid-fire exchange with the dialogue of the Macbeths after Duncan's murder), the scene poses a symmetrical, neoclassical dilemma, to which Jaffeir's failure of phallic authority provides only one solution – as did Otway's: he is doomed to choose Belvidera/Barry, and to be tormented by his choice.

This was the kind of part for which Barry was acclaimed: dignified in feeling, capable of turning private grief into public protest. Something of this Roman manner is conveyed in her portrait (Figure 5.3). Despising the Senate, Belvidera speaks the language of political indignation with a zest that equals Pierre's, yet the greatest 'ease' she can imagine is to lean submissively on Jaffeir's breast, so making and undoing his manhood in a moment. Cibber described this double facility of Barry's:

Mrs Barry, in characters of greatness, had a presence of elevated dignity, her mien and motion superb and gracefully majestic: her voice full, clear and strong, so that no violence of passion could be too much for her. And when distress or tenderness possessed her, she subsided into the most affecting melody and softness.

Good example.

Figure 5.3 Elizabeth Barry; anonymous

Cibber associated the former of the two registers with her roles for Dryden and Lee, the latter with 'the softer passions' of Otway.[45] As Otway's Monimia in his 1680 *The Orphan*, Cibber recalls, she would always shed real tears.[46] But it is heroic defiance, as well as a merciless racking of Jaffeir's sensitivity, that we hear in Belvidera's gruesome description of the 'bleeding bowels, and...broken limbs' that await Pierre, who is, after all, her rival. Otway's individuality as a dramatist is that these 'softer passions' often tend towards violent psychopathy – in this case literally, for Belvidera eventually goes mad and dies. The ideological containment Cibber identified by associating Barry and Otway with submissive, sentimental passions of character-ization is displaced by the sort in which students of Victorian fiction have revelled since Sandra Gilbert and Susan Gubar's *The Madwoman in the Attic*, but with a difference. Belvidera's final vision is of her husband and his friend reunited as ghosts: yet they 'pull so hard' to bring her down into an infernal threesome, the symmetrical dilemma merely deferred to another world.

Aphra Behn's *The Rover*: rival sisters

By the time Behn's most enduring comedy was first performed, in March 1677, the playwright had reached a secure understanding of her favoured Duke's Company, and they of her, not without diffi-culty. Depending on how adaptations are attributed, it was probably her seventh play for the Duke's, and before the year was out she had finished her eighth. But in her first three plays no actors' names are listed, and her third, *The Dutch Lover* (1673), condemns the slack discipline of the performers in a withering preface. A three-year break duly followed. With *Abdelazer* (1676), an exotic tragedy featuring the much-anthologized song 'Love in fantastic triumph sat', which sounds like a hymn by a Counter-Reformation monk, she found a way of writing for the company's major performers that suited their capacities and memories. For Betterton and Harris, *Abdelazer* must have seemed like a rerun of *The Siege of Rhodes*, with a villainous Moor pitted against a heroic Christian. For Betterton's wife, Mary, it was one of the first occasions she found herself matched with the novice who, according to stage legend, had been thrown out of the company and coached back into it by the Earl of Rochester. A year later the opening of *The Rover* captured perfectly the voice of the *ingénue* Hellena,

created by Elizabeth Barry, bridling in a private chamber against
the suspicions of her elder sister Florinda, played by Mary Betterton:

FLORINDA: What an impertinent thing is a young girl bred in a nunnery!
How full of questions! Prithee no more, Hellena, I have told thee more
than thou understandest already.

HELLENA: The more's my grief. I would fain know as much as you, which
makes me so inquisitive; not is it enough I know you are a lover, unless
you tell me too, who 'tis you sigh for.

FLORINDA: When you're a lover, I'll think you fit for a secret of that nature.

HELLENA: 'Tis true, I never was a lover yet – but I begin to have a shrewd
guess, what 'tis to be so, and fancy it very pretty to sigh, and sing, and
blush, and wish, and dream and wish, and long and wish to see the
man; and when I do, look pale and tremble; just as you did when my
brother brought home the fine English colonel to see you – what do you
call him? Don Belvile.

FLORINDA: Fie, Hellena.

HELLENA: That blush betrays you – I am sure 'tis so. Or is Don Antonio the
Viceroy's son? Or perhaps the rich old Don Vincentio whom my father
designs you for a husband? Why do you blush again?

FLORINDA: With indignation, and how near soever my father thinks I am to
marrying that hated object, I shall let him see I understand better what's
due to my beauty, birth and fortune, and more to my soul, than to obey
those unjust commands.

HELLENA: Now hang me, if I don't love thee for that dear disobedience. I love
mischief strangely, as most of our sex do, who are to come to love and
nothing else. But tell me dear Florinda, don't you love that fine *Anglese*
[Englishman]? For I vow next to loving him myself, 'twill please me
most that you do so, for he is so gay and so handsome.

FLORINDA: Hellena, a maid designed for a nun ought not to be so curious in
a discourse of love.

HELLENA: And dost thou think that ever I'll be a nun? Or at least till I'm so
old, I'm fit for nothing else. Faith no, sister; and that which makes me
long to know whether you love Belvile, is because I hope he has some
mad companion or other that will spoil my devotion; nay, I'm resolved
to provide myself this carnival, if there be ere a handsome proper fellow
of my humour above ground, though I ask first.

FLORINDA: Prithee be not so wild.

HELLENA: Now you have provided yourself of a man, you take no care for
poor me. Prithee tell me, what dost thou see about me that is unfit for
love? Have I not a world of youth, a humour gay, a beauty passable, a
vigour desirable? Well shaped? Clean limbed? Sweet breathed? And

sense enough to know how all these ought to be employed to the best advantage? Yes, I do and I will; therefore lay aside your hopes of my fortune, by my being a devote [nun], and tell me how you came acquainted with this Belvile, for I perceive you knew him before he came to Naples.

FLORINDA: Yes, I knew him at the siege of Pamplona; he was then a colonel of French horse, who when the town was ransacked, nobly treated my brother and myself, preserving us from all insolences; and I must own (besides great obligations) I have I know not what, that pleads kindly for him about my heart, and will suffer no other to enter...[47]

The interruption is caused by their brother, Pedro (note that the sisters don't interrupt each other, however playfully they may quarrel), who has come to lay down the parental law about Florinda's ancient intended and Hellena's gloomy fate in a nunnery. Behn appropriates conventions from male rakish comedy, making Hellena a smarter version of Margery Pinchwife who has learned to blazon her own physical charms with the particularity of an amorous poet. The woozy undulations of her language – 'it very pretty to sigh, and sing, and blush, and wish, and dream and wish, and long and wish to see the man' – create a character for whom imagination and experience are the same: a nun who was made to be an actress.

The staging of Barry's arrival as a performer contrasts with the trials of her sister, Florinda. Thanks to the intervention of the unimpeachable English colonel – surely a wink towards Mary Betterton's husband, who played Belvile – she has already been saved from the 'insolences' that follow invasions. When the 'mad companion' of Hellena's longings enters the fray, Belvile will have more rescuing to do. In a scene dripping with symbolism, Florinda goes into her garden at night 'with a key and a little box' and finds herself confronted by the Rover himself, Willmore, high in drink and with one thing in mind. Again, Belvile intervenes to prevent certain rape. Their subsequent dialogue shows Belvile chastising his friend in a language that sounds like the senior actor defending the professional credentials of his wife:

WILLMORE: By this light I took her for an errant harlot.
BELVILE: Damn your debauched opinion! Tell me, sot, had'st thou not so much sense and light about thee to distinguish her woman, and could'st not see something about her face and person to strike an awful reverence into thy soul?[48]

This negotiation of the person of the actress casts Mary Betterton as the uncannily dignified professional who has so far transcended the stigma of her profession as to be positively revered. Where Barry the *ingénue* is a nun becoming an actress, Mary Betterton the senior tragedienne is an actress metamorphosed into a saint.

Only three years on from *The Rover*, Behn's opening dialogue captured the relative trajectories of Elizabeth Barry and Mary Betterton. Mary's career declined as her younger colleague's accelerated. She continued to play long-standing signature roles such as Lady Macbeth but increasingly her appearances in new plays were limited to cameos, as though the burden of new challenges had become too great. In Lee's *Lucius Junius Brutus*, her character commits suicide at the end of Act I. The shadow of incapacity stalks her later career; when her husband died in 1710 it was said that the only thing preventing her from dying of grief was the fact that she had lost her wits.[49] Retreating from acting, she took up the role prescribed for her by the opening of *The Rover*: as a coach to younger actors, nurturing the next generation of entrants to the carnival world of theatre.

The Rover captured another actress's trajectory. In 1664 Ann Marshall had played the prostitute, Angellica Bianca, for Thomas Killigrew's King's Company production of his own Cavaliers-in-exile play, *Thomaso*. Behn's play is an adaptation of Killigrew's, and by 1677 Marshall had become sufficiently disenchanted with the King's Company to leave it. She played Angellica again in *The Rover*, under her new name of Ann Quin (or possibly Win). The maturity of the performance was matched by the complexity of the role: a woman who sells herself to the highest bidder, falls for the wandering Willmore, threatens to kill him and, ultimately, is left out of the happy resolution at the end of the play. Angellica provided Behn with an opportunity to reflect obliquely on the dilemmas facing the woman playwright. They share the same initials, submit themselves to the tribulations of the market, take on male behaviours when they have to and stage their own compromises. In Catherine Gallagher's words, Behn herself 'embraced the title of whore' in defining her position as a writer.[50] Some argue that the identification of writer and character is too simple; but that objection itself depends on a simple reading of one of the richly elusive, many-sided and shape-shifting characters in Restoration Drama, who like her creator learns to be protean as a means of survival.

Rival divas, rival queens

Restoration actresses and audiences also thrived on the staging of less harmonious double acts. In Nathaniel Lee's *The Rival Queens*, which opened in the same month as *The Rover*, they found a paradigm that would last long into the next century. The subject typified Lee's preference for using ancient history to sail close to the political wind: a dying king fought over by his former and current wives. Alexander the Great was played here by Charles Hart, another symbolic monarch who, as noted above, 'might teach any king on earth how to comport himself'.[51] The sentiment, safe in 1708 when Downes published *Roscius Anglicanus*, was risky in 1677. Like Dryden's *All for Love* the year afterwards, Lee's play takes the most conventional heroic plot motif – the dangers of ceding power to love – but spices it with further allusions to sexual politics at court. This was the period of rising anxiety about the influence of Charles II's French mistress, Louise de Keroualle, and *The Rival Queens* projects a future in which the ruler deals with the fallout from failing to discard a violently passionate first wife (Roxana) and turning to a steadier second one (Statira). It is *The Man of Mode* replayed in a strident minor key.

But the play has never been bound by its original courtly context. It remained popular in the eighteenth century because of the way its female roles allowed performers to stage their own complex identities, often in relation to changing political times.[52] Maximum electricity is achieved in the face-offs between two angry women. Here is Roxana falsely commiserating with Statira over the latter's decision to retire from public life:

ROXANA: Madam, I hope you will a Queen forgive,
   Roxana weeps to see Statira grieve:
   How noble is the brave resolve you make,
   To quit the world for Alexander's sake?
   Vast is your mind, you dare thus greatly die,
   And yield the King to one so mean as I:
   'Tis a revenge will make the victor smart,
   And much I fear your death will break his heart.
STATIRA: You counterfeit a fear, and know too well
   How much your eyes all beauties else excel:
   Roxana, who though not a princess born,
   In chains could make the might victor mourn.

Forgetting power, when wine had made him warm,
And senseless, yet even then you knew to charm:
Preserve him by those arts that cannot fail,
While I the loss of what I loved bewail.

ROXANA: I hope your Majesty will give me leave
To wait you to the grove, where you would grieve;
Where like the turtle, you the loss will moan
Of that dear mate, and murmur all alone.

STATIRA: No, proud triumpher o'er my falling state,
Thou shalt not stay to fill thee with my fate:
Go to the conquest which your wiles may boast,
And tell the world you left Statira lost.
Go seize my faithless Alexander's hand,
Both hand and heart were once at my command:
Grasp his loved neck, die on his fragrant breast,
Love him like me, which cannot be expressed,
He must be happy, and you more than blessed.
While I in darkness hide me from the day,
That with my mind I may his form survey,
And think so long, till I think life away.

ROXANA: No, sickly virtue, no,
Thou shalt not think, nor thy love's loss bemoan
Nor shall past pleasures through they fancy run;
That were to make thee blessed as I can be...

STATIRA: How frail, how cowardly is woman's mind?
We shriek at thunder, dread the rustling wind,
And glittering swords the brightest eyes will blind.
Yet when strong jealousy enflames the soul,
The weak will roar, and calms to tempest roll.
Rival, take heed, and tempt me not too far;
My blood may boil, and blushes show a war.

ROXANA: When you retire to your romantic cell
I'll make thy solitary mansion hell;
Thou shalt not rest by day, nor sleep by night,
But still Roxana shall thy spirit fright...[53]

To a greater degree than Dryden, this is baroque writing that soars above the particular moment in its very search for intimacy. Whereas Dryden deploys a language of rights and laws blended with the disconcerting similes that punctuate *The Conquest of Granada* and *All for Love*, Lee writes a bodily language of sentimental indulgence. He wrote in blank verse for most of *The Rival Queens* but returned

to rhyming couplets for this showpiece scene; thudding and incon-
sistently rhythmic, they enact the blows each woman lands on the
other. The passage builds to the crescendo of roused womanhood
Lee has Statira describe in her final speech. Just as Behn wrote what
some critics describe as a man's conclusion to *The Rover Part 1*, this
is *écriture feminine* imagined by a man.

The performers' identities were part of the effect. Rebecca Marshall,
as Roxana, had been with the King's Company since its inception.
Her line in feisty queens and mistresses (Berenice in *The Destruction
of Jerusalem*, Lyndaraxa in *The Conquest of Granada*, Poppaea in
The Tragedy of Nero) was complemented by a public form of private
life. When she accused Nell Gwyn of being 'my Lord Buckhurst's whore',
Gwyn is said to have retorted that 'I was but one man's whore, though
I was brought up in a bawdy-house to fill strong waters to the guests; and
you are a whore to three or four, though a Presbyter's praying daughter'.[54] Close to court circles, Marshall was reportedly privy to secrets
such as Hart's liaison with a real-life Roxana, Lady Castlemaine.[55]
Elizabeth Boutell, as Statira, embodied another side of the Restoration
actress's public persona: studious, enduring and professional, like Betterton, whom she followed into the Actors' Company in 1695 to conclude
a career that spanned over thirty years.[56] No Restoration actor, Betterton
included, was entirely free from the taint of scandal, but Boutell was
ideal casting for St Catherine in revivals of Dryden's *Tyrannick Love*
(1669) and as the first Fidelia in Wycherley's *The Plain Dealer* (1676).
It was a quality that could be exploited for comic ends too. She was the
first Margery in *The Country Wife*. The innocence of a woman who
fell for a company of actors was genuinely earned. *They* may not have
been the goodliest and properest, but *she* was.

Endnotes

1 Wycherley, *The Country Wife*, 15 (II.i.25–7).
2 See Mary Luckhurst and Jane Moody, eds., *Theatre and Celebrity* (London: Palgrave, 2006).
3 *The Diary of Samuel Pepys*, 16 October 1667.
4 Robert Gould, 'A Satyr against the Play-House', in his *Poems, Chiefly Consisting of Satyrs and Satirical Epistles* (London, 1689), 186.
5 State Papers 29/191, no. 31; in *Register*, no. 368.
6 Reverend Jeremy Collier, *A Short View of the Immorality and Profaneness of the English Stage* (London, 1698), 287.

7 Philip Stubbes, *The Anatomy of Abuses* (London, 1587).
8 Payne, 'Reified object or emergent professional?', 35.
9 *The Diary of Samuel Pepys*, 7 March 1667.
10 Ibid., 30 May 1668.
11 Ibid., 22 October 1662.
12 The amateur theatricals of Richard Norton MP are described by Le Neve, *The Lives and Characters*, 534–5.
13 See the letter to Weymouth's steward reproduced as the frontispiece to my *Thomas Betterton*.
14 The catalogue is available in my edition of Jacob Hooke's *Pinacotheca Bettertonaeana* (London, 1710), published as *Pinacotheca Betterton-aeana: The Library of a Seventeenth-Century Actor* (London: Society for Theatre Research, 2013).
15 For Kynaston, see *The Diary of Samuel Pepys*, 1 February 1669; for Lacy, and his subsequent quarrel with Howard, 15 April 1667.
16 See my *Thomas Betterton*, 156.
17 *The Diary of Samuel Pepys*, 12 November, 9 December 1662.
18 In 1660 and 1661 two loyal poems by John Crouch were published under the imprimatur 'Thomas Betterton'.
19 Patent granted to Thomas Killigrew, 25 April 1662, PRO c/66/3013; reprinted by David Thomas, *Restoration and Georgian England 1660–1788* (Cambridge University Press, 1989), 16–18.
20 Cibber, *An Apology*, 160–1.
21 For her singing, see Downes, *Roscius Anglicanus*, 94.
22 *The Diary of Samuel Pepys*, 11 November 1667. The play had premiered in 1665.
23 Ibid., 10 September 1664.
24 Downes, *Roscius Anglicanus*, 55–6.
25 Nokes played Bisket in Shadwell's *Epsom Wells* (1672), Buffoon in Behn's *The Feign'd Curtezans* (1679), Cocklebrain in D'Urfey's *A Fool's Preferment* (1688), Sir Credulous in Behn's *Sir Patient Fancy* (1678), Doodle in Edward Ravenscroft's *The London Cuckolds* (1681), Foppering in Edward Howard's *The Six Days' Adventure* (1671), Poet Ninny in Shadwell's *The Sullen Lovers* (1668), Noddy in the same author's *Bury Fair* (1689) and Puny in Abraham Cowley's *Cutter of Coleman Street* (1661).
26 Downes, *Roscius Anglicanus*, 64. In fact this was a very sensitive diplomatic occasion, and Nokes had been set up by the Duke of Monmouth to make fun of French fashions in front of the party of French diplomats who were negotiating the secret Treaty of Dover. See my *Thomas Betterton*, 124–8.
27 Cibber, *An Apology*, 85.

28 For 'stiff comportment', see Thomas Brown, *Amusements Serious and Comical* (London, 1702), 52; also Aubrey de la Motraye, *Travels Through Europe* (London, 1723), 143.

29 Judith Milhous counts 183 and concedes that to be an underestimate in 'An Annotated Census of Thomas Betterton's Roles, 1659–1710', *Theatre Notebook* 29 (1975), 33–45 (part 1), 85–94 (part 2). The sale catalogue of Betterton's books and pictures includes 264 'plays or parts of plays', which may well have been his personal collection of 'parts': Hooke, *Pinacotheca Bettertonaeana*, 22.

30 Steele, *The Tatler*, no. 10, 30 April 1709.

31 Anthony Aston recalls Betterton's 'corpulent body and thick legs with large feet' in *A Brief Supplement to Colley Cibber Esq.: His Lives of the Famous Actors and Actresses* (London, 1747), reprinted in R. W. Lowe's two-volume edition of Cibber's *An Apology* (London, 1889), vol. II, 299–303.

32 Cibber, *An Apology*, 39–40.

33 Ibid., 95.

34 On costumes in the Restoration Theatre, see LS1, xci–vciv. The basic approach was hybrid, with modern dress supplemented by items symbolizing history or place.

35 For a fuller account, see my introduction to *Pinacotheca Bettertonaeana*.

36 Cibber, *An Apology*, 55.

37 *The Diary of Samuel Pepys*, 7 December 1667, reports that the King's Company theatre had 'for some days been silenced upon some difference [between] Hart and Moone'.

38 Ibid., 22 July 1663, and subsequent entries.

39 I discuss this pairing at length in *Thomas Betterton*, 93–6.

40 Thomas Otway, *Venice Preserv'd* (London, 1682), 24 (II.ii.362–72).

41 In the preface to his *Love's Victim*, Charles Gildon praises the way Otway combined 'Nature and Propriety': English passion and French regulation.

42 Otway, *Venice Preserv'd*, 26–7 (III.i.100).

43 Cibber, *An Apology*, 49.

44 Otway, *Venice Preserv'd*, 55–6 (IV.ii.355–401).

45 Cibber, *An Apology*, 105–7.

46 Ibid., 106.

47 Aphra Behn, *The Rover* (London, 1677), 1–2 (I.i.1–71).

48 Ibid., 44 (III.iii.156–162).

49 *The Tatler*, no. 167, 2–4 May 1710.

50 Catherine Gallagher, 'Who was that masked woman? The prostitute and the playwright in the plays of Aphra Behn', *Women's Studies* 15 (1988), 23–42. For discussion of this association, see Susan J. Owen, *Perspectives on Restoration Drama* (Manchester University Press, 2002), 76–8.

51 Downes, *Roscius Anglicanus*, 41.
52 See Felicity Nussbaum, *Rival Queens: Actresses, Performance, and the Eighteenth-Century British Theater* (Philadelphia: University of Pennsylvania Press, 2010).
53 Nathaniel Lee, *The Rival Queens, or, The Death of Alexander the Great* (London, 1677), xxx.
54 *The Diary of Samuel Pepys*, 26 October 1667.
55 Ibid., 7 April 1668.
56 See LS1, 466.

6 | Playhouses

As for any house, the location and fabric of a playhouse create opportunities and risks as well as social capital or deficit. 'Improvement' was a concept cherished by dramatists who translated old masters for the modern stage, and Restoration theatre managers were correspondingly preoccupied by the need to modernize their playing spaces in order to attract not only the largest audience but the wealthiest. For this reason, although the mythology of Restoration Theatre is dominated by names that signal either gleaming continuity with the present or pastoral idylls – Drury Lane, Dorset Garden, Lincoln's Inn Fields, Haymarket – the history of playhouses in the period is that of everything else: of rapid development, a dash for riches, a haste to abandon the past. While most of the period's theatre history can be told in terms of pairs of companies operating under tightly controlled patents – the King's and the Duke's, Rich's and Betterton's – those companies and their offshoots operated from more than a dozen different premises, ranging from the glories of Dorset Garden to small 'nursery' accommodation in Hatton Garden and the Barbican.[1] Then there were the improvised spaces provided for court performances and summer tours, which brought financial rewards of their own: from Whitehall Palace to Dover Castle to the living room of a South Coast MP, and then, right at the bottom of the scale, the variety of [in]'convenient places' where touring companies were licensed to perform.[2] While it is tempting to think of the Restoration period as marking the invention of a prosperous, West End, institutionalized kind of theatre, Restoration actors had to be as adaptable to different kinds of playing space as any before or since.

Restoration playhouses therefore have a shadow history: one less of stable institutions than of buildings pressed into temporary service and then abandoned to other, often unlikely, uses. In November 1660 Thomas Killigrew renovated Gibbons' Tennis Court in Vere Street as a temporary home ahead of his planned move to a new

Theatre Royal in Bridges Street. Two and a half years later, soon after Killigrew's move, Samuel Pepys strolled down Vere Street and heard that fencing matches were being held in the old theatre; a fortnight later it boasted a full house once again, but the audience was a congregation and the stage commanded by a single performer in the shape of a Nonconformist preacher.[3] Six years on, Elizabeth Pepys went there to see a play by junior actors.[4] When Killigrew's Bridges Street theatre burned down in 1672, his King's Company went not to Vere Street but to Lincoln's Inn Fields, recently vacated by the Duke's and gathering dust while the new Dorset Garden, with its spectacular array of scenic effects, pulled in the crowds. 'Improving' the distant or uncomfortable past of civil strife, the restless traffic between theatre spaces created its own nostalgic mythologies, whose symptoms are the prototype theatre histories of the period such as John Downes's 1708 *Roscius Anglicanus*. When Betterton and his actors escaped the clutches of Christopher Rich in 1695 and set up in the old Lincoln's Inn Fields theatre, it was as though audiences were being returned to a golden age of theatrical purity: '[T]o our world, such plenty you afford,' said Betterton before the first performance of Congreve's *Love for Love*, which opened the new house. 'It seems like Eden, fruitful of its own accord.'[5] Yet the successor theatre to which Betterton moved in the 1704–5 season, the Queen's in Haymarket, was another grandiose improvement.

Even specially commissioned structures proved fragile. The Bridges Street theatre succumbed to fire, while the expensively assembled Dorset Garden playhouse was no sooner built (probably to a design by Robert Hooke) than it was the subject of an official inspection by the Clerk of the King's Works, Sir Christopher Wren himself. A flimsy retaining wall was to blame.[6] Just over a year later the theatre had to be closed temporarily for repairs to its stage machinery. Corners were cut during construction: it was erected at speed, in a labour market in which wages and raw material prices had risen steeply after the Great Fire, and on the basis of financing flimsier than any retaining wall. A new system of building shares was launched, with each share costing a staggering £450, or eight times the projected annual dividend, and it appears that Betterton and his fellow manager Harris used both their existing company shares and the promise of future income as collateral for loans to acquire building shares – a system of debt management that merits the epithet 'toxic'.[7] Betterton secured his position by lending the company money he himself had borrowed, but charging his own company a much higher rate of interest on it than he would pay himself.

Playhouses and scenes

Mutability notwithstanding, there was a broad consensus in the period as to what a mainstream playhouse should ideally look like and be equipped to do. The immediate inspirations were the rectangular hall of Shakespeare's Blackfriars Theatre, familiar to Davenant from his service to the King's Men, and the scenic innovations of the European stage, partly filtered through the pre-war theatre of Inigo Jones, who had designed elaborate scenes and costumes for the Jacobean and Caroline courts. In 1660 real tennis courts provided the structure needed to accommodate 600 to 700 spectators and a playing space that left as much room for movable scenery as for actors, and as much room for them as for the audience. A very similar design followed for purpose-built theatres. Richard Leacroft's reconstruction of the first Theatre Royal in Drury Lane is depicted in Figure 6.1.

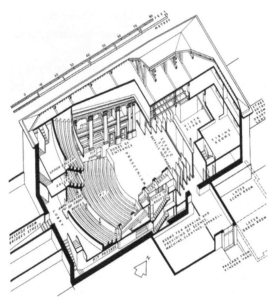

Figure 6.1 The Theatre Royal, Drury Lane; reconstruction by Richard Leacroft

Downstage, performers could interact cheek by jowl with the audience, as though on equal terms with them; upstage, they might seem both grander and more objectified – visual commodities for the audience to devour. It is natural to think of the downstage area as the vehicle for comedy: the side doors provided opportunities for surprise entrances, hurried exits, eavesdropping, hiding, forcible eviction and other conventions that came to be associated with the bodily chaos of farce. Aphra Behn was particularly resourceful in exploiting the structural relationships of doors to boxes, and of downstage to up.[8] Thus, in Act I of *The Rover Part 1*, there is a crafted image of carnival that borrows its language from the court masque:

Advances from the farther end of the scenes, two men dressed all over with horns of several sorts, making grimaces at one another, with papers pinned on their backs.[9]

The rover Willmore's friend, Belvile, interprets correctly: the cuckold's horns signify 'a satire against the whole sex'. In Act II, the adjacency of the side boxes and the doors literally and metaphorically aligns the glorious courtesan Angelica to the courtly ladies who were watching:

Enter two bravos, and hang up a great Picture of Angelica's, against the balcony, and two little ones at each side of the door.[10]

The script arises organically from the contours of the playing space.

Those examples show that the upper stage was as useful for comic writers as the lower, yet there is a tendency to associate the scenic vocabulary of the upstage area with the period's exotic tragedies, for which scene stores might be packed with Chinese pavilions, Mexican temples, Moroccan torture chambers or Mediterranean castles.

But that is partly because so much more evidence has survived of scenes for tragedies, from the sketches for Davenant's *The Siege of Rhodes* to the grisly engravings that accompanied the 1673 text of Elkanah Settle's *The Empress of Morocco* (see Figure 6.2) and the abundant stage directions that came with dramatic operas, specifying, for example, in the stupendous case of John Dryden's *Albion and Albanius*, a meeting of masque, opera and heroic drama:

[A] walk of very high trees; at the end of the walk is a view of that part of Windsor which faces Eton; in the midst of it is a row of small trees, which lead to the Castle-Hill. In the first scene, part of the town and part of the hill. In the next, the Terrace Walk, the King's Lodgings, and the

Figure 6.2 An engraver's imagined scene for Elkanah Settle's *The Empress of Morocco* (1673)

upper part of St George's Chapel; then the Keep; and lastly, that part of the Castle beyond the Keep.

In the air is a vision of the honours of the Garter; the Knights in procession, and the King under a canopy; beyond this, the upper end of St George's Hall.

FAME rises out of the middle of the stage, standing on a globe, on which is the arms of England: the globe rests on a pedestal; on the front of the pedestal is drawn a man with a long, lean, pale face, with fiend's wings, and snakes twisted round his body; he is encompassed by several fanatical rebellious heads, who suck poison from him, which runs out of a tap in his side.[11]

Grandiose naturalism and intricate symbolism sat side by side in Restoration scenography, in a marriage of epic cinematography and the densely packed pages of a Renaissance emblem book or court masque, all lit by candles.[12] The audience had to recognize Windsor, admiring the receding perspective of that 'walk of very high trees', but it also had to understand the significance of the gaunt, demonic figure whose appearance derives from ancient representations of envy, but whose unfortunate bodily malfunction recalls the Earl of Shaftesbury and his opposition to the Duke of York's succession to the throne. The sense of wonder Restoration audiences must have experienced in the face of such scenic splendour is almost palpable in the stage directions, but so is the extent to which their minds worked actively on politics. Of tragedy and comedy, moreover, that is often equally true.

Politics and the scene

From *The Siege of Rhodes* onwards, the stage pictures of Restoration Theatre engaged in public argument. Come the 1670s and 1680s, in Jean I. Marsden's words, playwrights and scenographers used 'spectacle and large-scale bloodshed to create bleak pictures of corruption [designed to] startle the audience into recognizing the potential ramifications of topical problems'.[13] Like the horror films of McCarthyite America, Marsden suggests, such images were intended to scare people into compliance with authority.

A less bracing purpose has been proposed by Cynthia Wall for the many scenes in Restoration Comedy that depicted London's royal parks. Such scenes are often, as in *The Man of Mode* or *The Way of the World*, the parts of the play where plans drawn up in a private apartment or corner of a coffee house falter or become subject to unwelcome scrutiny; they typically show us characters on parade yet deep in discussion about strategy and stratagem. They also owe something to a tradition that had never seemed more reassuring to Londoners ravaged by the experience of plague and fire: pastoral, with its invitation to annihilate everything, as Andrew Marvell put it, to a green thought in a green shade.[14] Marvell's verb was prophetic, for annihilation was what threatened all of London in 1666, except the wide open spaces of the parks, stage images of which offered audiences, in Wall's words, a comforting 'retreat into the *known*, the secure, the green spaces of uninterrupted social life'.[15] Park scenes, in other words, turned the gaze of the audience away from the misery of urban destruction.

An older misery, still vivid and as likely to repeat itself, lurked in the green shades. St James's Park, a popular backdrop for many Restoration comedies, had witnessed Charles's I's last walk before his execution in 1649 ('He was brought from Saint James about ten in the morning, walking on foot through the Park, with a Regiment of Foot for his guard, with colours flying,' reads one sober newsletter report).[16] During the Republic the parks, once playgrounds for the royal hunt, were either sold off or pillaged for wood, and it became easy to draw analogies between what Simon Schama has described as the 'raw and grimy stumps' of elm trees and the violence inflicted on the king's body at the executioner's block.[17] New planting followed the Restoration. 'Bold sons of earth' was how Edmund Waller hailed the fresh growth,

> that thrust their arms so high,
> As if once more they would invade the sky.
> In such green palaces the first kings reigned,
> Slept in their shades, and angels entertained.[18]

Kingship and greenery went together, ancient but violable. Roy Strong has described Inigo Jones's backdrop sketches for court masques of the 1630s as 'stage garden pictures…of the king's peace', and the green spaces of the Restoration Theatre might be described less in terms of a retreat into the reassuringly known than as stage garden pictures of the king's turmoil. Waller's poem celebrated another sphere of improvement. Charles II not only replanted St James's Park but tried to turn it into another Versailles, with a great canal and French-style 'goose-foot' design.[19] He ran out of money before the scheme was complete, leaving the sort of half-baked compromise of English and French values that typified his rule. It is fair to conclude that, when they saw St James's Park on stage, Restoration audiences looked at images of the space as it had been restored and improved: an airbrushing of history that kept the ghosts alive by hinting that the restored king's dearest wish was to share the glamour, riches and power of his French cousin Louis.

Actors and scenery

How did actors respond to this new world of scenic technology? In the theatres of Shakespearean London the actor's body and the playwright's words counted for everything; now they had to contend with this compelling new sign system. Contemporary performers can be suspicious of design-led productions. Recalling in a Channel 4 documentary Philip Prowse's spectacular baroque set for his 1985 National Theatre production of *The Duchess of Malfi*, Ian McKellen mournfully reflected that his Bosola had no hope of rising to the same heights, and reviewers tended to agree. Jonathan Hyde, on the other hand, as Ferdinand, struck a note and a pose that did fit: his was a sculpted performance that in another production might have looked wooden. Statuesque and so vocally commanding as to border on the operatic, this haughtily deranged prince was completely at home in the grand, looming chambers of Prowse's imagination.

It is no accident that the most successful actor of the Restoration period, Thomas Betterton, was also one of the foremost advocates of elaborate design. While his loyal biographer, Charles Gildon, felt bound to report a common anxiety that spectacular scenery would lead to 'the destruction of good playing', Betterton evidently found a way of reconciling them. His use of stage technology, in Francis Manning's poetic tribute, nurtured the ghost in the machine, giving mechanical 'motions' the 'soul' that came of interaction with performers.[20] In turn, that interaction bequeathed to actors so inclined and talented the quality that breathes out of every page of Gildon's book and all the rhetorical manuals on which it was based: the craft of a demonstrable art that, taking its bearings from the finest European painting and sculpture, craved and began, at least, to acquire their discipline and prestige. The company discipline instilled by William Davenant, scene maker *extraordinaire*, was the discipline not just of learning lines and turning up on time but of suiting the action to the scene as well as to the word.

No scenic effect such as the entrance of the cuckolds from *The Rover* could work with actors in a loose rabble in front of it. The denouement of Southerne's dark comedy *The Wives' Excuse* (1691), in which an errant husband is finally exposed, would go for nothing if the rest of the company were not mindful of the stage picture:

Scene draws, shows Friendall and Wittwoud upon a couch.[21]

Pepys regularly found that it was hard enough seeing perspective effects from the cheap seats without having the extra nuisance of actors standing in the way. If the examples from Behn show how the anatomy of the theatre necessarily became an extension of the anatomy of the actor, the crafting of the many park scenes of Restoration Comedy indicates how performers learned to manoeuvre their way around a scenic stage in a way that also imitated the studied motions of polite behaviour. 'A constant and direct foot is the index of a steady, certain, constant and right study and aim of our designs,' Betterton allegedly told Gildon, and acting from the feet up was just what was required of moments such as this, in *The Man of Mode*: 'Walk on,' says Dorimant to Sir Fopling; 'we must not be seen together...the next turn you will meet the lady.'[22] Here, the rituals of theatre and everyday life become hard to distinguish: the role of the actor is to use movement and scene to capture the social performance that was 'High Mall'.[23]

Shakespeare improved with scenes: *The Fairy Queen* (1692)

The routines of everyday life, however fashionable, were remote indeed when theatre scenery and financial risk reached their apogee in the multimedia spectaculars for which the Dorset Garden theatre in particular had been designed. In *The Fairy Queen*, an adaptation of *A Midsummer Night's Dream* thought to be the work of Betterton, and with a series of magnificent masque-like episodes by Henry Purcell, Shakespeare's cast list is infiltrated by some conspicuous strangers, all of them there to provide musical interludes and additions. They mix symbolism, satire, mythology and armchair tourism: personifications of Night, Sleep, Secrecy, Mystery and the four seasons rub shoulders with nymphs, haywains, Juno, Hymen – who at least has a Shakespearean forebear in *As You Like It* – and, most disconcertingly, a group of Chinese. Betterton owned a copy of John Ogilby's sumptuous coffee-table folio *Atlas Chinensis*, a translation of a work by Montanus, and was perhaps struck by the illustrations, though he may also have had in mind the first known Chinese visitor to London, Shen Fu-Tsung, a Jesuit and friend of the actor's former patron, James II. This was Betterton's last hurrah before Christopher Rich pressurized him into quitting, and the loyal Downes's account suggests that he was prepared to blow everything in the interests of outdoing the earlier successes of *King Arthur* and *The Prophetess*:

This in ornaments was superior to the other two... The court and the town were wonderfully satisfied with it; but the expenses in setting it out being so great, the company got very little by it.[24]

According to one report, those 'expenses' came to £3,000, or more than half the year's production budget. No wonder *The Gentleman's Journal* of May 1692 found the 'music and decorations extraordinary'.

The effect builds slowly, like a well-run firework display. A routine 'first music' and overture are the prelude to what might, but for a major cut, have looked like any scenically designed version of Shakespeare's play: the palace of Theseus, decked not for its owner's wedding but only with Egeus complaining about Hermia and Lysander. The first act ends with the flight into the wood and a vision of Titania. Then comes a conventional duet for soprano and bass to words that turn Shakespeare's forest into a classical arcadia (in Jonathan Kent's 2009 Glyndebourne production it was the Garden of Eden itself, just after the fall):

In pleasant shades upon the grass
At night ourselves we'll lay;
Our days in harmless sport shall pass,
Thus time shall slide away.[25]

Now the fun begins. A drunken, blind poet musically defuses any anxiety the audience may feel at the doggerel additions to Shakespeare: 'If you will know it,' he confesses to a group of fairies, 'I am a scurvy poet.'[26] Catch this in a fine recording such as the one conducted by William Christie and the contrast of lumbering, stammering poet and the brilliantly precise coloratura singing of the fairies (itself hopelessly imitated by the poet) is as insightful as it is funny, with the earthbound, malfunctioning writer overwhelmed by supernatural fizz. It is a fine defence of the kind of theatre Betterton and Purcell championed, with words panting in the effort to keep up with music and dance.

After Demetrius mistakenly receives the love potion, a 'heavenly choir' of fairies reinforces the power of music over nature by lulling Titania to sleep, and here Purcell brings off the first great set piece of *The Fairy Queen*. Night enters, an ethereal soprano hovering over light violins, and introduces Mystery, whose tones darken over viols (instruments like a modern cello). The interlude concludes way down the scale with Sleep, a deep bass whose lines are interrupted by silence. 'Hush,' he intones, before a bar's rest; 'no more' (another rest), 'be silent' (rest again) 'all.'[27] Finally, there is the wonderful conceit of an entire chorus of fairies taking up the same lines and singing them, magically, with still quieter intensity.

At the end of Act III, Titania lays on an entertainment for Bottom that would make Prospero – or Inigo Jones himself – envious. As in the court masque, the spirits of rebellion (here in the shape of a dance of wild green men) are banished and give way to a vision of conventional country swains. Mopsa defies Corydon's attempts to kiss her, while a nymph concludes that a woman is entitled to be as 'false and inconstant' as her husband. The hybrid theatrical language, in which Elizabethan pastoral and the court masque touch noses with libertine comedy, embodies a complex fantasy of possession: Titania, mooning over her simple lover, runs through a series of dramatic tropes that attempt and fail to describe him. The interlude ends with a juxtaposition that is both ironic and sexually charged: as the queen takes her ass-headed favourite to bed, a chorus sings a hymn to erotic love that echoes Marlowe and Rochester:

> A thousand, thousand ways we'll find
> To entertain the hours...[28]

A masque of the seasons, reminiscent of *The Tempest*, concludes Act IV. At the end of the final act, Theseus expresses incredulity at the tales he has been told of the lovers' adventures in the wood, and the fairies take it upon themselves to convince him. The baroque wonders of this final sequence set out to surpass the supernatural mysteries of the play, not least in visual complexity. This was one of Betterton's most elaborate conceptions, plausibly drawn from one of John Ogilby's illustrations (see Figure 6.3):

As the stage darkens a dance is presented. Then a symphony is heard and the stage suddenly lights up, discovering a Chinese garden. The architecture, trees, plants, fruits, birds and animals are quite unlike those we know in our part of the world. There is a large arch through which can be seen other arches with close-set trees and an arbour. Above, a hanging garden rises in terraces surrounded by pleasant bowers, with a variety of trees and numerous strange birds circling about. From the topmost platform the water from a spurting fountain falls into a large pool.[29]

With exoticism came a local *cri de coeur*. A Chinese man and woman start to sing of the creation, when the 'gloomy world / At first began to shine'. *The Prophetess*, a comparable spectacle mounted two years beforehand, and only days before the Battle of the Boyne, had run into trouble because Dryden's prologue was suspected of casting aspersions

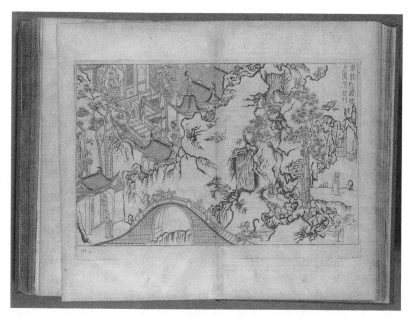

Figure 6.3 A Chinese garden, from John Ogilby's *Atlas Chinensis* (London, 1671), 570; Betterton owned a copy

on William III's accession.[30] The conclusion to *The Fairy Queen* uses the mythology of a paradisal orient to hope for a fresh start in domestic politics, an 'innocence secure / Not subject to extremes'. So doing, the show seemed to pave the way for future self-reincarnations, lavishly appointed for a leisurely class by actors free from the routines not just of daily labour but of business responsibility. 'Thus wildly we live,' sings the chorus,

> Thus freely we give
> What Heaven as freely bestows.
> We were not made
> For labour and trade
> Which fools on each other impose.[31]

It was a premonition of the dispute with the slave-driving Christopher Rich. Scenic spectaculars such as *The Fairy Queen*, then, were not simply exploitations of a new style of theatre architecture but idealized responses to texts, to politics and to the condition of actors themselves.

Staging the stage: Buckingham's *The Rehearsal* (1671)

A play about a play is subject to, but also free from, the observer's paradox. The audience recognizes the dimensions of what is being represented, but representing it necessarily distorts the usual configurations of stage performance; in the distortion, however, we see the outlines of conventional practice, for the dramatist must still work within the conventions the space allows.

In the case of *The Rehearsal*, a satire of the fashion for heroic drama that held the stage until Richard Brinsley Sheridan wrote *The Critic* in 1779, the stage action is mediated through two men named for their anonymity: Smith and Johnson. Smith has just arrived in London from the country, and Johnson is eager to share with him 'the impertinent, dull, fantastical things' that have been going in the capital. Chief among them are 'hideous, monstrous' plays, in particular high-minded heroic dramas such as *The Conquest of Granada* and *The Indian Queen*. Smith and Johnson chat as though they were in the audience, mediating the event for us like the speaker of a prologue. Then, what screenwriters call the 'inciting action' happens, prompting Johnson to exclaim, as though he has seen an escaped chimpanzee, 'God so, this is an Author.' The intimate conversation of the two friends gives way to that spectacle: *Mr. Bayes passes o'er the stage*. In turn, like the layers of an onion peeling away, Bayes promises to take Smith and Johnson to the playhouse; they exit, and three actors appear *upon the stage*, which this time means both the stage of the playhouse in the story and the one the audience is actually looking at, except that they are doing something – comparing notes about the play – which wouldn't normally be seen on stage.

Bayes proceeds to orchestrate a series of ludicrous scenes: a tritely rhyming dialogue between Thunder and Lightning; a pair of Francophile kings of Brentford; four soldiers who kill each other and straightaway rise again to the sound of mysterious music; and, finally, what Bayes describes as 'the scene of scenes...an heroic scene', which turns out to be an ugly mash-up of scenes, songs, swords, dance, hobby horses and general mayhem. The heroic rant Buckingham assigns to the warrior Drawcansir parodies the excesses of 1660s tragedy, a Terminator speaking in couplets:

> Others may boast a single man to kill;
> But I, the blood of thousands daily spill.
> Let petty kings the names of parties know:
> Where'er I come, I slay both friend and foe.[32]

But Buckingham's finest sense of the absurd is reserved for the moment when Bayes shows us how to embody the conflict of love and honour through the motions of the feet:

> My legs, the emblem of my various thought,
> Show to what distraction I am brought.
> Sometimes with stubborn honour, like this boot,
> My mind is guarded, and resolved, to do't:
> Sometimes again, that very mind, by love
> Disarmed, like this other leg does prove.
> Shall I to honour or to love give way?
> Go on, cries honour; tender love says nay:
> Honour aloud commands, put both boots on;
> But softer love does whisper put on none.
> What shall I do? What conduct shall I find
> To lead me through the twilight of my mind?
> For as bright day with black approach of night
> Contending, makes a doubtful puzzling light;
> So does my honour and my love together
> Puzzle me so, for I can resolve for neither.
>   *Goes out hopping with one boot on, and the other off.*[33]

The joke is partly in the replacement of body parts. In Bulwer's *Chirologia*, foundation of the rhetorical school of acting, the hand is a crucial instrument of rhetorical expressiveness; here its functions are usurped by what Shakespeare called the 'lowest, basest, poorest part of the anatomy', the part that even the greatest actors apparently ignored.[34] The clumsy actor is a metaphor for the hapless writer struggling in the twilight of his mind with stale metaphors and rigidly binary thought, marching out to the thumping beat of his lines.

Buckingham achieved his effect not only through ingenious parody. He succeeded because the play uses the resources of the Restoration stage space so skilfully. We move from the everyday world of Smith and Johnson, chatting to each other at the corners of the forestage, to the fantastic nonsense of the scenic stage, while accepting that Smith and Johnson are not really on the stage being represented. The play consistently exploits the visual joke of its happening both here and on that other stage. At the end, the disgruntled Bayes, who has suffered multiple humiliations in his attempt to rehearse his new play, resolves to give up on the theatre altogether. 'And so farewell to this stage,' he says, leaving it. Two actors enter, planning to 'set up bills' for another play. But they decide to call two others, Haynes and Shirley, to perform the closing dance: '[T]hey are but in the tiring room.' The dance is completed, and they go off to dinner.

This quality of double vision parallels a controversy surrounding the play. Judith Milhous and Robert D. Hume have argued that it is an accurate representation of Restoration rehearsal practice, along with the anonymous chamber piece *The Female Wits* (1697). But Tiffany Stern argues, persuasively, that it reflects more accurately the circumstances Buckingham might have observed during his long stay in France, where authors were typically in charge of rehearsals; in England, that was left to managers and senior actors. Stern also concludes that the historic association of Bayes with Dryden is simplistic; in practice he appears to have been a hybrid concoction of writers both professional and amateur.[35] Yet the strangest thing about this unexpectedly complex play is that Buckingham's absurd anti-hero verged on self-portraiture. A contemporary wrote,

> But when his poet John Bayes did appear
> 'Tis known to more than half that were there
> The greatest part was his own character...[36]

A fine mimic, Buckingham was a meticulous rehearser of the actors in *The Rehearsal*. What generations of readers have taken for a disdainfully aristocratic satire of a parvenu playwright's collision with the theatre may instead be an act of joyous self-mockery.

John Vanbrugh's *The Provok'd Wife*: first principles (1697)

When Betterton and his troupe escaped the 'slavery' of working for Christopher Rich in 1695 and set up in the old Lincoln's Inn Fields theatre, they were returning to a performance space Betterton's own experiments at Dorset Garden had rendered almost obsolete. The difficulties his new company faced might be traced to his inability to scale down his thinking about the scenic effects that could be achieved in a Restoration playhouse – to return, in effect, to the less extravagant technologies of 1660. But that is to underestimate his ingenuity, or, rather, his ability to coax from dramatists plays that were suited to a particular theatre environment. One such is Vanbrugh's *The Provok'd Wife*, first performed in April 1697 and carefully contrived to extract the greatest value from the limited stage resources of one of the original

Restoration playhouses: a sort of return to the first principles of Restoration staging, but in the form of a play designed to capture the mood of the 1690s.

The Provok'd Wife has been described as 'one of the harshest marital discord plays in the whole period', and it begins with the foul grump Sir John Brute lamenting his state: 'What cloying meat is love – when matrimony's the sauce to it!'[37] Whereas George Etherege's Dorimant gives up his wild oats to marry (or so we may suppose), Brute travels the other way, his marriage prompting him to outbursts of classic Restoration rakishness, with friends to match. 'Why did you marry then?' asks Heartfree. 'Why did I marry?' replies Brute. 'I married because I had a mind to lie with her, and she would not let me.' The dialogue continues in the same vein:

HEARTFREE: Why did not you ravish her?
BRUTE: Yes, and so have hedged myself into forty quarrels with her relations, besides buying my pardon. But more than all that, you must know I was afraid of being damned in those days, for I kept sneaking cowardly company, fellows that went to church, said grace to their meat, and had not the least tincture of quality about 'em.
HEARTFREE: But I think you are got into a better gang now.
BRUTE: Zoons, sir, my Lord Rake and I are hand and glove. I believe we may get our bones broke together tonight; have you a mind to share a frolic?[38]

Jeremy Collier was appalled by the play because he did not appreciate what seems obvious now: that Brute is a comic throwback, a man out of his time who fails miserably as a result. Partly as a result of pressure from the moral lobby, Vanbrugh changed the scene in which Brute tries to escape the watch by dressing as a clergyman, and instead had him wear women's clothes, the version pantomime traditions lead modern directors to prefer.[39] Yet the plot shows a remarkable degree of restraint: the wife is endlessly provoked but does nothing about it. Like the heroine of another paradigmatic 1690s play examined in the next chapter, Southerne's *The Wives' Excuse*, Lady Brute ends the play no better off than she began it.

To this modern plot Vanbrugh brings resources of language and scenic invention that characterize, and in some respects outdo, the high Stuart style of Etherege and Wycherley; when Brute revisits the worst of Restoration rakishness, Vanbrugh extracts its finer essence.

His dialogue avoids self-conscious elegance, tersely pinpointing the heart of disputes between characters in a manner perfectly shaped to mood and the motion of actors across the stage:

LADY BRUTE: What reason have I given you to use me as you do of late? It once was otherwise: you married me for love.
BRUTE: And you me for money: so you have your reward, and I have mine.
LADY BRUTE: What is it that disturbs you?
BRUTE: A parson.
LADY BRUTE: Why, what has he done to you?
BRUTE: He has married me. (*Exit Sir John*)

Vanbrugh then has Lady Brute reflecting on the way social conventions lead to bad decisions: 'I thought I had charms enough to govern him, and that where there was an estate, a woman must needs be happy.'[40]

Vanbrugh realized his mordant treatment of married life through a dialogue not just of disenchanted partners but of complementary scenic pictures. The play unfolds through a series of contrasts between private schemes and public tests that reinflect the scenic language of *The Man of Mode*.

ACT I: first the exposition in the Brute household, then the dressing room of Lady Fancyfull, a precious Francophile.
ACT II: cut to the same two characters – Lady Fancyfull and her maid, Mademoiselle – in St James's Park, where Heartfree and Constant present libertine threats to her composure; they are later joined by Brute. The act concludes with Lady Fancyfull consoling herself with music back at her house.
ACT III: a switch to the Brute household is signalled by *Scene opens*, which shows that the contrast between private and public space is not automatically marked by the invisible line between forestage and rear stage. The Brute family rise from dinner and Brute leaves to go drinking. Constant arrives and attempts to woo Lady Brute. Then the *Scene opens* again to reveal Brute and Lord Rake at the Blue Posts Tavern, presumably indicated with a sign since the dialogue does not mention it. Spatially, this takes us to a different part of the rear stage; again we see Brute at table, this time in his preferred milieu, singing a drinking song with Lord Rake. Use of the same scenic device therefore counterpoints the futility of his domestic life with the ugliness of his public one. The peace he has left behind is accentuated by the next scene change, which shows Lady Brute in her bedchamber, preparing to sleep. There is a political resonance here as well: the Blue Posts was a noted resort

for Jacobites, so emphasizing Brute's regressive tendencies. Good patriots stay at home in their beds.

ACT IV: Now the play cuts back to Brute, this time out in the street at Covent Garden, sword drawn and looking for trouble; again, the scene changes create a contrast between the domestic sphere and the feral existence Brute craves. Scene 2 takes us to another bedchamber, which shows the 'real' man's work of devotion, with Heartfree mulling over his passion for Bellinda. Scene 3 goes back to the public sphere, with Brute drunk, under arrest and dressed as a parson (or a woman in the revised version). The final scene of Act 4 morphs to another public space, the Spring Garden, a respectable revival of the place previously 'contrived to all advantages of gallantry' but still prone to the kind of mishaps that duly happen in the play: Brute blunders in drunk, while Constant nearly rapes a masked Lady Brute.

ACT V: All the characters return to their domestic spheres and unsatisfactory lives: we move between the Brute and Fancyfull households and Constant's chambers, the latter embodying his ambiguous isolation from settled bourgeois existence.

Vanbrugh's rich interplay of scenes shows that, whatever economies Betterton's company had to suffer after 1695, it could still produce work that used a classic Restoration language of scenic form and extracted maximum meaning and colour from the physical resources of the Lincoln's Inn Fields theatre. For the playwright, effective narrative was partly a function of observing this balance between conventionally realized spaces, between the contrasting contingencies of the public and private worlds. Yet *The Provok'd Wife* is a subtle reworking of the contingencies found in *The Man of Mode* and *The Country Wife*. There, plans laid confidently in the safe spaces of the domestic world are either challenged or affirmed in public. In Vanbrugh's spatial world, both dimensions prove equally claustrophobic.

Endnotes

1 For details, see LS1, xxxviii–xxxix.
2 Licence to John Rhodes. LC 5/138, p. 387, in *Register*, no. 265. For sample lists of court performances, see Nicoll, *A History of Restoration Drama*, 305–14. Both the King's and the Duke's Companies played at Dover Castle in May 1670 (see LS1, 170).
3 *The Diary of Samuel Pepys*, 1 June 1663; BL Add MSS 31916, fol.104; reported in LS1, xxxv.
4 *The Diary of Samuel Pepys*, 23 April 1669.

5 'Prologue', spoken at the opening of the New House, by Mr Betterton, in Congreve, *Love for Love*.

6 LC 5/14, p. 73; in *Register*, no. 659.

7 See the Chancery document dated 18 July 1674; in *Register*, no. 853.

8 For detailed analysis, see Dawn Lewcock, 'More for seeing than hearing: Behn and the use of theatre', in Janet Todd, ed., *Aphra Behn Studies* (Cambridge University Press, 1996), 66–83; and Derek Hughes, *The Theatre of Aphra Behn* (Basingstoke: Palgrave, 2001).

9 Behn, *The Rover*, 9 (I.ii.137).

10 Ibid., 18 (II.i.120).

11 John Dryden, *Albion and Albanius* (London, 1685). Betterton is credited with designing the scenes.

12 Candles – first tallow, then wax – have been estimated to supply the theatres with power equivalent to that of a single 100 watt bulb: see Donald Mullin, 'Lighting on the eighteenth-century London stage', *Theatre Notebook* 34 (1980), 73–85, 74. For more on this topic, see LS1, xciv–xcv.

13 Jean I. Marsden, 'Spectacle, horror, and pathos', in Deborah Payne Fisk, ed., *The Cambridge Companion to English Restoration Theatre* (Cambridge University Press, 2000), 174–90, 179.

14 Andrew Marvell, 'The Garden', in Elizabeth Story Donno, ed., *Andrew Marvell: The Complete Poems* (Harmondsworth: Penguin Books, 1972), 100–1, 101.

15 Cynthia Wall, *The Literary and Cultural Spaces of Restoration London* (Cambridge University Press, 1998), 149.

16 *A Perfect Diurnall of Some Passages in Parliament*, no. 288 (29 January–5 February 1649).

17 Simon Schama, *Landscape and Memory* (London: Fontana, 1996), 159.

18 Edmund Waller, 'On St James's Park, as lately Improv'd by His Majesty', in Thomas Park, ed., *The Poetical Works of Edmund Waller*, 2 vols. (London, 1806), vol. I, 87–91, 88.

19 Guy Williams, *The Royal Parks of London* (London: Constable, 1978), 21–9.

20 Gildon, *The Life of Mr Thomas Betterton*, 6; Francis Manning, 'To Mr Thomas Betterton', in *Poems upon Several Occasions and to Several Persons* (London, 1701).

21 Thomas Southerne, *The Wives' Excuse* (London, 1692), 53; in Robert Jordan and Harold Love, eds., *The Works of Thomas Southerne*, 2 vols. (Oxford: Clarendon Press, 1988), vol. I, V.iii.264.

22 Etherege, *The Man of Mode*, 49 (III.iii.184–6).

23 I explore the political implications further in my article 'Caesar's gift: playing the park in the late seventeenth century', *English Literary History* 71 (2004), 115–39.

24 Downes, *Roscius Anglicanus*, 89.
25 Henry Purcell, *The Fairy Queen*, sleeve notes to the recording by Les Arts Florissants, cond. William Christie (Arles: Harmonia Mundi, 1989), 31.
26 Ibid., 35.
27 Ibid., 43.
28 Ibid., 57.
29 Ibid., 69.
30 *The Muses Mercury*, January 1707, 4–5; reprinted in LS1, 382.
31 Purcell, *The Fairy Queen* sleeve notes, 71.
32 Duke of Buckingham, *The Rehearsal* (London, 1671), 53 (V.i.343–6).
33 Buckingham, *The Rehearsal*, 30 (III.v.81–104).
34 Aston, *A Brief Supplement to Colley Cibber Esq.*
35 Stern, *Rehearsal*, 130.
36 Anon., cited in ibid., 138.
37 Hume, *The Development of English Drama*, 414; John Vanbrugh, *The Provok'd Wife* (London, 1697), 1; in John Vanbrugh, *Four Comedies*, ed. Michael Cordner (Harmondsworth: Penguin Books, 1989), I.i.1.
38 Vanbrugh, *The Provok'd Wife*, 20 (II.i.251–63).
39 For critical discussion, and a reprint of the parallel scenes, see Vanbrugh, *Four Comedies*, 247–51.
40 Vanbrugh, *The Provok'd Wife*, 2 (I.i.41–8).

7 | *Audiences and critics*

The Way of the World ends with a conflict of pen and sword. Mirabell flourishes the will that dashes forever Fainall's hopes of a financial settlement, and Fainall's reaction is to offer to run through his estranged wife. It is tempting to call it a triumph of the pen, of law and civility, over violence; except that Mrs Fainall is really saved not by a waft of parchment but by the bulk of Sir Wilful Witwoud, a country cousin who has learned some of the rules of drawing room behaviour and can sound, for all his physical presence, as haughtily disapproving as any dowager: 'Hold, Sir,' he interjects, 'now you may make your *Bear-Garden* flourish somewhere else, Sir.'

If Fainall's defeat is that of Stuart *droit de seigneur*, Sir Wilful's lecture in manners charts how far the theatre had come since the days when playhouses abutted less civilized forms of entertainment. Yet Restoration playgoers occasionally lived as much as Mrs Fainall in fear of the sword, and without Sir Witwouds to accompany them. In 1712 *The Spectator* dramatized the tension between violence and civility. Here, a respectable citizen – an invention worthy of Mr Pooter in the Grossmiths' *Diary of a Nobody* – recalls an encounter with an arrogant toff:

> I do not wear a sword, but I often divert myself at the theatre... I was in the pit the other night, (when it was very much crowded) a gentleman leaning upon me, and very heavily, I very civilly requested him to remove his hand; for which he pulled me by the nose. I would not resent it in so public a place, because I was unwilling to create a disturbance; but have since reflected upon it as a thing that is unmanly and disingenuous, renders the nose-puller odious, and makes the person pulled by the nose look little and contemptible.[1]

The narrator would probably not have preferred the manly candour of a drawn sword, which, he implies, was a familiar passport into the auditorium. Resisting his literal suppression by the hand of this 'gentleman', he endured the tug on his nose for fear of creating something much worse than 'a disturbance'. Yet there he was in the pit, notionally on a level with his antagonist even as he was being pressed into the floor and then humiliated. For all his soreness at feeling 'little and contempt-ible', he appreciated things could easily have turned as ugly as this:

On Saturday last, at the Duke's playhouse, Sir Thomas Armstrong killed Mr Scrope... Their quarrel is said to [be] about Mrs Uphill, the player, who came into the house masked, and Scrope would have entertained discourse with her, which Sir T. Armstrong would not suffer, so a ring was made wherein they fought.[2]

Bear-Garden flourishes indeed: this 'ring' sounds like an improvised forum for entertainment, a playground fight rather than a mass of panicked spectators fleeing danger. The notional play was *Macbeth*, in which Betterton's stage death at the hands of Harris probably looked tame in comparison.

Sir Thomas Armstrong killing *Mr* Scrope underlines the class antag-onism witnessed by the *Spectator* article. While reported instances of playhouse violence in the period are relatively rare, the most civil playgoers worried about who was entitled to sit where, if at all. In December 1662 Pepys came back from the theatre dissatisfied with

the company of the house today, which was full of citizens, there hardly being a gentleman or woman in the house, but a couple of pretty ladies by us, that made sport at it, being jostled and crowded by prentices.[3]

The pretty ladies sound less anxious than Pepys; perhaps they remin-isced fondly about their day with the plebs. Going to the theatre helped Pepys to look up as well as down in measuring his status. By October 1667, with more money and no less leisure, he could afford not to worry about crowds of apprentices from the safety of a box – his first ever. Even so, the experience was hardly free from prickling doubt:

And in the same box came by and by, behind me, my Lord Berkly and his Lady; but I did not turn my face to them to be known, so that I was excused from giving them my seat. And this pleasure I had, that from this place the scenes do appear very fine indeed and much better than in the pit.[4]

Every theatre is an image of the society that built it, but the image is in motion. The pricing of different seats, from twelve pence for the upper gallery to five shillings for a box, may appear to reinforce an established grid of social distinctions, but, as Pepys's experiences show, pricing also had the opposite effect: it reminded people of how disorderly the grid might appear in the face of such a mixed audience. Even drama at court succumbed to the trend, the poet and MP Andrew Marvell complaining of

all sorts of people flocking [to plays at court], and paying their money as at a common playhouse; nay even a twelve-penny gallery is builded for the convenience of His Majesty's poorer subjects.[5]

What was good policy for the king, throwing open the royal pleasure grounds to paying customers, was disturbing for those such as Marvell who still had some distance to travel up the social ladder and needed to use the language of 'sorts', 'flocking', 'common' and 'poorer' to reassure themselves that *up* was where they were going.

Numerous comedies enacted the same disturbance, often in belated memory of a civil war that had threatened the certainties of social privilege. 'Tupping the enemy' is how J. Douglas Canfield candidly describes the ethos of much rakish comedy, in which gentlemen lean 'very heavily' on the shoulders of their social inferiors, and still more heavily on those of their wives. Theatricality, no less than tension, crossed the boundary between stage and auditorium. The boxes that gave the best view of the 'Scenes' in turn became miniature proscenium arches where views were available of the theatre of courtly sexual politics. At Richard Brome's *The Jovial Crew* in 1661 Pepys witnessed the beginnings of the king's infatuation with Barbara Palmer, Lady Castlemaine, noting that 'my wife, to her great comfort, had a full sight of them all the while'; seven years on Castlemaine was suffering a reversal of fortune comparable to Mrs Loveit's in *The Man of Mode*, only worse, since her rival was a mere showgirl:

[I]t vexed me to see Moll Davis, in the box over the King's and my Lady Castlemaine's, look down upon the King and he up to her; and so did my Lady Castlemaine once, to see who it was; but when she saw Moll Davis, she looked fire.[6]

Castlemaine's determination to outdress and outvamp any actress attracted fire of its own; it was, in its own theatrical extravagance, as deliberate an affront as the pulling of a nose. On 'Shrove-Tuesday last,' drawls the imaginary Castlemaine of an anonymous squib,

Splendidly did we appear upon the Theatre...being to amazement wonderfully deck'd with jewels and diamonds, which the (abhorr'd and to be undone) subjects of this Kingdom have payed for.[7]

This Castlemaine may be imaginary, but the 'amazement' of her spectators is just the emotion that was inspired by the theatre's most baroque indulgences.

For Pepys, the breathtaking object of male desire that could be 'all the pleasure of the play' was not the only species of theatre to be found in the audience.[8] If Castlemaine rivalled the wonders of scenic spectacle, Sir Charles Sedley and his masked interlocutor held their own with the wittiest protagonists of comedy, turning a Beaumont and Fletcher staple into a dull sideshow:

> [T]o the King's to *The Mayds Tragedy*; but vexed all the while with two talking ladies and Sir Charles Sedley, yet pleased to hear their discourse, he being a stranger; and one of the ladies would, and did, sit with her mark on all the play; and being exceedingly witty as ever I heard woman, did talk most pleasantly with him; but was, I believe, a virtuous woman and of quality. He would fain know who she was, but she would not tell. Yet [she] did give him many pleasant hints of her knowledge of him, by that means setting his brains at work to find out who she was; and did give him leave to use all means to find out who she was but pulling off her mask. He was mighty witty; and she also making sport with him very inoffensively, that a more pleasant rencontre I never heard. But by that means lost the pleasure of the play wholly, to which now and then Sir Charles Sedley's exceptions against both words and pronouncing was very pretty.[9]

Pepys's indecision anticipated on a different palette the grievance of the *Spectator's* sore-nosed citizen. 'Vexed...yet pleased', he was suspended between two forms of drama, the first his right as a paying customer on the same terms as any baronet, the second forced upon him by a superiority both social and intellectual. His eagerness to stress how 'inoffensively' this 'pleasant rencontre' was played out may be laying to rest the ghost of Sedley's previous misdemeanours (in addition to his public genital bathing, 'abusing of scriptures and...saying that there he hath to sell such a powder as should make all the cunts in town run after him').[10] But Pepys's emphasis on the civility of Sedley and the masked lady also defended the idea of performance in terms that any opponent of the Reverend Collier might have used; it was the more pronounced for fear that an opposing interpretation of the 'rencontre' was potentially as valid. Where Pepys saw innocent 'sport', others might find in the 'exceedingly witty' woman a foreshadowing of the pert, convention-defying heroines of Aphra Behn. The poor *Spectator* citizen had no power to prevent a gentleman pulling his nose; this

woman dared to dangle before the legendary Sedley the prospect of
another humiliating pulling, of mask from face, only to snatch it
from him.

Episodes such as these may suggest that it was impossible to go to
the Restoration theatre without status consciousness of one sort or
another getting in the way of the play. Not so. Pepys's diary is a record
both of close attention to text and performance, shared between
the Navy Office man and his wife, and of the restless intuition that is
the privilege of someone conscious of purchasing luxury goods. His
sensibility needed time to develop. In the early 1660s he seems to have
lacked a language to differentiate between live performance and reading: he watches Shakespeare's *1 Henry IV* with a text in his lap and
finds the experience predictably unsatisfactory; he describes Betterton's
Hamlet as the 'best part that ever man played', leaving us wondering
whether he is referring to the role, the performance or both; on reading
Davenant's *The Siege of Rhodes*, which he had previously seen in
the theatre, he finds it 'the best poem that ever was wrote'.[11] Yet the
individual attractions – and in some cases the disadvantages – of
performance broke through the mist. Betterton's Hamlet was also
'beyond imagination', in excess of anything the experience of reading
the play could suggest; Jonson's *Catiline* was emphatically to be
reserved for the library:

[A] play of much good sense and words to read, but that doth appear the
worst upon the stage, I mean the least divertising, that I saw any, though
most fine in clothes and a fine scene of the Senate and of a fight, that ever
I saw in my life – but the play is only to be read.[12]

Pepys evidently resisted flashy effects we might call 'theatrical'; he
sought in performance a range of qualities distinct from those he might
expect to find by reading. His key critical coordinates of 'plot', 'design',
'language' and 'variety' looked to principles of scenic and narrative
structure that Jonson's 'good sense and words' however admirable in
themselves, failed to fulfil. With the growth in printed plays emerged a
stronger differentiation between the performed and the printed text,
each having its own sphere of value. Corneille's *Le Cid* might be a
'most dull thing acted' but a 'great delight' to read, and it follows that
Pepys's library of approximately 3,000 items included a number of
plays, both English and Continental, that – as far as we can tell – he
never saw performed.[13]

All the same, he veered between liking and disliking the same plays and productions. The sumptuous New Year entertainment of *Henry VIII* he found 'a thing made up of a great many patches' that all the 'shows and processions in it' could not redeem; the memory of his first reaction lingered during a revival five years later, when he was 'mightily pleased, better than I ever expected, with the history and the shows of it'.[14] Jonson's *Epicoene* he hailed as 'an excellent play' in 1661 (as he did *The Alchemist* in the same year) before giving it a lukewarm response in 1664 then praising it in 1668 as 'the best comedy, I think, that ever was wrote'.[15] These shifts in opinion may have something to do with the variable quality of performance but it is striking that when Pepys saw repeat showings in quick succession they tended to be near the beginning of a long initial run in the theatre, as though something clicked between players and playwright. *The Tempest*, Dryden's *Secret Love* and Dryden and Newcastle's *Sir Martin Mar-All* are examples of plays Pepys saw repeatedly in a short space of time, and in each case he seemed struck by the longevity of his preferences: '[A]s often as I have seen it,' he wrote of *The Tempest*, 'I do like it very well.' Yet even in these cases, perhaps, he was subconsciously justifying to himself the expense of seeing something familiar. The period's rage for novelty took a new twist: the cash-rich, burgeoning metropolitan culture produced its own guilt about revisiting the known.[16]

Pepys's intuitive reactions to plays cohabited with a set of critical benchmarks deployed with varying degrees of consistency. The plot – often referred to as 'design' – was the main reason for the hint of a preference for Sir Samuel Tuke's *The Adventures of Five Hours* over *Othello*. The kind of narrative pleasure of the detective novel, the paced interlocking of apparently discrete elements leading to a *denouement*, was what he found in 'the best comedy...that ever was wrote', *Epicoene*, and what he evidently found lacking in *A Midsummer Night's Dream*.[17] Shakespeare's resistance to the ancient notion of humours made his comic output as a whole seem flimsy and fanciful, with the single exception of the play most audiences today rate lowest among his comedies, *The Merry Wives of Windsor*, parts of which Pepys admired for its 'humours' while finding the rest ponderous.[18] Plotting also informed his judgements about tragedy but the highest standards of what he valued as variety and profundity were found in Shakespeare, and especially in *Hamlet* and *Macbeth*.

Criticism over the past two decades has dealt with the progressive 'institutional' recognition of Shakespeare as a national treasure through print, portraits, repertory, criticism and, ultimately, festivals, such as David Garrick's Jubilee.[19] Such work carries the risk that the power of the plays themselves to grip the imaginations of audiences and readers gets lost, as the though the making of the national poet were a political conspiracy aimed at fending off the French, with their false religion, bottomless exchequer, massed armies and snooty preference for the lucid delights of neoclassical drama. In Pepys's reactions to *Macbeth* lie the seeds of another narrative.

The diary shows the play stealing upon him: across a period of three years it reveals something less predictable, more mysterious, like a ceaselessly unfolding flower that confounds every previous judgement. Here, repeated viewing cannot be put down to mere pleasure in plot, since the most complex plot can be mastered by reason. In 1664 the performers stood out: it was merely 'a pretty good play, but admirably acted'. Two years on performance and play enjoyed equal supremacy. It was 'most excellently acted, and a most excellent play for variety', a quality etched in high definition by Davenant's additions; this version, with singing witches and a more heart-rending Lady Macduff, was narratively as well as theatrically more diverse than the 1623 First Folio text. But by January 1667 it was clear that variety did not come at the expense of seriousness. Multiple surprises awaited Pepys:

[T]hence to the Duke's house and saw *Macbeth*; which though I saw it lately, yet appears a most excellent play in all respects, but especially in divertisement, though it be a deep tragedy; which is a strange perfection in a tragedy, it being most proper here and suitable.[20]

It is not only the Davenant version that has this appeal, of balancing profundity with entertainment. In his fine edition of Shakespeare's play Nicholas Brooke remarks that, while a trip to see *King Lear* might be harrowing, *Macbeth* should, because of its virtuosic delight in the thrills and horrors of illusion, be fun.[21] Taken together, Pepys's experiences of the play show how its significance has dawned on him, until this point at which he bestows on it a term of almost Shakespearean richness that befits any classic – 'strange perfection' – as though the play's distinction were both formally explicable and numinously uncanny. It is no wonder, then, that Pepys's own terms for theatrical excellence were a little inconsistent. He was devoted enough as a playgoer to be surprised into new kinds of aesthetic pleasure.

If the Restoration playhouse encouraged the growth of an interiorized, connoisseurial appreciation of classic theatre, it was also a place where opinion was shouted loud, and not only by men such as Sir Charles Sedley and the 'wits' and 'criticks' cited in hundreds of prologues and epilogues. For organized vocal indignation it was hard to beat a group of women offended by the sexual frankness even of stock plays such as Fletcher and Massinger's *The Custom of the Country*, mistakenly revived as a New Year treat on 2 January 1667. According to one observer it was 'so damned bawdy that the ladies flung their pears and fruits at the Actors' (Pepys, who saw the same performance, did not comment but simply found it 'the worst play that ever I saw or I believe shall see').[22] Commentaries sometimes represented such intervention as a reprisal for embarrassment, another response to which was the widespread wearing of masks in the theatre to prevent anyone from concluding that, if a woman blushed at a dirty joke, she therefore had to have understood it.

Militant action by female spectators persisted throughout the period. Wycherley's last two plays, *The Country Wife* and *The Plain Dealer*, drew abuse from a group of women identifiable as the court maids of honour. The maids were debutantes, the daughters of aristocrats or senior professionals associated with the court and engaged in their own, highly rarefied theatricals through masques and court entertainments. One such was John Crowne's *Calisto*, a work that, contemporary with *The Country Wife*, might be described as its polar opposite by virtue of being an irony-free, mythological celebration of chastity. Treasury warrants indicate that the maids formed a sort of theatre-going club, with numerous records specifying 'a box for the Maids of Honour'.[23] On 25 November 1682 the maids (by then rather differently constituted, so presumably protests had become something of a tradition with them) took a box for Edward Ravenscroft's racy comedy *The London Cuckolds*, subsequently panned as 'a heap of vice and absurdity'.[24] Towards the end of the 1680s such protests had turned into a movement. Different constituencies of women, aristocratic and merely genteel, went to theatre to protest against the indecency of rakish, male-oriented comedy. Backed by a new wave of journalism and domestic literature aimed at a group called 'the ladies' that was in part culturally created, these women helped realize the progressive change in the values of comedy that saw out the aggressive, discredited ideology of the Stuarts, to be replaced by a reformed comedy of 'sentimental' sociability.[25] So doing, they prepared the ground for the bitter assault on the theatre mounted by Jeremy Collier.

The narrative of vocal and outraged female spectators obscures their sophistication. Numerous playwrights drew a connection between the kind of plot discoveries Pepys so admired and the capacity of plays to move their female audience. Writing to Catherine Trotter about her final play, *The Revolution of Sweden*, Congreve shows why:

> One thing would have a very beautiful effect in the catastrophe, if it were possible to manage it through the play: & that is to have the audience kept in ignorance, as long as the husband (which sure they may as well be) who Fredage really is, till after her death.[26]

The husband's tragic knowledge is the audience's, and the proposed marriage of rational 'design' and emotional release is offered as the perfection of a reformed, sentimental approach to drama derived from narratives of secrecy. The tears of what Peter Motteux has described as 'the fairest eyes' might be hard won.[27] If such reports still construe women spectators as emotionally vulnerable, it is clear from Pepys's accounts of his own wife's theatre-going that a woman such as Elizabeth Pepys, with no particular privileges of birth or education, went to the playhouse with a scepticism as lively as her husband's, alert to nuances of performance and attuned to sources.[28] So what did plays written to pacify this changing group of spectators look like?

A play for the ladies? Thomas Southerne's *The Wives' Excuse* (1691)

A character called Wellvile steps forward in Thomas Southerne's comedy *The Wives' Excuse* to announce a new kind of play, written in the aftermath of political revolution:

> I have a design upon a play... I am scandalized extremely to see the women upon the stage make cuckolds at that insatiable rate they do in our modern comedies; without any other reason from the poets, but, because a man is married he must be a cuckold: now, sir, I think the women are most unconscionably injured by this general scandal upon their sex; therefore to do 'em what service I can in their vindication I design to write a play, and call it...*The Wives' Excuse, or, Cuckolds Make Themselves.*[29]

Among Wellvile's companions, Friendall feels the intended play is 'very like to be popular among the women'. Whether Friendall knows that the joke is on him – or whether it really is – is not clear. 'And true among the men,' adds a third character, Wilding, perhaps under his breath, because in *The Wives' Excuse* it is Friendall whose flirtations give his long-suffering wife every justification – in fact, encouragement – to take her revenge in the arms of a smooth-talking libertine called (who would have guessed?) Lovemore. Repeatedly, she declines the opportunity, like the heroine of Madame De Lafayette's great novella *La Princesse de Clèves*, Nathaniel Lee's dramatization of which had been first published two years beforehand. Southerne's play ends in partial stalemate (or 'Peace...Treaty', as Wilding calls it) after Friendall has been caught, by a parting of scenes, *in flagrante* with Mrs Witwoud, a woman of unfashionable maturity. By agreeing to separate rather than divorce, the unhappy Friendalls leave Lovemore stuck in his obsession to gain another conquest. Southerne's play revises many of the conventions of Restoration Comedy but recalls an earlier play, Thomas Heywood's 1603 *A Woman Kill'd With Kindness*, in which a cuckolded husband punishes his wife not with threats or murder, as in the nearly contemporaneous *Othello*, but cold, pious separation. The arrangement the Friendalls envisage at the end of the play is certainly chilly, but hardly pious. 'There's yet a lady to declare herself,' says the predatory Lovemore, hoping to find Mrs Friendall rushing into his embrace:

MRS FRIENDALL: Mr. Friendall, I'm sorry you thought it necessary to your pleasures, to make me a witness of my ill usage: you know I can and have passed [over] many things, some women would think wrongs, as such resent 'em, and return 'em too: but you can tell how I've behaved myself.

MR FRIENDALL: Like a gentlewoman always, madam, and my wife.

MRS FRIENDALL: The unjust world,
Let what will be the cause of our complaint
(As there is cause sufficient still at home)
Condemn us to a slavery for life:
And if by separation we get free,
Then all our husband's faults are laid on us:
This hard condition of a woman's fate,
I've often weighed, therefore resolv'd to bear:
And I have born; O! what have I not born?
But patience tires with such oppressing wrongs,

> When they come home, to triumph over me;
> And tell the town, how much I am despis'd.

MR FRIENDALL: I see we are both disappointed in this affair of matrimony; it is not the condition you expected; nor has it the advantages I proposed. Now, madam, since 'tis impossible to make it happy between us, let us even resolve to make it as easy as we can.

MRS FRIENDALL: That must be my business now.

MR FRIENDALL: And mine too, I assure you: look you, madam, your own relations shall provide for you at pleasure, out of my estate; I only article that I may have a freedom of visiting you, in the round of my acquaintance.

MRS FRIENDALL: I must be still your wife, and still unhappy.

LOVEMORE: What alteration this may make in my fortune with her, I don't know; but I'm glad to have parted 'em.

MR FRIENDALL: Well, gentlemen, I can't be very much displeased at the recovery of my liberty, I am only sorry Witwoud was the occasion of it. For an old blown-upon she-wit is hardly an intrigue to justify the separation on my side, or make a man very vain of his fortune.[30]

This is 'true among the men' to the extent that it is hard to decide which man comes out of it worse. Refracting Heywood, the play also recalls Wycherley, for, if Lovemore is a Horner figure, Friendall is a Sparkish, but by deliberation rather than accident. Dismantling the assumptions of the proposal scene Congreve brought to perfection in *The Way of the World*, the conclusion of *The Wives' Excuse* takes us back to an earlier stage of the Friendalls' life in which the groom has conceived of his 'proposal' of marriage as a set of 'advantages' to himself. An 'easy' resolution is what he has always sought, and the smooth 'round of…acquaintance' is barely disturbed by separation. The bachelor joke he ends with combines fatuity and stomach-turning vanity: if only he had been found bedding some luscious young A-lister, it would have been worth the minor inconvenience. Lovemore's final words seem merely destructive: he is content to have engineered what amounts to a divorce. Speaking the epigraph, he lays claim to an authority the play denies him:

> This must you all expect, who marry fools;
> Unless you form 'em early in your schools,
> And make 'em, what they were design'd for, tools.[31]

'Schools' betrays a debt to Molière's *L'Ecole des Maris*, from which the lines have been adapted, but, where that play assigned a similar closing sentiment to a plain-speaking maid, Lisette, Southerne gave it to someone the audience had been coached to mistrust, as though he either intended the play to cause moral confusion or had lost his plot.

Southerne soon acquired a reputation for capturing a 'spirit of conversation in everything he writes', and in the language of Mrs Friendall he explored a range of registers that both imitate and elevate the tone and diction of natural speech.[32] She can be dignified but cutting ('I'm sorry you thought it necessary...') or determined in resignation ('That must be my business now'), or she can deploy a classical caesura to emphasize the inescapability of her fate ('I must be still your wife, and still unhappy'). Breaking into blank verse, she identifies the 'home' that is supposed to be her natural abode as the site of the worst indignity that could befall her. For eleven lines, this is a tragic heroine from Otway lamenting her 'hard condition' in sweeping proto-Romantic cadences: 'And I have born; O! what have I not born?' Casting played its part, and Elizabeth Barry brought to Mrs Friendall the impassioned dignity of Monimia in Otway's *The Orphan* or Belvidera in the same writer's *Venice Preserv'd*, just as Betterton brought to Lovemore a long history of playing libertines used to having their own way.

Those complex messages got in the way of the play's success. Dryden wrote Southerne a consolatory prologue that reports that *The Wives' Excuse* was, 'with a kind civility, dismiss'd'. The problem, he implied, was the 'tale' rather than the 'wit'; Southerne's language was lively but his reversal of the narrative conventions of libertine drama was too strange, with not enough scope for laughter.[33] So much is clear from the conclusion, with its unresolved tightrope walk between tragic and comic traditions accentuated by the profiles of the actors. The epilogue, spoken by Barry as Mrs Friendall, admits that the main character is 'not...much in vogue' and suggests that men of a certain sort were bound to feel disappointed by Lovemore:

> Damn me, cries one, had I been Betterton,
> And struts, and cocks, I know what I had done;
> She should not have got clear of me so soon.[34]

But why did the play not appeal more strongly to 'the ladies' it was Southerne's (and his mouthpiece Wellvile's) intention to please? They had damned the kind of play Southerne's turns on its head, but they did not rescue this one. The dedication suggests that audiences had found the satire too pointed, while modern editors point to the cast's inability to 'deal convincingly with the elaborate ensemble scenes', which are indeed highly complex and innovative in their use of the 'discovery' device.[35] A more obvious explanation is the discrepancy between the title of the play and what actually happens in it. Pepys was sensitive to such things, and doubtless others were too, since a title creates expectations that audiences expect to see fulfilled. Watching Dryden's *The Wild Gallant*, Pepys found it

ill acted and the play so poor a thing as I never saw in my life almost, and so little answering the name, that from the beginning to the end I could not, nor can at this time, tell certainly which was the wild gallant.[36]

Southerne's *The Wives' Excuse* breaches the contract that is formed of familiar conventions not just in its plot and casting but in the way its title implies a conclusion that never happens, and an ideology that is never endorsed or really clarified (the title and epilogue imply that women can be libertines as well as men, if the cause if right). The odious Friendall fails, in spite of his best efforts, to make a cuckold of himself; his wife needs no excuse, for she *does* nothing. Refusing the humiliating means of escape represented by sex with Lovemore, she has no other options: a prisoner moved from shared quarters to solitary confinement, as though the only answer to an unhappy marriage was a monastery. Amid that civilly dismissive audience of December 1691 there was, conceivably, a longing for something bolder, less submissive: a longing for the sound that would begin to echo round the theatres of Europe two centuries later when another frustrated woman, Ibsen's Nora Helmer, left her husband not with a peace treaty and the promise of a continuing round of acquaintance but with the slamming of a door. Elizabeth Barry may have spoken in impassioned iambs of woman's 'hard condition', but, as far as even the most elastic conventions of Restoration Comedy were concerned, solutions were in short supply. Another self-declared play for 'the ladies', Colley Cibber's 1696 *Love's Last Shift*, results in a pious reunion of an estranged couple: no slam of the door here either, merely a gentle click of the latch as the sanctity of marriage is restored.

Something for everybody? Colley Cibber's *Love's Last Shift* (1696) and its legacy

The Wives' Excuse was a well-documented flop, *Love's Last Shift* a well-attested hit – and partly thanks to Southerne, who 'had the Patience to hear [Cibber] read it to him' and 'immediately recommended it to the patentees'. Cibber's uncertainty persisted beyond his surprise at Southerne's patience, and, when Congreve gave his verdict, Cibber was forced to agree that the play 'had only in it a great many things that were *like* wit, that in reality were *not* wit'.[37] Even Southerne was not so certain of Cibber's acting talent. Cibber had cast himself as the foppish Sir Novelty Fashion, and Southerne administered a dose of brusque encouragement just as the first performance was about to start: 'Young Man!' he said. 'I pronounce thy play a good one; I will answer for its success, if thou dost not spoil it by thy own action.' Cibber saved his smug riposte for when he wrote up the incident more than forty years later: 'I succeeded so well in both, that people seemed at a loss which they should give the preference to.'[38] What the audience liked in the play was its 'purity of plot, manners and moral'; this comedy of reformed manners was such a success that it could be described as 'the Philosopher's Stone' because it 'did wonders' at the box office.[39]

Critics have attributed its popularity to its mixing of styles, to a happy resolution of the old and new comic ideologies that had produced a frustrating dead end for Southerne; Robert D. Hume describes it as a 'potpourri' with 'something for everybody'.[40] This summary reveals a consistent immersion in the business of reformation: all the male leads are 'new men', for good or ill, either as reformed rakes or, in the case of Cibber's role, fashion-obsessed airheads. The main plot begins with reminiscences of Otway and Behn. Amanda, an impeccably dignified heroine abandoned ten years ago by her wastrel husband, Loveless, has since come into an inheritance but remains loyal to her roving man. When Loveless returns, deep in debt and believing her dead, she disguises herself and makes him believe she is merely another of his conquests. The morning afterwards, though, all is revealed and the floodgates open:

AMANDA: The conflict's past, and heaven bids me speak undaunted. Know then, even all the boasted raptures of your last night's love, you found in your Amanda's arms: – I am your wife.
LOVELESS: Ha!
AMANDA: For ever blest or miserable, as your next breath shall sentence me.
LOVELESS: My wife! Impossible! Is she not dead? How shall I believe thee?
AMANDA: How time and my afflictions may have altered me, I know not: but here's an indelible confirmation. (*Bares her Arm*) These speaking characters, which in their cheerful bloom our early passions mutually recorded.

LOVELESS: Ha! 'tis here; – 'tis no illusion, but my real name; which seems to upbraid me as a witness of my perjured love: – Oh, I am confounded with my guilt, and tremble to behold thee. – Pray give me leave to think. (*Turns from her*)

AMANDA: I will. (*Kneels*) But you must look upon me: for only eyes can hear the language of the eyes, and mine have sure the tenderest tale of love to tell, that ever misery, at the dawn of rising hope, could utter.

LOVELESS: I have wronged you. Oh! Rise! Basely wronged you! And can I see your face?

AMANDA: One kind, one pitying look cancels those wrongs for ever: And oh! Forgive my fond presuming passion; for from my soul I pardon and forgive you all: all, all but this, the greatest, your unkind delay of love.

LOVELESS: Oh! seal my pardon with thy trembling lips, while with this tender grasp of fond reviving love I seize my bliss, and stifle all thy wrongs for ever. (*Embraces her*)

AMANDA: No more; I'll wash away their memory in tears of flowing joy.

LOVELESS: Oh! Thou hast roused me from my deep lethargy of vice! For hitherto my soul has been enslaved to loose desires, to vain deluding follies, and shadows of substantial bliss: but now I wake with joy, to find my rapture real – thus let me kneel and pay my thanks to her whose conquering virtue has at last subdued me. Here will I fix, thus prostrate, sigh my shame, and wash my crimes in never-ceasing tears of penitence.

AMANDA: O rise! This posture heaps new guilt on me! Now you overpay me.

LOVELESS: Have I not used thee like a villain? For almost ten long years deprived thee of my love, and ruined all they fortune! But I will labour, dig, beg, or starve to give new proofs of my unfeigned affection.[41]

Loveless is spared the indignity of his promise, since the next revelation is that Amanda has been made rich by her inheritance. He may speak as though he has undergone some feverish Low Church conversion, but his reward would have made Dorimant content: money and the woman who can settle his emotional and financial debts. But, while Dorimant and Harriet are drawn to each other by wit, it is tears that ultimately unite Loveless and Amanda – and, indeed, their first audience. The saccharine excesses of Cibber's language derive partly from his topical wish to subsume the erotic into the pious. Loveless's waking 'with joy, to find [his] rapture real', recalls Adam's discovery of Eve, while his promise to 'dig, beg or starve' is the labour of love assigned to the postlapsarian couple. Cibber's attempts at poetry – 'shadows of substantial bliss' – likewise resemble offcuts of Milton.[42] But he also mines a different kind of ancient narrative language. As Frank H. Ellis points out, Loveless re-embodies the folkloric archetype of a man awakened from a magic sleep by his wife.[43] Still in thrall to archetypes, Cibber hijacks the mythical scar of Odysseus that launched a thousand recognition scenes by transforming it into a lover's tattoo.[44] The 'speaking characters' that Amanda has engraved on her arm record, in a multiple revelation, his name, his historic nature and her historic situation, now transformed. The real wonder is how on earth Loveless missed them during the night.

The play – and its reconciliation scene in particular – was successful enough to spawn imitations, fond, satirical or both. Vanbrugh's *The Relapse* (1696) shows Loveless backsliding in a stew of guilt and falling for his wife's best friend, Berinthia; Sir Novelty Fashion has been elevated into the majestic Lord Foppington, whose absurd idiolect replaces every long 'o' with an 'a' ('A man gets so many heats and colds, 'twould destroy the constitution of a harse,' he complains).[45] George Farquhar's second play, *The Constant Couple*, was such a success for Rich's company in 1699 that it almost took out the competition at Lincoln's Inn Fields.[46] It makes fun of its hero's instruction at the hands of Lady Darling and her daughter Angelica, whom he mistakes for a prostitute; the rakish Sir Harry Wildair, whose popularity saw his life continue into a second, less successful play, is reduced to a sweating schoolboy sent to the corner for his errors:

ANGELICA: Now sir, I hope you need no instigation to redress our wrongs, since even the injury points the way.
LADY DARLING: Think, sir, that our blood for many generations has run in the purest channel of unsullied honour.
SIR HARRY: Ay, madam. (*Bows to her*)
ANGELICA: Consider what a tender blossom is female reputation, which the least air of foul detraction blasts.
SIR HARRY: Yes, madam. (*Bows to Angelica*)
LADY DARLING: Call then to mind your rude and scandalous behaviour.
SIR HARRY: Right, madam. (*Bows again*) ...Was ever man so catechised?[47]

Yet at the end of the play Sir Harry speaks a language of piety worthy of Cibber, moving from chatty prose to incantatory verse:

In vain are musty morals taught in schools,
By rigid teachers, and as rigid rules.
Where virtue with a frowning aspect stands,

And frights the pupil from its rough commands.
But woman –
Charming woman, can true converts make;
We love the precepts for the teacher's sake.
Virtue in them appears so bright, so gay,
We hear with transport, and with pride obey.[48]

The epilogue claims the play as a 'whole compliment' to 'the ladies', but like *The Wives' Excuse* and *Love's Last Shift* it exorcises negative images of manhood by indulging them. In the sequel, *Sir Harry Wildair*, the indulgence is taken to extremes. Believing his Angelica dead in her travels through France, the hero – in Hume's droll description – 'roar[s] through the country impregnating nuns in revenge'.[49] In fact, Angelica has disguised herself as Sir Harry's younger brother, and it is her reappearance as her own ghost that sparks the (by then) customary scene of tearful reconciliation.

Outrage in print: Jeremy Collier

Paper succeeded vocal outrage as a means of intervening in the affairs of the stage. It is an irony of the history of Restoration Drama that, just as dramatists were well into a process of reform nourished by a wider social movement, they were torpedoed by a formidable critical mind who, to all appearances, had not noticed. The work of the Reverend Jeremy Collier, like the managerial career of Christopher Rich, holds an ambiguous place in theatre history. Both men appeared to share an antipathy towards everything interesting in their period's theatre; for this reason, both are paradoxically integral to an understanding of Restoration plays and players. *A Short View of the Immorality and Profaneness of the English Stage* (1698) had a greater material impact on Restoration plays and players than any defence or apology, as witnessed by a series of reports by the news-monger Narcissus Luttrell. In May 1698 he wrote,

The justice[s] of Middlesex have presented the playhouses to be nurseries of debauchery and blasphemy.

Two days later Luttrell caught up with the details:

The justices of Middlesex did not only present the playhouses, but also Mr Congreve, for writing the Double Dealer; Durfey, for Don Quixot; and

Tonson and Brisco, booksellers, for printing them: and that women frequent-ing the playhouses in masks tended much to debauchery and immorality.

Over the next three years actors found that they could not take refuge in the obvious defence that they were merely speaking words scripted for them:

> An information is brought in the Kings Bench against 12 of the players, *viz.* Mrs Bracegirdle, Mrs Barry, Mr Betterton, Mr Verbruggen, &c for using indecent expressions in some late plays, particularly The Provok'd Wife, and are to be tried the latter end of the term.[50]

The twelve were fined £5 each (a little more than a month's salary for a tenured actor) and obliged to 'give good security not to commit the like again'. Now they would be cautious of the zealot gangs who brought their notebooks to the day's performance. The editor of the *Post Man* hoped the verdict would 'deter for the future such as shall write plays, from using any lewd and immoral expressions'. Presumably to the disgust of Betterton and his troupe, their Drury Lane rivals were acquitted of the same offence the following week.[51]

What motivated Collier? For all its rage, his work transcends the puritan, anti-theatrical tradition partly because it is not fundamentally anti-theatrical any more than Collier was a puritan. The full title is significant: *A Short View of the Immorality and Profaneness of the English Stage, Together with a Sense of Antiquity upon this Argument.* While Collier's book is a manifestation of other pious movements of the late 1680s and 1690s, it is also coloured by a question that had preoccupied some of his adversaries for much longer: were modern writers inferior to their ancient forebears? But the book is also the product of Collier's controversial past.

The son of a Cambridgeshire clergyman, he became a minister before moving to London to lecture at Gray's Inn; what impresses in his critiques of Congreve, Vanbrugh and D'Urfey is their forensic tenacity. Loyal to James II, Collier was ousted during the revolution of 1688 and engaged in a pamphlet war over the legality of William III's succession (he was thus a 'non-juror', or a person who would not swear allegiance to the new king). When James's flight to France was construed as legal abdication, Collier entered the fray with the energy of a man as convinced of his law as his Latin etymology. Take, for example, *The Desertion discuss'd in a letter to a country gentleman* (1689):

[S]ince His Majesty had sufficient reasons to withdraw, these can be no
pretence for an abdication: for we are to observe, that to abdicate an office,
always supposes the consent of him whom quits it. That this is the significa-
tion of the word *abdico*, appears from *Tully*, *Salust*, and *Livy*; to which I shall
only add the learned *Grotius*, *De jure Belli*, &c. *Libr*. 1. *Cap*. 4. *Sect*. 9.[52]

Collier was sent to Newgate for his efforts. Released without trial after
months of detention, he remained under surveillance and was repeatedly
suspected of communicating with the exiled James. He officiated with
two other non-juror clergymen at the executions of two anti-Williamite
plotters and dared to give them absolution. After his lodgings were
searched, he replied with a learned pamphlet, *A Defence of the Absolution given to Sir William Perkins* (1696). Forbidden by the Church to
minister, he began a collection of his writings, publishing *Essays
on Several Moral Subjects* in 1697. This included a piece from the
revolutionary year called *The Office of a Chaplain enquir'd into and
vindicated from servility and contempt* (1688), the expression of a
fiercely independent habit of mind:

He does not receive this commission from the master of the family, or from
any human authority, but from God himself, whose deputy he is in things
pertaining to religion: he is not entertained upon any secular account, or to
manage any other business but what relates to another world; and is conse-
crated to this function by the divine warrant and appointment, and consequently he is God's minister not man's.[53]

As Collier was preparing his *Essays* for publication, Betterton's
company at Lincoln's Inn Fields was mounting a new comedy whose
boorish hero, drunk in the street, dresses up as a clergyman so that, in
the ensuing brawl with the London watch, 'the scandal may light upon
the church'.[54] For Collier, Vanbrugh's *The Provok'd Wife* (of particular interest to the Middlesex magistracy) was a personal insult, an
assertion of the 'servility and contempt' from which he had hoped for
the past ten years to rescue his profession. The third chapter of *A Short
View* is called 'The Clergy Abused by the Stage', and it ends with a
quotation from 'The Office of a Chaplain'.

A Short View was therefore a complex opportunity for Collier: a
chance to assert Christian principles in the public sphere without fear of
prosecution. So doing, he could draw on convictions about the dignity
of the ministry and his right to speak for God. In this sense, *A Short
View* is both an attack on the Restoration Stage and a self-justification.

The book has six chapters. First, Collier sets out the general case against the malign influence of contemporary drama on society and in particular on the status of women: '[N]othing has gone farther in debauching the age than the Stage Poets, and Play-House.' He then argues that the dramatists of pagan Greece and Rome had more excuse for 'immodesty' but did not indulge it, supporting his case with reference to Aeschylus, Sophocles, Euripides, Plautus and Seneca, but concluding with some admonitions for Aristophanes. In a Christian society, he suggests, the irreverence of modern drama is particularly 'insufferable'. Jonson, Beaumont and Fletcher, and Corneille, are brought in to demonstrate that modern drama need not be profane. Chapter 2 is devoted to swearing, both in plays and among the audience; Collier cites the legal sanctions against it, discusses examples from a range of plays and again contrasts contemporary English with ancient Greek practice. In Chapter 3 he turns to representations of the clergy.

Chapters 4 and 5 deal with the more general question of immoral conduct and influence, and in particular the tendency to make heroes of libertines and whores of women. As we have seen, the theatre he attacked increasingly represented his libertine targets as cultural poltergeists to be mocked and exorcised, symptoms of the very dynasty he had gone to prison to defend. Even so, Collier makes a strong contribution to the *fin de siècle* debate, witnessed in a range of plays and other publications, about the rights and status of 'the ladies'. Chapter 5 includes a particularly pointed attack on D'Urfey's *Don Quixote*, which fuelled the prosecution of the dramatist that year. Closing his *Short View*, Collier explores the statutory and philosophical basis for theatre as a basis for promoting civic virtue, both in the ancient world and in contemporary London; the founding patents of the Restoration Stage had, after all, been issued on the basis that plays 'well managed might serve as moral instructions in human life'.

A Short View is therefore no clergyman's rant but a reasoned and well-evidenced polemic. For all its moments of hysteria – '[T]o compliment vice, is but one remove from worshipping the Devil,' concludes the preface – it often outmanoeuvres the many counterblasts it spawned. From some of its targets it drew contrition, from others revision: '[I]n many things he has taxed me justly,' wrote Dryden in his preface to *Fables Ancient and Modern*, while the offending scene in *The Provok'd Wife* was changed so that Sir John puts on women's clothes. The effectiveness of the many rebuttals is arguable, but what is certain is that Collier rose to his own defence with the same vigour he had brought to the first onslaught, publishing *A Defence of the Short View* and *A Second Defence* in successive years after 1698.

A Short View made Collier the symbolic leader of moral revival movements and led to calls for him to rejoin the Church of England. But vindication, not rehabilitation, had always been his aim. He continued to preach to fellow non-jurors effectively as part of a parallel Church with its own bishopric. Seeking justification in history, he worked on revisions to Louis Moreri's monumental *The Great Historical, Geographical, Genealogical and Poetical Dictionary*, adding to the two-volume edition of 1701 with a supplement in 1705. The scale of that project inspired him to further heights, his two-volume folio *Ecclesiastical History of Great Britain* appearing in 1708 and 1714. The second volume, dealing with the Reformation, incited what was probably to Collier a pleasing degree of irritation among Anglican bishops, for whom his non-juring history told an obvious truth: that he was really a closet papist who had all along liked James II for his religion. He died on the fringes of sanity, managing to upset even the small minority of people who shared his views. His last major project before his death, in April 1726, was an attempted union between non-jurors and the Eastern Church, involving a visit from the Archbishop of Thebes and correspondence with the Russian court in which he was prone to describe himself as 'Jeremias, Primus Anglo-Britanniae Episcopus'. Bordering on fantasy, this designation manifested the most abiding – and least appealing – quality of this ferociously disciplined, intelligent and combative critic of Restoration Drama: a conviction, in the words of his *Office of a Chaplain*, that he did not answer to 'any human authority, but. . .God himself, whose deputy he is'.

Critics in defence

Not surprisingly given the threat represented by Collier, it was theatre people who first began to write critically about theatre in formats suited for rapid consumption either daily or weekly, as a way first of justifying, then analysing, their business. Peter Motteux, Huguenot exile, dramatist and man of letters, wrote short notices of recent plays in *The Gentleman's Journal* between 1692 and 1694; in 1702 *The Daily Courant* picked up the baton, and the occasional playwright John

Oldmixon's *Muses' Mercury* continued the practice in 1707. The same period saw a host of publications rebutting and defending *A Short View*. Two memorial works entered the fray by insisting that performances and performers were as respectable a subject for publication as any other. John Downes's *Roscius Anglicanus* (1708) is a tribute by a retired prompter to the companies, and in particular the great actor, Thomas Betterton, he had served for nearly half a century. Charles Gildon lent his support with his 1710 *Life of Mr Thomas Betterton*, which presents the recently deceased actor, who had appeared in Gildon's plays and helped him write for the stage, as a prosperous country gentleman of wide learning. Downes defines in far more vivid detail than Motteux or Oldmixon the quality and impact of individual performances, while providing key insights into how they came into being as cultural artefacts handed down from before the civil war.

The ubiquity of Betterton in early theatre criticism argues that the genre could not have developed in the same way without him. His craft and intelligence as a performer, not to mention the peculiar charisma of his stocky figure and magisterial voice, gave educated critics something remarkable to write about. In the appreciation of Richard Steele, another playwright frank in his defence of the theatre, Betterton's performances of Shakespearean roles made a sense that the words on the page did not: what on the page seemed 'dry, incoherent and broken sentences' seemed natural and intelligible in the actor's performance. Throughout *The Tatler* (1710–11), Steele showed how audiences were moved to sympathy, so portraying theatre-going as a secular congregational experience, a living instance of sentiment's power to create and reinforce sociability.

But the path to maturity in theatre criticism was jagged and broken. Succeeding *The Tatler*, *The Spectator* turned away from its nascent attempts at performance criticism, with no real attempt to record a new play or performance. Joseph Addison was more concerned to bewail the threats to serious drama presented by Italian opera, circus-type exhibitions and pedantic classicists. Other publications, such as the *Female Tatler* (1709–10) and Theobald's *Censor* (1715 and 1717), promised regular theatre criticism but failed to publish any of note. The genre would not reach maturity for another thirty years, at least. A different kind of criticism lay outside the scope of emergent metropolitan journalism: in the apparatus made available to playwrights by the appearance of their work in print.

Endnotes

1 *Spectator*, no. 268 (7 January 1712).
2 Letter from John Verney to Sir Ralph Verney, 30 August 1675; reprinted in LS1, 235.
3 *The Diary of Samuel Pepys*, 27 December 1662.
4 Ibid., 19 October 1667.
5 Andrew Marvell to William Popple, 24 July 1675; in H. M. Margoliouth, ed., *The Poems and Letters of Andrew Marvell*, 2 vols. (Oxford: Clarendon Press, 1952), vol. II, 320.
6 *The Diary of Samuel Pepys*, 27 August 1661, 21 December 1668.
7 *The Gracious Answer of the most Illustrious Lady of Pleasure the Countess of Castlemaine to the Poor-Whores Petition* (London, 1668).
8 *The Diary of Samuel Pepys*, 3 April 1665.
9 Ibid., 18 February 1667.
10 Ibid., 1 July 1663. For further information, including the £500 fine Sedley incurred, see the Latham and Matthews edition, vol. IV, 209, n. 3.
11 For *1 Henry IV*, see *The Diary of Samuel Pepys*, 31 December 1660; for *Hamlet*, 24 August 1661; for *The Siege of Rhodes*, 1 October 1665.
12 Ibid., 19 December 1668.
13 Ibid., 1 December 1662. For the catalogue of Pepys's library, see C. S. Knighton, ed., *Catalogue of the Pepys Library at Magdalene College Cambridge: Supplementary Series I: Census of Printed Books* (Martlesham: D. S. Brewer, 2004).
14 *The Diary of Samuel Pepys*, 1 January 1664, 30 December 1668.
15 Ibid., 7 January 1661 (22 June 1661 for *The Alchemist*), 1 June 1664, 19 September 1668.
16 On the idea of novelty in the Restoration period, see J. S. Peters, 'The novelty; or, print, money, fashion, getting, spending and glut', in Canfield and Payne, *Cultural Readings*, 169–94.
17 *The Diary of Samuel Pepys*, 29 September 1662.
18 Ibid., 5 December 1660.
19 See, for example, Michael Dobson, *The Making of the National Poet* (Oxford: Clarendon Press, 1992); Robert D. Hume, 'Before the Bard: "Shakespeare" in early eighteenth-century London, 1660–1740', *Huntington Library Quarterly* **64** (1997), 41–75; Kewes, *Authorship and Appropriation*, 180–224.
20 *The Diary of Samuel Pepys*, 7 January 1667. Previous references are dated 5 November 1664 (the play's historic association with the Gunpowder Plot survived the Restoration) and 28 December 1666.
21 Shakespeare, *Macbeth*, ed. Nicholas Brooke (Oxford University Press, 1990), 32.

22 Richard Legh to his wife, 3 January 1667; in LS1, 100; *The Diary of Samuel Pepys*, 2 January 1667.

23 As reprinted, for example, in Nicoll, *A History of Restoration Drama*, 305–14. For the identification of these women, see Roberts, *The Ladies*, 108–9.

24 *The Tatler*, no. 8, 28 April 1709.

25 This narrative was established by J. H. Smith's 'Shadwell, the ladies and the change in comedy', *Modern Philology* **46** (1948), 22–33.

26 William Congreve to Catherine Trotter, dated 2 November 1703; in *The Mourning Bride Poems, and Miscellanies*, ed. Bonamy Dobree (Oxford: Oxford University Press, 1928), 528. Trotter went on revising her play until late 1705, ahead of its premiere in February 1706.

27 Peter Motteux, 'Preface', *Beauty in Distress* (London, 1698).

28 See, for example, *The Diary of Samuel Pepys*, 20 June 1668. For further discussion, including analysis of the frequency of Elizabeth's theatre visits, see Roberts, *The Ladies*, 49–64.

29 Southerne, *The Wives' Excuse*, 33–4 (III.ii.225–31).

30 Ibid., 54–5 (V.iii.298–332).

31 Ibid., 55 (V.iii.333–5).

32 *A Comparison Between the Two Stages*, 19. See also Motteux's *The Gentleman's Journal*, January 1693, 28.

33 John Dryden, 'To Mr Southerne; on his Comedy, Called the Wives Excuse'; in Jordan and Love, *The Works of Thomas Southerne*, vol. I, 270.

34 Thomas Southerne, 'Epilogue [to *The Wives' Excuse*]', spoken by Mrs Barry; in Jordan and Love, *The Works of Thomas Southerne*, vol. I, 341.

35 Thomas Southerne, Dedication 'To the Right Honourable Tho. Wharton, Esq, Controuler of His Majesty's Household'; in Jordan and Love, *The Works of Thomas Southerne*, vol. I, 268; for complex scenes, see ibid., 264.

36 *The Diary of Samuel Pepys*, 23 February 1663.

37 Cibber, *An Apology*, 124 [emphasis in original].

38 Ibid.

39 *A Comparison Between the Two Stages*, 16.

40 Hume, *The Development of English Drama*, 412. See also Paul E. Parnell, 'Equivocation in Cibber's *Love's Last Shift*', *Studies in Philology* **57** (1960), 519–34.

41 Colley Cibber, *Love's Last Shift* (London, 1696), 91–2 (V.ii.212–66).

42 See, for example, the following lines from *Paradise Lost*, IV 483–5: '[T]o give thee being I lent / Out of my side to thee, nearest my Heart / Substantial Life.'

43 Frank H. Ellis, *Sentimental Comedy: Theory and Practice* (Cambridge University Press, 1991), 32.

44 For a brilliant study of the device in Western drama and literature, see Terence Cave, *Recognitions: A Study in Poetics* (Oxford: Clarendon Press, 1988).

45 John Vanbrugh, *The Relapse* (London, 1697), 41 (III.i.10–12).

46 See Shirley Strum Kenny, 'Theatrical warfare, 1695–1710,' *Theatre Notebook* **27** (1973), 130–45.

47 George Farquhar, *The Constant Couple* (London, 1699), 45.

48 Ibid., 52.

49 Hume, *The Development of English Drama*, 446.

50 Narcissus Luttrell, *A Brief Historical Relation of State Affairs from September 1678 to April 1714*, 6 vols. (Oxford, 1857), vol. IV, 378, 379 (10, 12 May 1698), vol. V, 111 (20 November 1701).

51 *Post Man*, 17–19 February 1702; *Post Boy*, 24–6 February 1702.

52 Reverend Jeremy Collier, *The Desertion discuss'd in a letter to a country gentleman* (London, 1689), 4.

53 Reverend Jeremy Collier, *The Office of a Chaplain enquir'd into and vindicated from servility and contempt* (London, 1688), 14.

54 Vanbrugh, *The Provok'd Wife*, 45 (IV.i.33).

8 | *Texts and publishers*

In 1668 the dramatist Edward Howard observed that

> the impression [i.e. printing] of plays is so much the practice of the age,
> that few or none have been acted, which fail to be displayed in print; where
> they seem to put on the greater formality of authors.[1]

The phrasing teases: 'display' reads like a continuation of 'acted', yet
it is an act of metamorphosis that produces a new 'formality'. No one,
he implies, would be interested in reading a play that had not made it
to the stage. Even so, closet dramas from the period have survived,
none more precariously or notoriously than the Earl of Rochester's
Sodom, which some believe was not printed until 1904, for the obvious
reason that it was close to unprintable.[2] Its roster of roles (King
Bolloxinian, Queen Cuntigratia and the maids of honour Cunticula,
Clitoris and Fuckadilla, etc.) is often held to announce a satire on
Charles II's willingness to wield the member of state over any woman
he chose. As the title declares, however, it is more obviously obsessed
with a pastime Charles that did not favour but that was all the rage in
the circle of his brother-in-law, the Duke of Orléans, and aptly captured in the antics of the man Rochester describes as 'General of the
Army', Buggeranthus.

The promiscuity of printed plays was of greater interest to Howard,
and it is reflected in the popularity of another Restoration novelty,
the book auction. London saw its first one in 1676, and soon there
were dozens every year. Sale catalogues of the time reveal plays as a
marginal but not insignificant component of major collections. The
gentleman's library, which prescribed a core diet of classical texts in
their original languages and, at the pinnacle of prestige, in lush folio
format, might nevertheless find room for more disposable quarto
play texts. The quality and dimensions of that space varied, even
among theatre people.

Congreve kept a library in which Aristophanes, Plautus, Sophocles and Terence rubbed shoulders insouciantly not only with Corneille, Racine and Molière, but with Davenant, Dryden, Etherege, Otway, Southerne and Wycherley.[3] Curiously, the collection kept by Thomas Betterton relegated plays to a less exalted station. The sale catalogue of his books and pictures reflects a shelving system of nine separate categories in which 'English Plays in Quarto' and 'French and Italian Plays in Octavo and Duodecimo' come almost the bottom of the list, ahead only of 'Bundles of Pamphlets'. It was as though he had heeded Sir Thomas Bodley's advice to keep classical drama but 'hardly one in forty' modern plays.[4]

Nevertheless, going into print was, Howard suggests, like acquiring a smarter set of clothes. Printing was in theory the point at which the multiple, accidental agency of theatre gave way to the singular and controlling voice of the author. Many Restoration performances 'staged' the person of the author, and not just in pieces such as Buckingham's *The Rehearsal*. Prologues and epilogues were frequently written by playwrights themselves and refer to their plans or wishes, but their performance by actors often shrank the author to a bystander pleading vicariously for charity. The apparatus of the printed text, on the other hand, gave authors the chance to flex their own vocal cords. An epistle dedicating the play to – usually – a noble patron advertised connections; a preface or essay guided readers' interpretation of the text and puffed its triumph in the theatre or sought to shift blame for its failure. Either way, there was a pervasive assumption that readers would know which was in order, because they were believed also to be theatre-goers.

How were those opportunities taken? This chapter considers three aspects of Howard's mass 'impression': first, the visual qualities of Restoration play texts, a subject increasingly beset, like so much else in the period, by differentiation between English and French practice; second, the relationship between playwrights and booksellers, the people who published their work; finally, the pieces of Restoration play texts modern readers are most likely to skim over. Dedicatory epistles described and helped form playwrights' relationships to people of influence; not just arbiters of taste, but agents (and sometimes victims) of regime change. As such, while they promoted the name, market value and cultural symbolism of the author, they might also advertise his or her abject failure of authority.

Seeing double: Congreve's *The Double Dealer* in 1694 and 1710

Compare Jacob Tonson's luxury folio edition of Congreve's plays (1710) with the handy quarto editions of *The Double Dealer*, *Love for Love*, *The Mourning Bride* and *The Way of the World* he published within a year of each of those plays opening in the 1690s, and the differences are stark. The folio has short, French-style scenes, whereby a new scene artificially marks every entrance and exit; prompt-book directions and character names have been tidied up; the whole book breathes 'the greater formality of authors', and with it the greater prosperity of readers. Open the quartos and the impression is of texts that act as memorials or perhaps anticipations of live performance, with its fluid motion, provisionality and dependence on the benign control of the prompter and his book.

The 1694 and 1710 texts of Congreve's *The Double Dealer* (both published by Jacob Tonson) complicate the distinction; for legibility's sake they are reproduced here both in their original form (Figures 8.1 and 8.2) and in transcription. Modern editors prefer to represent this scene as IV.ii, in which Mellefont, in love with Cynthia but an object of desire for his own aunt, Lady Touchwood, conceals himself to eavesdrop on a conversation his aunt is having with Maskwell, whom he suspects has been deceiving him. As Fainall is to Mirabell in *The Way of the World*, so Maskwell is to Mellefont: a Iago-like shadow or double who professes friendship while being attracted to the same women (he too pursues Cynthia and disguises his intentions through a liaison with Lady Touchwood), and who is ultimately punished because he reminds us that even the greatest virtue may be accompanied by the lowest degree of animal cunning; this is another attempt to exorcise scheming Stuart masculinity, all the more dramatic because, as in *The Way of the World*, it is incomplete. *The Double Dealer* compresses time and place to Aristotelian order, and then some: the 'scene' is defined as 'A Gallery in the Lord Touchwood's House' and the time 'from Five o'clock to Eight in the Evening'. Such intensity of focus means that the play in performance unfolds with a breathtaking – and sometimes confusing – narrative energy as plot meets counterplot and hero confides in anti-hero.

Here is Tonson's quarto text of a passage in which the conventions of the comedy of manners are pushed to the borders of farce or melodrama (in these two extracts, original spelling and punctuation are integral to the effect):

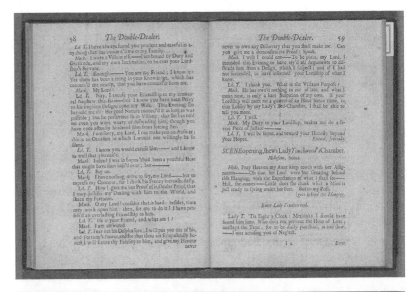

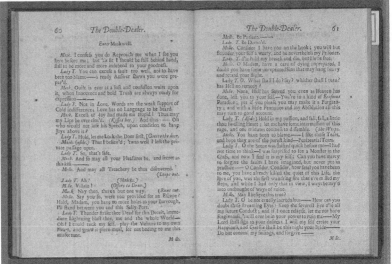

Figure 8.1 1694 quarto text of William Congreve's *The Double Dealer*

SCENE opening, shows Lady *Touchwood's* Chamber.
Mellefont, Solus.

MELLE. Pray Heaven my Aunt keep touch with her Assignation – Oh that her
Lord were but sweating behind this Hanging, with the Expectation of
what I shall see – Hist, she comes – Little does she think what a Mine is
just ready to spring under her Feet. But to my Post.

(*goes behind the Hanging.*
Enter Lady Touchwood

LADY T. 'Tis Eight a Clock: Methinks I should have found him here. Who does not prevent the Hour of Love, outstays the Time; for to be dully punctual, is too slow – I was accusing you of Neglect.

Enter Maskwell

MASK. I confess you do Reproach me when I see you here before me; but 'tis fit I should be still behind hand, still to be more and more indebted to your goodness.

LADY T. You can excuse a fault too well, not to have been to blame – a ready Answer shows you were prepar'd.

MASK. Guilt is ever at a loss and confusion waits upon it, when Innocence and bold Truth are always ready for expression –

LADY T. Not in *Love*. Words are the weak support of Cold indifference; Love has no Language to be heard.

MASK. Excess of Joy had made me stupid! Thus may my Lips be ever clos'd. (*Kisses her*) And thus – Oh who would not lose his Speech, upon condition to have Joys above it?

LADY T. Hold, let me lock the Door first.

(*Goes to the door.*

MASK. (*aside*) That I believ'd; 'twas well I left the private passage open.

LADY T. So, that's safe.

MASK. And so may all your Pleasures be, and secret as this kiss –

MELLE. And may all Treachery be thus discovered.

(*Leaps out.*

LADY T. Ah!

(*shrieks*)

MELLE. Villain!

(*Offers to Draw*)

MASK. Nay then, there's but one way.

(*Runs out.*

MELLE. Say you so, were you provided for an Escape? Hold, Madam...

This quarto text does not give a scene marking: the play runs on from a conversation between Maskwell and Lord Touchwood at the end of which they *exeunt, severally.*

Compare the effect of the 1710 folio text, which conducts a stately progress from one set piece to another:

SCENE XV
      SCENE *opening, shows Lady* TOUCHWOOD's *Chamber.*
MELLEFONT, *Solus.*

260   *The* DOUBLE-DEALER.

Mask. My Duty to your Lordſhip, makes me do a ſevere Piece of Juſtice. —

Ld. Touch. I will be ſecret, and reward your Honeſty beyond your Hopes.

SCENE XV.

SCENE *opening ſhews Lady* TOUCH-WOOD's *Chamber.*

MELLEFONT *Solus.*

Mel. PRAY Heav'n my Aunt keep touch with her Aſſignation. —— Oh that her Lord were but ſweating behind this Hanging, with the Expectation of what I ſhall ſee —— Hiſt, ſhe comes —— Little does ſhe think what a Mine is juſt ready to ſpring under her Feet. But to my Poſt.   [*Goes behind the Hangings.*

SCENE XVI.

Lady TOUCHWOOD.

L. Touch. 'TIS Eight a Clock: Methinks I ſhould have found him here. Who does not prevent the Hour of Love, outſtays the Time; for to be dully punctual, is too ſlow. — I was accuſing you of Neglect.   SCENE

The DOUBLE-DEALER.   261

SCENE XVII.

Lady TOUCHWOOD, MASKWELL,

MELLEFONT *abſconding.*

Mask. I Confeſs you do reproach me when I ſee you here before me; but 'tis fit I ſhould be ſtill behind hand, ſtill to be more and more indebted to your Goodneſs.

L. Touch. You can excuſe a Fault too well, not to have been to blame — Already Anſwer ſhews you were prepar'd.

Mask. Guilt is ever at a Loſs, and Confuſion waits upon it; when Innocence and bold Truth are always ready for Expreſſion --

L. Touch. Not in Love; Words are the weak Support of cold Indifference; Love has no Language to be heard.

Mask. Exceſs of Joy has made me ſtupid! Thus may my Lips be ever clos'd. [*Kiſſes her.*] And thus —— Oh who would not loſe his Speech, upon Condition to have Joys above it?

L. Touch. Hold, let me lock the Door firſt.   [*Goes to the Door.*

Mask. (*Aſide.*) That I believ'd; 'twas well I left the private Paſſage open.

S 3   L. *Touch*

Figure 8.2 1710 folio text of William Congreve's *The Double Dealer*

MEL. Pray Heav'n my Aunt keep touch with her Assignation. – Oh that her Lord were but sweating behind this Hanging, with the Expectation of what I shall see – Hist, she comes – Little does she think what a Mine is just ready to spring under her Feet. But to my Post.

[*goes behind the Hangings*

SCENE XVI

Lady TOUCHWOOD

L. TOUCH. 'Tis Eight a Clock: Methinks I should have found him here. Who does not prevent the Hour of Love, outstays the Time; for to be dully punctual, is too slow – I was accusing you of Neglect.

SCENE XVII

Lady TOUCHWOOD, MASKWELL,

MELLEFONT *absconding.*

MASK. I Confess you do reproach me when I see you here before me; but 'tis fit I should be still behind hand, still to be more and more indebted to your Goodness.

262   *The* DOUBLE-DEALER.

L. *Touch.* So, that's fafe.
Mask. And fo may all your Pleafures
be, and fecret as this Kifs——
Mel. And may all Treachery be thus
difcover'd.   [*Leaps out.*
L. *Touch.* Ah!   [*Shrieks.*
Mel. Villain!   [*Offers to draw.*
Mask. Nay then, there's but one Way.
                               [*Runs out.*

❀❀❀❀❀❀❀❀❀❀❀❀❀❀❀❀❀❀❀❀❀❀❀❀❀

S C E N E   XVIII.

Lady TOUCHWOOD, MELLEFONT.

Mel. SAY you fo, were you provided
for an Efcape? Hold, Madam,
you have no more Holes to your Bur-
rough, I'll ftand between you and this
Sally-Port.
L. *Touch.* Thunder ftrike thee dead for
this Deceit, immediate Lightning blaft
thee, me and the whole World—— Oh!
I could rack my felf, play the Vulture to
my own Heart, and gnaw it piece-meal,
for not boding to me this Misfortune.
Mel. Be Patient.——
L. *Touch.* Be Damn'd.
Mel. Confider I have you on the Hook;
you will but flounder your felf a weary,
and be neverthelefs my Prifoner.
                          L. *Touch.*

Figure 8.2 (*cont.*)

L. TOUCH. You can excuse a Fault too well, not to have been to blame –
    A ready Answer shows you were prepar'd.
MASK. Guilt is ever at a Loss, and confusion waits upon it, when Innocence
    and bold Truth are always ready for Expression –
L. TOUCH. Not in *Love*; Words are the weak Support of cold Indifference;
    Love has no Language to be heard.
MASK. Excess of Joy had made me stupid! Thus may my Lips be ever clos'd.
    (*Kisses her*) And thus – Oh who would not lose his Speech, upon Condition
    to have Joys above it?
L. TOUCH. Hold, let me lock the Door first.
[*Goes to the Door.*
MASK. (*Aside*) That I believ'd; 'twas well I left the private Passage open.
L TOUCH. So, that's safe.
MASK. And so may all your Pleasures be, and secret as this Kiss –
MEL. And may all Treachery be thus discovered.
[*Leaps out*

L. TOUCH. Ah!
[*shrieks*
MEL. Villain!
[*Offers to draw*
MASK. Nay then, there's but one Way.
[*Runs out.*

SCENE XVIII
   Lady TOUCHWOOD, MELLEFONT.
MEL. Say you so, were you provided for an Escape? Hold, Madam...

The 1710 text observes French conventions: instead of 'enter' and
'exit', a new scene for every fresh configuration of characters, with a
reminder that a character who is hidden ('Mellefont, absconding')
remains part of the scene. The use of an enlarged initial letter for each
scene draws analogies with the structuring unit of expository prose, the
paragraph; the earlier text has been tidied so that capitalization
observes the normal conventions of printed text in the period, with
nouns so distinguished. This shift in textual practice has been described
by Julie Stone Peters as one of tense: imagined future and past performances yield to 'the eternal present...[of] events happening in the
now, on the page and in the reader's imagination'.[5]
   Messy, hurried and transient, the theatre gives way to the uphol-
stered permanence of the gentleman's library – a transition Congreve
himself was only too anxious to make. It is possible to overstate the
difference, for the 1710 folio includes cast lists, a reminder that the
plays were conceived with a particular pool of acting talent in mind
(if such luxury items as the 1710 folio gilded the names of authors,
presumably actors felt a little of the benefit too). Peters's procession of
nouns – from 'now' to 'page' to 'imagination' – also raises the question
of why Tonson bothered with his fussy, French-style division of scenes
if not to provide a textual metaphor for the cognitive effect of live
performance. All those scenes keep reminding the reader as to which
characters are in play at a given point, substituting the sign of the
actor's body with the symbols deployed by the printer. Certainly, the
effect is to slow down the process of perception; but, then, the quarto
text arguably takes it at such a rush in the absence of live performance
that readers struggle to decode what is happening. The very title of
Peters's study, *Theatre of the Book*, indicates how publishers were
less concerned to turn plays into pseudo-novels than to present the
book itself as a kind of living theatrical entity, with illustrations and

other textual conventions that recorded the non-verbal aspects of performance and their impact on the reader/spectator.[6]

Booksellers and their playwrights

The 1660 patents had assigned the rights in plays to companies, so there was no reason for companies to stand in the way of publication, as there had been before the civil war. If the King's Company put on *The Conquest of Granada*, the Duke's could not. Hence the pervasive 'impression' noted by Howard: playwrights had everything to gain, their companies nothing to lose, and plays typically appeared in print between six months and a year after the first performance. The fees paid by publishers ('booksellers' in the language of the period) began to rise from about £10 per play in the 1660s to between £15 and, in some cases, more than £50 by the early eighteenth century.[7] As the commodity became more valuable, producers naturally began to assert their rights: the 1710 Act for the Encouragement of Learning identified authors as copyright holders, although it would take another sixty-four years to dismiss rival claims to perpetual copyright by booksellers.[8] Sensing the shift of power, booksellers began to compete for publishing rights ever earlier, sometimes before a play had been tested in performance, and longer-term relationships developed that secured the interests of both parties. The more successful the dramatist, the more likely s/he was to be published by a restricted number of booksellers; the more exclusive the relationship, the greater the chance of a complete edition – a luxury item for libraries and a badge of honour for playwrights – free from a messy trail of rights transfers. How did playwrights emerge? The answers lie on a spectrum from 'authority' to 'desperation'.

John Banks (c. 1653–1706) wrote eight plays in twenty-seven years. He is believed to have abandoned a legal career for the theatre 'till experience convinced him of his error', and a recent biographer finds 'no evidence that he profited much by his plays'.[9] *The London Stage* records only around a dozen performances of his plays between 1660 and 1700, and no benefit days but for the 'six days together' enjoyed by *Cyrus the Great* in 1695.[10] He did not enjoy a steady relationship with a single theatre company, while his relationship to booksellers was hard won. His first play, *The Rival Kings*, a response to the success of Nathaniel Lee's intensely baroque dramas, was performed by the King's Company and published by William

Cademan in 1677. Cademan was probably drawn to Banks's work by his eleven-year experience of publishing **Elkanah Settle** (1648–1724), for whom he had taken the unusual step of printing 'sculptures' or engravings of the opulent scenery for *The Empress of Morocco* in 1673. But Cademan did not stick with his new man any more than the King's Company did, and Banks's second play, *The Destruction of Troy*, was performed by the Duke's Company in 1678, then published the following year by Charles Blount, who did not publish a single other major dramatist of the period.

With *The Unhappy Favourite* Banks began to find his voice, focusing on Tudor history and, in this case, the fall of the Earl of Essex. Back with the King's Company, he found two booksellers who were sufficiently sympathetic towards his work to want to keep publishing it, even in extreme adversity. Richard Bentley was so popular with another of his writers, Thomas Otway, that he was the dedicatee of Otway's 1681 comedy *The Souldier's Fortune*, and there are similarities between Otway's explorations of female heroism and the tenor of Banks's plays. Bentley was known as 'Novel' because he published so many of them: the huge French romances beloved of female readers that supplied many dramatists with plots.[11] In 1678 Bentley entered into partnership with John Magnes and then with Magnes's widow, Mary, so one of the chief promoters of Banks's historical 'she-tragedies' was, fittingly, a woman. There is scant evidence of women – even Lady Mary Davenant – exercising such entrepreneurial power in the theatres; yet Mary Magnes published no plays by women.

By the time Banks's next play was produced, the ground had shifted. *Vertue Betray'd, or, Anna Bullen* was one of the first new plays to be performed by the new United Company. Bentley and Magnes published it a matter of months afterwards, in 1682, but the play showed how history snapped at the heels of the present. The Duchess of York, alarmed by the Popish Plot crisis and the threat to her own and her husband's position, 'kept her bed the day after seeing *Anna Bulloigne* acted'.[12] In such circumstances a playwright needed to be sure of his publisher, since the theatres might find their hands tied. Tudor history became too potent, and Banks's next two plays, the first about Mary Queen of Scots (*The Island Queens*), the second on the subject of Lady Jane Grey (*The Innocent Usurper*), were banned at a time when sensitivities about legitimate succession were raw, although this did not prevent Bentley from publishing them. It was perhaps with a sense of allegiance to a once popular form of drama that Betterton produced *Cyrus the Great* for the breakaway company in 1695; Bentley stuck by Banks as well, and the playwright's career ended – but for a 1704 revision of *The Island Queens* – on a note of stability that had largely eluded him for the previous seventeen years.

Aphra Behn worked with one theatre company – the Duke's – but her publishing history was much less predictable. Only her posthumous play, *The Younger Brother* (1696), was not premiered by a company headed by Thomas Betterton, but her eighteen plays appeared under thirteen different imprimaturs. Good times were punctuated by periods when she was published by booksellers such as Thomas Benskin, John Harris and John Amery, who were better known for political and pamphlet works. Her association with Richard Bentley and John Magnes came to an end just before the former entered into partnership with Magnes's widow, Mary. At the height of her productivity, during the Popish Plot years, her plays carried the prestigious Tonson imprint four times, but when she returned to playwriting with *The Luckey Chance* in 1686 she was published by William Canning, who took such risks with his political imprints (he kept a separate, private press for really dark matter) that he was arrested several times.[13] Her remaining three plays came out through three different booksellers.

She must have envied the consistency enjoyed by **John Crowne**, surely her inferior as a writer, and for whom Richard Bentley had a hand in publishing eleven out of his seventeen plays. In Crowne's case there was a relatively smooth transition from Bentley and J. Magnes to Bentley and M. Magnes. **William Congreve** was nothing like as prolific as either Banks, Behn or Crowne, but sat in the Kit Kat Club with the man who published all his five plays except the first, but then bought the rights to it for the 1710 folio, Jacob Tonson the Elder. Tonson's friend Betterton, painted by Kneller as though he were a Kit Kat member, produced and starred in all Congreve's plays; this was a charmed circle of influence from which the playwright could really profit.

In the same circle sat **John Dryden**, who managed enduring relationships with both companies and booksellers; yet even he suffered some sharp twists of publishing fortune. Between 1663 and the end of 1677 he was house dramatist to the King's Company, writing thirteen plays for them, including signature successes such as *An Evening's Love* and the two parts of *The Conquest of Granada*. His one effort during this period for the Duke's, *Sir Martin Mar-All*, was a Molière adaptation thought to be the joint work of the Duke of Newcastle. Throughout this period his plays and poems were published by Henry Herringman, one of the most successful and influential booksellers of the century; Master of the Stationer's Company from 1685, Herringman is often described as the first wholesale publisher in England, with 532 titles to his name. This was no mass-market business, however, but a reflection of a literary culture in which production and patronage were intertwined. In the words of James A. Winn,

> Poets depended for their support upon gentlemen who amused themselves by writing verses, just as musicians depended on such gentleman amateurs as Pepys, who enjoyed taking part in sacred and secular music, and was painted holding one of his compositions, as if he were a professional composer. Booksellers like Herringman [recognized] that literary amateurs would be even better customers if they, too, had books in print...[14]

Dryden had probably lodged with Herringman in the late 1650s and written prefaces and occasional verses for his books; the bookseller had in effect been his patron, bringing him to the attention of 'gentlemen who amused themselves by writing verses' such as the man who would become Dryden's collaborator and brother-in-law, Sir Robert Howard. Herringman published Howard's poems in 1660 and, in a 1664 project that smacked of vanity, a folio of his four plays, and he was the natural publisher for the comedies of another gentleman who amused himself by writing, Sir George Etherege.[15]

At the end of the 1670s Dryden's charmed association with Herringman faltered. *All for Love* (1678) was the last Dryden play to be performed by the King's Company, by then in turmoil, and the last to be published by Herringman. Winn suggests that money was behind the writer's decision to abandon his twenty-year relationship with his bookseller; Dryden's court payments for his Poet Laureateship were badly in arrears, and he needed a quick remedy. The theatrical context looks just as important. Dryden severed his ties with the King's Company at this time because the company could not be relied on to produce his plays with the same professionalism as the Duke's, but his first two plays for the Duke's were controversial for different reasons. *The Kind Keeper* (March 1678), a satirical sex farce, was 'stopped, when it had but thrice appeared on the Stage', because it caused widespread offence.[16] *Oedipus* (November 1678), a collaboration with Nathaniel Lee, was published by Lee's booksellers, Bentley and

Magnes; a year later, and without Dryden's approval, they published *The Kind Keeper*.[17] Dryden may have been short of cash, but there is no obvious reason why he should have despaired of finding it from the biggest publisher in England. On the other hand, it is very easy to see why Herringman might have been disturbed by Dryden's recent output and come to feel that a writer who had been an asset was no longer so dependable. The Duke's Company, financially and professionally sound, had long been lambasted by its rivals as an advocate of showy, middle-brow entertainment – precisely the kind of thing that would not transfer well to the medium of print. Herringman had cultivated the young writer as any patron would, and, like any patron, he also had the power to drop him.

With *The Kind Keeper* in mind, it is worth noting that Herringman published the first two plays of **William Wycherley**, but, when it came to the sexual frankness of *The Country Wife*, the playwright had to look elsewhere. It is possible that Herringman was turned off plays altogether at a time when, thanks to the Popish Plot crisis, audiences were starting to shrink: **Thomas Shadwell**, published by Herringman for nine of his first ten plays, also moved to another bookseller in 1678. Although a Duke's Company playwright, Shadwell's comedies were serious attempts to develop a distinctively English tradition, and his prefaces essays of some critical worth. When, ten years after his last play with Herringman, he again found a long-term partner in James Knapton, Knapton took over his backlist.

Dryden's experience of stable associations led to others on the stage and in the bookshop. 'With his next play, *Troilus and Cressida*,' writes Winn, 'he began an association with Jacob Tonson that would last the rest of his life.'[18] The transition was not quite so straightforward, in fact. Tonson shared business in *Troilus* with the lesser-known Abel Swall, while the banned *The Duke of Guise* (1682) was shared with Richard Bentley, and *Don Sebastian* (1689) published under another name altogether, Joseph Hindmarsh. But it was Tonson who saw Dryden, like his protégé Congreve, through a series of plays culminating in the magnificent 1693 *Works*, which bestowed on him the status of a modern classic and confirmed bookseller and playwright in their place at the centre of literary culture. Even when it was not in folio format, the existence of a volume of 'works' conferred dignity not just on the writer but on the bookseller, a sign that the transient world of one-off quartos marking premieres and revivals had transmuted into the permanent capital of the gentleman's library. Such was the status conferred afterwards on **Nathaniel Lee** by his lifelong associate Richard Bentley, who published a one-volume *Works* in 1687, albeit in humble quarto.

With Bentley's predilection for publishing 'she-tragedies' went a tendency to attract awkward cases such as Lee and **Thomas Otway**. Otway wrote nine plays, all for companies led by Betterton, but under five different imprimaturs. Betterton appears to have paid him in advance to help him stay afloat; Jacob Tonson lent him money.[19] From *Don Carlos* to *Friendship in Fashion* (1676–78) Otway published with Jacob's brother Richard, who brought out his editions with a speed that shows how the bookseller's wish to capitalize on theatrical success was entirely consonant with the playwright's dire need for cash. Then, presumably hoping for more, he transferred to a newcomer, Thomas Fletcher, before moving to Bentley for the high watermark of his achievement: *The Orphan, Venice Preserv'd* and the two parts of *The Souldier's Fortune*, the latter of which was published jointly with Jacob Tonson, the two publishers having perhaps decided that the time had come to share the risk of dealing with a man unhinged by infatuation with Elizabeth Barry. Otway was in some respects a prototype of the Romantic artist, his work compounding the intensity of his obsessions, and it was fitting that when he died he should leave his minders with the very Romantic problem of a manuscript that had probably been paid for in advance and that was not only incomplete but lost. Nineteen months after his death, probably after a great of deal of fruitless rummaging, the following newspaper advertisement appeared:

Whereas Mr Thomas Otway some time before his death made four acts of a play, whoever can give notice in whose hands the copy lies, either to Mr Thomas Betterton, or Mr William Smith at the Theatre Royal, shall be well rewarded for his pains.[20]

Otway was an exasperating writer to work with, but even an incomplete play was valuable enough to warrant a reward. Worked up, it could turn out to be as lucrative as *The Orphan*. This was another 'she-tragedy' on the ever popular subject of Iphigenia; perhaps Otway died imagining the scene yet to be written in which Agamemnon would plunge a dagger into the palpitating bosom of one last Elizabeth Barry heroine. In the hope of restoring a lost project,

Betterton commissioned a young John Dennis to write another Iphigenia play thirteen years later.

When assessing the rise of the author in the Restoration period, it is sobering to reflect that, while the period between 1616 and 1647 saw the production of three folio editions on behalf of people who could be described as professional writers – Jonson, Shakespeare, and Beaumont and Fletcher – so did the period from 1660 to 1714. For the rest, it was a story of attempting and largely failing to do as the most successful did: moving from bookseller to bookseller or company to company in search of stability and long-term profit, but finding instead penury, the madhouse or the gaol. It is in the nature of play publishing that the trajectory of elevation was just as conspicuously enjoyed, if not more so, by those who did the commissioning: by Henry Herringman, who became Master of the Stationer's Company, and Thomas Betterton, who would beat any of the playwrights he championed to the ultimate textual accolade, a single-volume biography.

Special pleading: the art of the dedication

Since the start of the seventeenth century dramatists had confronted the relative novelty of publishing their plays by introducing them with what began as variants of the Renaissance 'familiar letter': the dedication, usually written to a specified patron or friend; and the preface, addressed to a largely unknown mass of readers.[21] Gérard Genette has called such letters 'paratexts', those written at the margin of the text that, like an acknowledgements page, prescribe yet invite: a required cultural practice but also an attractive opportunity to characterize the work, its genesis and potential impact.[22] It is tempting to see the different audiences for these texts as symptomatic of a broader shift in patronage and cultural value: court gives way to marketplace, aristocracy to bourgeoisie, paid servant to autonomous author. Such narratives invest prefaces with the fragrance of the new and dedications with the less appealing aroma of the obsolete, which may explain the relative lack of attention paid to them as a body of writing.

Dramatists themselves are partly to blame. Lamenting the insufferable hypocrisy of the dedication was, from the start of the seventeenth century to the close, almost as popular as writing it. In 1602 John Marston dedicated *Antonio and Mellida* to that 'bounteous Maecenas of poetry, Nobody', while in 1695 William Congreve wrote disdainfully of the 'common form of poetical dedications, which are generally made up of panegyrics'; the only example of the form that met with his approval was the one that most daringly unmasked its polite conventions, Wycherley's dedication of *The Plain Dealer* to Mother Bennett, who, nothing if not plain in her dealings, kept a brothel.[23] The most trenchant denunciation of all was Dryden's. Dedications, he complained, tested any sensible writer's skill to the limit:

'Tis difficult to write justly on anything, but almost impossible in praise.[24]

But dedications survived long after writers were able to make a living from seeing their works performed and published; with the rush for 'impression' went a rush for dedication. Complaints about dedications are most often found in dedications themselves. Bemoaning the 'common form of poetical dedications' was a common form of self-advertisement, a way of demonstrating superiority in social and authorial skill. John Crowne drew attention to this vice in 1671. When he declined to indulge in 'the common practice of dedications' it was because, he said, in saying so little about their recipients, they merely gave scope to their authors' 'skill in writing characters and essays'.[25] All the same, Crowne played the very game he decried, his own self-promotion subverting the subservience he proclaimed in offering his first play, *Juliana*, to the Earl of Orrery.

All paratexts, in other words, furthered a single economic agenda, that of better book sales. The patronage of a duke or duchess was part of the commodity exchange enacted by the business of printing: letters to My Lord *X* or My Lady *Y* lent authors and their readers the glamour of a Gramscian 'symbolic capital' that, for authors, might in turn translate into bigger and better book deals in the future.[26] Starker finance clinches the point: dedications might yield instant rewards of money or hospitality that no taking up of cudgels in a preface could match. Thomas Otway spoke for many in 1676 when he used the preface to *Don Carlos* – the only play preface by this compulsive dedicator – to complain that prefaces just didn't pay.[27] Others, such as Thomas D'Urfey, were also sparing in their prefatory endeavours, saving them in order to prolong a controversy, whether for his political stance in *The Royalist* (1682) or for the suspicion that he had attended an establishment of the sort depicted in his 1691 comedy *Love for Money, or, the Boarding School*. So reluctant was D'Urfey to frame critical defences of his plays that, when he felt one was required for *The Marriage-Hater Match'd*, his friend Charles Gildon did it for him.[28] A few dramatists, Dryden and Crowne included, saw a higher value in the preface, while the less productive and well connected saw little point in attempting either form – a helplessness that encouraged Abraham Bailey to a feeble, sub-*Tristram-Shandy* joke in 1667: 'Epistles and Prologues,' he observed, were 'for the most part skipped over without reading', and he addressed the reader only to spare his stationer the embarrassment of charging for 'a blank page'.[29]

It was not all about money. Dedications were the door to state politics. Claiming to find their composition impossible, Dryden diced with the equally impossible task of securing his footing in the volatile politics of the 1680s. *The Spanish Fryar* was dedicated during the Popish Plot crisis to John Holles, Lord Haughton, a militant Protestant, four years before Dryden's conversion to Catholicism ('[A] Protestant play to a Protestant patron,' as Dryden put it); the gap between playwright and dedicatee would widen further by the end of the decade, when Holles embraced the new Williamite regime with the same fervour Dryden had invested in its predecessor. As Holles made his political entrance, Dryden was heading towards the door.[30]

Addressing a patron, the dramatist often conjures up not just a public figure but an ideal interpreter. In this respect, dedications announce the rise of authors (albeit as abject servants), prefaces their demise in the imminent babble of readership. The protected space of the dedication goes with a kind of intimacy: 'confess' is a familiar term in the genre. But the intimacy is partly an illusion, since the 'confessor' is really every reader. So, dedications are occasions for authorized eavesdropping to which the general reader, nominally directed below stairs to the preface, listens in as author talks to patron. These are what Jacques Derrida has called 'circumfessions' – personal histories told through detour, in relation to others.[31] The vivid textual presence of the dedicatee leaves traces of another's voice, body, mind, family or career that give shape to the author's; inscribing these traces, the author both measures his own social distance from them while striving to be closer to them. The result is a form of life-writing in which the self is created not through lonely interrogation but social relation and aspiration.

The Restoration play's life cycle was in many ways a thing of threads and patches: actors' parts, detachable prologues, epilogues and songs, and other features of its apparatus that renders it, in Tiffany Stern's words, a 'play made of patches of varying fixity'.[32] Towards the end of the cycle dedications offered a redeeming unity in the person of the dedicatee. Prologues might be occasional; once dedicated, a play was never rededicated. The body of the author, the biological parent often invoked to assert the text's unity, shared its duties with the honoured, illustrious and renowned person of the patron and ideal reader.

What did this mean in practice? Dedications by three major dramatists show contrasting approaches to the form.

Thomas Otway, pilgrim

Otway found solace in religious diction. If he is guilty of the usual self-promotion in his dedications, his route is self-abasement, and his characteristic image of ritual not confession but pilgrimage:

[A]s poorest pilgrims, when they visit shrines, will make some presents where they kneel: so I have here brought mine, by your own goodness only made worthy to be preserved...[33]

The metaphor is historically significant, emphasizing links with the religious and family past, to pre-war England and a concept of the poetical golden age built upon it; this was also a theme pursued by the royalist Aphra Behn in her dedication of *The Luckey Chance* to Laurence Hyde. Otway dedicated *Caius Marius* to Lord Falkland in 1680 because of the allegiance of his father, Lucius Cary, to Crown and poetry; the Italian ancestry of the second Duchess of York, dedicatee of *The Orphan*, is honoured by references to Tasso and Ariosto; his own family history as a dispossessed royalist emerges in his proud complaint to the Duchess of Portsmouth that

a steady faith and loyalty to my prince was all the inheritance my father left me...[34]

But these conventional royalist and High Church sentiments took a different direction in his 1680 tragedy *The Orphan*. The occasion for the dedication of *The Orphan* is an absence, and Otway's desire to fill it. Alarms caused by the Popish Plot meant that the Duchess of York, an Italian Catholic, had left London for her own safety;[35] she missed both the opening and subsequent revivals later in the season.

Though fortune would not so far bless my endeavours, as to encourage them with your Royal Highness's presence, when this came into the world: yet, I cannot but declare it was my design and hopes it might have been your divertisement in that happy season, when you returned again to cheer all those eyes that had before wept for your departure, and enliven all hearts that had drooped in your absence...[36]

Conventionally, Otway describes his play as a child who comes 'into the world' with performance; by the time the duchess had the opportunity to see the piece it had become a 'little mite'. Another metaphor registers the transformation of his play into a text. He continues by observing, with conventionally stodgy gallantry, that 'all the applauses of the world' could not make up for his patroness's absence from the theatre, but turns to the printed text and the occasion of dedicating it as a consolation:

Nevertheless, I thought myself not quite unhappy, so long as I had hopes this way yet to recompense my disappointment past; when I consider also that poetry might claim right to a little share in your favour. For *Tasso*, and *Ariosto*, some of the best, have made their names eternal, by transmitting to after-ages the glory of your ancestors.

Within a sentence, consolation turns to glorification. Only the printed form is capable of 'transmitting to after-ages': Otway realizes the possibility of his own future through the dedicatory mode, his patron's glory and his own inextricably linked. The duchess's absence is transformed by the occasion of print into the perpetual presence conferred by 'poetry', a literary rather than a dramatic art. The fitting metaphor for the way Otway's work will be similarly transformed is not infantine – the baby or little mite of the play in performance – but classically vegetable, lesser than a mite and yet greater:

And under the spreading of that shade, where two of the best [Tasso and Ariosto] have planted their laurels, how honoured should I be, who am the worst, if but a branch might grow for me.

The ancient associations of laurel make it an unavoidable choice, but Otway modifies it into a fantasy of literary history in which he will be organically (if humbly) linked to a tradition made possible by patronage and articulated by patronage's exclusive mode, the dedication.

Joining the club: William Congreve

William Congreve's dedication of *The Way of the World* to Ralph, Earl of Montagu, envisaged a different future altogether. If Voltaire is to be believed, indeed, the aim of Congreve's desire for distinction was to eliminate the memory of the work that produced it: to rise so far as an author that he would cease to be one. Congreve had, according to Voltaire,

one defect, which was, his entertaining too mean an idea of his first profession, (that of a writer) though it was to this he owed his fame and fortune. He spoke of his works as of trifles that were beneath him; and hinted to me in our first conversation, that I should visit him upon no other foot than that of a gentleman... I answered, that had he been so unfortunate as to be a mere gentleman I should never have come to see him...[37]

Voltaire later retracted the accusation of vanity that followed,[38] but the mud stuck: in Mark S. Dawson's study of gentility and the Restoration Theatre, the anecdote introduces discussion of how Congreve was derided as a 'fop' for his social ambition. Of that, there is no shortage in his address to the Earl of Montagu.[39]

Congreve begins conventionally enough by contemplating the awesome social difficulties involved in dedicating a play at all: wondering whether he will be accused of vanity in addressing himself to such an eminent man, he concludes that even to wonder about it is a sign of vanity – of course he is being presumptuous. But this is nothing to the puzzle that follows. Contrary to the conventions of the dedication, he doesn't need Montagu's protection in the critical sense, since the play, much to his surprise, 'succeeded on the stage':

[L]ittle of it was prepared for that general taste which seems now to be predominant in the palates of our audience.[40]

Yet the reception of the play provided more than enough evidence that Congreve's 'design' of characters had not been understood as he would have wished, even after two or three showings.[41] Presenting the play to Montagu was a means of privatizing the reception, of seeing his designs realized in the reading where they could not be in the playing, and here this wish is expressed in terms that are aesthetic as they are social: '[O]nly by the countenance of your Lordship, and the *few* so qualified, that such who write with care and pains can hope to be distinguished.' Indeed, the play is incomplete without its patron:

[W]hatever value may be wanting to this play while yet it is mine, will be sufficiently made up to it, when it is once become your Lordship's.

Unable to place the same faith in the simple term 'poetry' as Otway had, Congreve craves distinction among the rest, 'for the prostituted name of *poet* promiscuously levels all that bear it'. His desire for writerly distinction is, unmistakably, a desire for social advancement: 'Poetry, in its nature, is sacred to the good and the great; the relation between them is reciprocal.' The symmetry is proved by extended reference to the works of Terence, whose 'purity', 'delicacy' and 'just-ness' are models for how Congreve hopes his own works might be evaluated, but also how he might transcend altogether the prostitution of poetry. This longing is crowned in his classical language of narra-tive. He figures the apex of critical recognition as a narrative reso-lution, so that to be a true connoisseur is to value not 'two or three unseasonable jests' in the last act but the 'artful solution of the *fable*'. Congreve's critical language rehearses the biography he aims to achieve, in which the impeccable last act will see him released from the sordid business of being accountable to a general audience of readers and theatre-goers.

The virtuosic writer: John Dryden

In his dedication of *The Spanish Fryar*, Dryden articulates pride in his own accomplishments. Convinced that the dedication and the pref-ace are distinct genres, he paradoxically sets about blending them in an extraordinary display of paratextual virtuosity. In doing so, he started a fashion. Hybrid dedications increased in number towards the end of the Restoration period, with a rush in the 1690s, as if the dedication served as an incentive to critical thought even as the 'author' was becoming more identifiable in agency and value. A combination of criticism and compliment is found in the dedications of three out of the five plays Congreve wrote in the 1690s (*The Double Dealer*, *The Mourning Bride* and *The Way of the World*), in four out of South-erne's five plays of the decade (*Sir Anthony Love*, *The Wives' Excuse*, *The Fatal Marriage* and *Oroonoko*) and in one of Crowne's (*The Married Beau*), while Dryden continued to write in the mixed dedicatory form, the best example of which is the section on stoic virtues from the dedication of *Don Sebastian* in 1690.[42] In recent criticism of Restoration Drama, a particular interest has been attached to such mixed forms.

Buckingham may have mocked the tendency among Restoration playwrights to make audiences laugh at tragedy and cry at comedy,[43] but, for scholars such as Laura Brown and Nancy Klein Maguire, such blending of conventions is a sign of engagement with central ideological questions; mixed forms are by definition 'sites of anxiety'.[44] In Maguire's work in particular, tragicomedy supplies the means by which to reconcile the tensions between the 'old mythical values' associated with the royal martyr Charles I and the 'new and secular ones' ushered in by his son.[45] For Dryden, however, it is perhaps less anxiety than writerly confidence that characterized his mixing of forms.

The dedication of *The Spanish Fryar* is the finest example of stylistic hybridity, because, fusing both forms, it advances the best-developed case both for and against the dedication. Concluding his dedication to Holles, Dryden declared that he had deliberately exceeded his brief:

And now, my Lord, I must confess, that what I have written looks more like a preface, than a dedication; and truly it was thus far my design, that I might entertain you with somewhat in my own art which might be more worthy of a noble mind, than the stale exploded trick of fulsome panegyrics. 'Tis difficult to write justly on anything, but almost impossible in praise.[46]

Since the dedicatee's nobility of mind and body are the lingua franca of the genre, the playwright's professed disdain for such language is, typically, a subtler instance of it. Even so, the distinction he offers between the genres of 'preface' and 'dedication' appears emphatic enough. It turns on powerful oppositions and associations. Dryden's word 'design' ('truly it was thus far my design') comprehends both the disguised intentions of the dedicator and the well-turned plot of his play. The parallel drew on his deepest instincts about dramatic structure, which he shared with Congreve but to different effect. The moment when the master playwright's hidden design is revealed to an audience Dryden had defined in his *Essay of Dramatick Poesie* during a passage on Ben Jonson's *Epicoene*. There, the achievement of Jonson's plot is mirrored in the critic's syntax, which memorably delays its own disclosure until the last possible moment:

I will observe yet one thing further of this admirable plot; the business of it rises in every act. The second is greater than the first; the third than the second; and so forward to the fifth. There too you see, till the very last scene, new difficulties to obstruct the action of the play; and when the audience is brought into despair that the business can naturally be effected, then, and not before, the discovery is made.[47]

By disguising his dedication to *The Spanish Fryar* as a preface, Dryden shows how his 'art' can be used to entertain the most discerning audience, so aligning the form of the preface with the play itself, and that of the dedication with an altogether shoddier kind of entertainment. His 'own art' is, by definition, his or it is no one's: its deep, slow design, food for the 'noble mind' of his patron, outdoes the tawdry magic of conventional praise, which anyone can practise and anyone else can spot.

For all the charges laid against the form, Dryden even gives the impression that he enjoys making it work for his own ends. The result is so impressively hybrid that it is hard to tell whether it is a preface disguised as a dedication or the other way round. It complements the play not simply in its satisfying conclusion but in a mixing of styles:

When I first designed this play, I found, or thought I found, somewhat so moving in the serious part of it, and so pleasant in the comic, as might deserve a more than ordinary care in both; accordingly, I used the best of my endeavour, in the management of two plots, so very different from each other, that it was not perhaps the talent of every writer to have made them of a piece.[48]

In turn, this brag is justified by the dedication as much as by the play: the twin plots of compliment and criticism converge at the end with a skill such 'that it was not perhaps the talent of every writer to have made them a piece'. The critical language of the dedication proves to be an instance of the 'art' one should not expect to find there: Dryden's hesitant 'I found, or thought I found, somewhat so moving in the serious part' does its own finding, illuminating in a single phrase layers of authorial self-consciousness in the process of discovering and fashioning the play's raw material. The 'confession' that he has actually written not a dedication but a preface is, properly, a confession of the self-conscious means and processes by which he has come to write the play.

Dryden's dedicatory confessions are self-conscious in their allusion not only to the style, content and genesis of the play they are attached to but also to his other works. In the dedication of *Don Sebastian*, Dryden reflects on the nature of contentment: 'How much happier is

he...who, centring on himself, remains immovable...he puts it out of
fortune's power to throw him down.'[49] The allusion is to his own
translation from Horace, published five years beforehand:

> Enjoy the present smiling hour,
> And put it out of fortune's power...
> Happy the man, and happy he alone,
> He who can call today his own...[50]

The effect is to make this dedication an agent of self-articulation,
the playwright's works the fruit of a consistent world view. Speaking of
and through his own writings, Dryden shows how future criticism might
address not just his qualities as a writer but his coherence as an author.

Such an idea would have seemed astonishing to Dryden at the start
of his playwriting career; the art of the dedication was another instance
of the constantly evolving world of Restoration Theatre. In the late
1660s he seemed only dimly aware that there was a history, especially
a specifically English history, to the question of what happens to a play
when it is printed and what sort of prefatory material should go with it.
Indeed, at times he approached the whole question of play publication
from scratch. His first play, *The Wild Gallant*, had premiered in
1663 to a hostile reception. According to Pepys, who saw it at court
on 23 February,

> it was ill acted and the play so poor a thing as I never saw in my life
> almost...The King did not seem pleased at all, all the whole play, nor
> anybody else, though Mr Clerke whom we met here did commend it to us.[51]

Such was the failure that the play did not make it into print until 1669,
when Dryden assumed that a work that had flopped before an audience could not be justified to a readership:

> It would be a great impudence in me to say much of a comedy which has had
> but indifferent success in the action. I made the town my judges; and the
> greater part condemned it.[52]

A French precedent came to mind, only to be discarded: Dryden
contrasted his own diffidence with the 'more resolute' Corneille,
who in his preface to *Partherite* (1651) had declared his play,
though 'condemned more universally than this', to be 'well, and
regularly written; which is more than I dare say for mine'.[53] In this
account, any prefatory material is a vain endeavour, but the opposite
case proves the point: the biggest theatrical success of his early

career, *Sir Martin Mar-All* (1668), had no prefatory material, because it needed none.

He represented these paratextual writings as yet another French import. In the preface to *Secret Love* (1668), he used that grudging fact to explain his latest play's *lack* of a dedicatee:

It has been the ordinary practice of the French poets, to dedicate their works of this nature to their King, especially when they have had the least encouragement to it, by his approbation of them on the stage.[54]

Having received such encouragement from his king, Dryden preferred not to seek protection for the play 'from any subject'; but nor could he presume to use 'the tedious form of a dedication' to his royal master Charles II, since that would entail

presuming to interrupt those hours which he is daily giving to the peace and settlement of his people.[55]

Was there a more outrageous fiction perpetrated by any dedication of the period? Skating over the paratext's English history, Dryden performed the familiar Restoration trick of making it new while struggling to accommodate its allegedly unEnglish floridity, as if its generic challenges were inherently alien to his own formative designs as a writer.

Overall, however, his early experiments with prefatory material suggest that attention to print as a cultural form should not obscure its power as a *personal* one; the transition from performance to page was negotiated by different dramatists at different times and speeds. In this sense it remains an autobiographical genre, though elusively: a means of criticism that assists the writer in announcing the moment when the stage gives way to the forever new world of print. But only, of course, before print gives rise to the unending business of revivals.

Endnotes

1 Edward Howard, 'Preface', *The Usurper* (London, 1668).
2 For a textual history, see Lyons, *Rochester: Complete Poems and Plays*, 312–14.
3 See John C. Hodges, *The Library of William Congreve* (New York Public Library, 1955).
4 Cited by Julie Stone Peters, *Congreve, the Drama and the Printed Word* (Stanford University Press, 1990), 36.

5 Julie Stone Peters, *Theatre of the Book 1480–1880: Print, Text and Performance in Europe* (Oxford University Press, 2000), 62.

6 Ibid., 65.

7 Kewes, *Authorship and Appropriation*, 30–1. Peters, *Theatre of the Book*, 55, cites a number of cases: Dryden's £31 10s for *Cleomenes* (1691); Southerne's £36 for *The Fatal Marriage* (1694); then the eye-watering £50 and £75 Nicholas Rowe received from Bernard Lintott for *Jane Shore* (1714) and *Lady Jane Grey* (1715). Yet these sums still lagged behind the very large amounts paid to the most successful French dramatists: see Peters, *Theatre of the Book*, 55–6.

8 See Shirley Strum Kenny, 'The publication of plays', in Robert D. Hume, ed., *The London Theatre World, 1660–1800* (Carbondale: Southern Illinois University Press, 1980), 309–36.

9 David Wykes, 'John Banks', in Backscheider, *Dictionary of Literary Biography*, vol. LXXX, 5. The 'Error' quotation is from Wykes, citing Charles Gildon's 1699 revision of Gerard Langbaine's *An Account of the English Dramatick Poets* (London, 1691).

10 Langbaine, rev. Gildon, *An Account of the English Dramatick Poets* (London, 1699), 6.

11 H. R. Plomer, *A Dictionary of the Printers and Booksellers Who Were at Work in England, Scotland and Ireland from 1668 to 1725* (Oxford University Press, 1922), 31.

12 Historical Manuscripts Commission, Twelfth Report, Rutland Manuscripts; cited in LS1, 311.

13 Plomer, *A Dictionary of the Printers and Booksellers*, 64.

14 James A. Winn, *John Dryden and His World* (New Haven, CT: Yale University Press, 1987), 97–8.

15 Winn, *John Dryden and His World*, 95.

16 Langbaine, *An Account of the English Dramatick Poets*, 164.

17 Winn, *John Dryden and His World*, 314.

18 Ibid.

19 *Register*, no. 1113, records a loan of £11. For Betterton's charity, see 'A Satyr against Poetry'.

20 *London Gazette*, 25–29 November 1686. The advertisement reappeared in *The Observator* the following week.

21 Among the extensive critical literature on this subject of seventeenth-century drama in print, see Douglas Brooks, *From Playhouse to Printing House: Drama and Authorship in Early Modern England* (Cambridge University Press, 2000); Martin Butler, 'Jonson's folio and the politics of patronage', *Criticism* 35 (1993), 377–90; Kevin Dunn, *Pretexts of Authority: The Rhetoric of Authorship in the Renaissance Preface* (Stanford University Press, 1994); Lukas Erne, *Shakespeare as Literary*

Dramatist (Cambridge University Press, 2003); David Scott Kastan, *Shakespeare and the Book* (Cambridge University Press, 2001); Zachary Lesser, *Renaissance Drama and the Politics of Publication: Readings in the English Book Trade* (Cambridge University Press, 2004); Robert S. Miola, 'Creating the author: Jonson's Latin epigraphs', *Ben Jonson Journal* 6 (1999), 35–48; Peters, *Theatre of the Book*; and Wendy Wall, *The Imprint of Gender: Authorship and Publication in the English Renaissance* (Ithaca, NY: Cornell University Press, 1993).

22 Gerard Genette, *Paratexts: Thresholds of Interpretation*, trans. Jane E. Lewin (Cambridge University Press, 1997).

23 John Marston, 'To the only rewarder...', *The History of Antonio and Mellida* (London, 1602); William Congreve, 'To the Right Honourable Charles, Earl of Dorset and Middlesex', *Love for Love*; Congreve's 'To the Right Honourable Charles Mountague...', *The Double Dealer* (London, 1694), refers to William Wycherley's 'To My Lady B___', *The Plain Dealer* (London, 1676).

24 John Dryden, 'To the Right Honourable John, Lord Haughton', *The Spanish Fryar*.

25 John Crowne, 'Epistle Dedicatory to the Earl of Orrory', *Juliana, or, The Princess of Poland* (London, 1671).

26 See, for example, Joseph Loewenstein, *Ben Jonson and Possessive Authorship* (Cambridge University Press, 2002); Max W. Thomas, 'Eschewing credit: Heywood, Shakespeare, and plagiariam before copyright', *New Literary History* 31 (2000), 277–93; David M. Bergeron, *Textual Patronage in English Drama, 1570–1640* (Aldershot: Ashgate, 2006); Deborah C. Payne, 'The Restoration dramatic dedication as symbolic capital', *Studies in Eighteenth-Century Culture* 20 (1990), 27–42.

27 Otway, 'The Preface', *Don Carlos*, np.

28 Thomas D'Urfey, 'Letter to the Author from Mr Charles Gildon', *The Marriage-Hater Match'd* (London, 1692).

29 Abraham Bailey, 'To the Reader', *The Spightful Sister* (London, 1667).

30 For a survey of the debate, see Derek Hughes, *English Drama 1660–1700* (Oxford: Clarendon Press, 1996), 236 n.49.

31 Jacques Derrida, 'Circumfession', in Derrida and Geoffrey Bennington, *Jacques Derrida* (University of Chicago Press, 1993).

32 Tiffany Stern, 'Repatching the play', in Peter Holland and Stephen Orgel, eds., *From Script to Stage in Early Modern England* (Basingstoke: Palgrave Macmillan, 2004), 151–77, 170.

33 Otway, 'To the Right Honourable Charles Earl of Middlesex', *Alcibiades*.

34 Dedication to *Venice Preserv'd*.

35 Kenyon, *The Popish Plot*, 120.

36 Thomas Otway, 'To her Royal Highness the Dutchess', *The Orphan* (London, 1680), np.

37 Cited from J. C. Hodges, ed., *William Congreve: Letters and Documents* (London, 1964), 242–3. Voltaire allegedly made his remarks in the middle of the 1720s, and they first appeared in *Letters concerning the English Nation by M. de Voltaire* (London, 1733).

38 See D. F. McKenzie, '*Mea culpa*: Voltaire's retraction of his comments critical of Congreve', *Review of English Studies* 49 (1998), 461–5, 462.

39 Dawson, *Gentility and the Comic Theatre*, 251–4.

40 Congreve, 'To the Right Honourable Ralph, Earl of Montagu, &c.', *The Way of the World*.

41 Congreve writes scornfully in the dedication that 'this play has been acted two or three days before some of these hasty judges could find the leisure to distinguish betwixt the character of a Witwoud and a Truewit'.

42 John Dryden, 'To the Right Honourable Philip, Earl of Leicester Etc', *Don Sebastian* (London, 1690).

43 Buckingham, 'Prologue', *The Rehearsal*, II.13–14.

44 Laura Brown, *English Dramatic Form, 1660–1700* (New Haven, CT: Yale University Press, 1981); Maguire, *Regicide and Restoration*.

45 Maguire, *Regicide and Restoration*, 217.

46 Dryden, 'To the Right Honourable John, Lord Haughton', *The Spanish Fryar*.

47 John Dryden, *An Essay of Dramatick Poesie* (London, 1668).

48 Dryden, 'To the Right Honourable John, Lord Haughton', *The Spanish Fryar*.

49 Dryden, 'To the Right Honourable Philip, Earl of Leicester Etc', *Don Sebastian*.

50 John Dryden, 'The Twenty-ninth Ode of the Third Book of Horace', in Keith Walker, ed., *John Dryden: A Critical Edition of the Major Works* (Oxford University Press, 1987), 302–5, 303–4, lines 51–2, 65–6.

51 *The Diary of Samuel Pepys*, 23 February 1663.

52 John Dryden, 'Preface', *The Wild Gallant* (London, 1669), A2.

53 Ibid.

54 John Dryden, 'Preface', *Secret Love, or, The Maiden Queen* (London, 1668), A2.

55 Ibid.

9 | Revivals and adaptations

Revivals of Restoration comedies up to the end of the seventeenth century were often coloured by politics; the Collier crisis initiated a long period in which decency became their chief controversy. Recoiling in shock from *The Rover Part 1* in 1757, the reviewer for *The London Chronicle* recommended that 'all managers [should remember] that this play was written in the dissolute days of Charles the Second; and that decency is, or at least ought to be, demanded at present'.[1] The recoil did not happen suddenly, however, as the fortunes of *The Country Wife* illustrate.

Wycherley's play was performed in London at least 150 times between 1700 and 1753.[2] For twelve years it disappeared from the repertory, to be replaced by John Lee's truncated version of 1765, which lopped all the bawdy jokes, and with them Horner himself. Pinchwife was reinvented as a sentimental hero gradually overcome with guilt at his ill-treatment of Margery. If Lee's version was less adaptation than amputation, David Garrick's 1766 *The Country Girl* went for total makeover. Horner becomes Young Belville, a sensitive soul who falls with melting sweetness for the innocent ward Peggy Thrift and eventually releases her from the clutches of her grumpy guardian, Moody. It took more than 150 years for *The Country Wife* to wriggle away from *The Country Girl*, and its first experience of freedom was in the airless confines of a museum-style theatre designed to reproduce minute details of period performance style (the text remained filleted, however). The Phoenix Society revival of 1924 and a subsequent performance at the Everyman Theatre in 1926 were historical reconstructions that focused on contrivances of gesture, intonation, scenery and costume – an approach that some would argue has been insidiously influential ever since. A similar production at the Ambassadors Theatre in 1934 prompted the critic of *The Daily Telegraph* to observe that it was only the mass display of Restoration camp that saved the play from being banned; the man

217

from *The Times*, not noticing the cuts, was surprised at how clean the play was given its reputation.[3]

Style and contemporary relevance have, in turn, succeeded decency in arguments about the revival of Restoration plays. Conceived in times of rapid urban expansion, the canonical comedies have in the past eighty years provided directors and audiences with rich metaphors for the impact of socio-economic change on human behaviour. A Broadway production of *The Country Wife* in 1936 refracted the vortex of indulgence that had led to the Great Depression. Laurence Harvey's predatory Horner in the Royal Court's 1956 production anticipated his star turn in the film of John Braine's *Room at the Top* (1959), embodying a post-conflict masculinity heedless of class distinction and convinced of its right to pleasure on equal terms with anyone else. Robert Chetwyn's 1969 production at the Chichester Festival, conceived in the wake of *Hair* and other expressions of 1960s liberation, gave full rein to the homosocial world of Horner and his coterie; the Restoration camp of museum performance flowered into gay politics.

Since the 1980s *The Country Wife* has surfed waves of economic optimism and despair, seeking out hybrid styles of performance and design that often quote the museum tradition rather than ditching it. Nicholas Hytner's pulsating revival at the Manchester Royal Exchange in 1986 exposed the dark side of roaring Reaganomics, with rising commodity prices revealing the price of rising commodification. Gary Oldman's Horner was a barrow-boy trader on the make, a fitness freak obsessed with his own performance (see Figure 9.1); even more disturbing was Ian McDiarmid's Pinchwife, a rancid paedophile. Punk chic twitched nervously alongside silk waistcoats and breeches; a thumping soundtrack sent Handel skidding into the Clash.

Hytner set dizzying standards of innovation and energy that others subsequently aimed at but largely failed to meet. Garry Hynes's 1988 *Man of Mode* for the Royal Shakespeare Company was pastiche Hytner but divorced from any clear sense of social context, except by showing that golden boxer-shorted types such as Dorimant treat women with contempt. Phyllida Lloyd's 1995 *The Way of the World* at the National Theatre set the play among devotees of contemporary art and fashion, but this catwalk Congreve indulged the superficiality it affected to observe. Hytner's 2007 *Man of Mode* at the National repurposed the visionary thrill of his *Country Wife* in the context of

Figure 9.1 Nicholas Hytner's 1986 *The Country Wife*, with Gary Oldman as Horner

the conspicuous consumption of the 'noughties', the design concept breaking free of period hybridity in a sea of designer shades, puffer jackets and flash nightclubs. A new kind of hybridity emerged, with British Asian casting serving a play built partly on arranged marriages.

This modernizing trend has proved too much for some audiences and reviewers. A rock star revival of *The Way of the World* at the Sheffield Crucible prompted Charles Spencer of *The Daily Telegraph* to wonder whether the really radical approach to a Restoration play would be to 'stage the play in period, complete with fans, beauty spots, huge wigs and elegant diction'.[4] Arguably, any play capable of only one performance style is by definition moribund, but that does not entirely dispense with Spencer's argument. The excitement of Nicholas Hytner's productions gives them canonical status in the recent stage history of Restoration Comedy, yet a great deal of fine work sits between them and the museum tradition. Productions such as Peter Gill's 1992 *Way of the World* at the Lyric Hammersmith, Max Stafford-Clark's 1993 *Country Wife* for the Royal Shakespeare Company and Roger Michell's 1990 production for the same company of Farquhar's *The Constant Couple* made the plays fresh and immediate without squeezing them into miniskirts and leather trousers. Individual performances stood out even amid the stronger directorial visions (Oldman and McDiarmid in 1986, Geraldine McEwan and Fiona Shaw as the 1995 Lady Wishfort and Millamant, Rory Kinnear as Sir Fopling in the 2007 *Man of Mode*), but they were – rightly – the principal story in a number of other recent productions that managed to create space for acting rather than mannerism, sometimes in spite of themselves. This theatre-goer has not seen finer performances in Restoration Comedy than in three productions that otherwise fell into a trio of classic traps.

Peter Wood's 1980 National Theatre *Provok'd Wife* took scenic extravagance to levels Thomas Betterton could only have dreamed of, with skaters traversing a frozen Thames to the sound of 'Winter' from Vivaldi's *Four Seasons* and a disappearing play. But the peculiarly cerebral spontaneity of John Wood and Geraldine McEwan made the battling Brutes as funny (and the rebarbative Sir John as cranky) as they can ever have been. A different register had been struck by Michael Bryant in the same director's *Double Dealer* at the National in 1978, a fine chamber production swallowed by the epic breadth of the Olivier Theatre. Sir Paul Plyant is, to put it mildly, Sir John Brute's opposite, though no less unhappy in his marriage, since every night he is bound hand and foot by his lady, and not for pleasure. The Act Three speech in which Bryant's Plyant explained to his friend Careless with halting, smiling, self-deprecation why he had not fathered a son was psychologically complex, tearfully hilarious:

You'll scarcely believe me, when I shall tell you – my lady is so nice – it's very strange, but it's true; too true – she's so very nice, that I don't believe she would touch a man for the world – at least not above once a year; I'm sure I have found it so; and, alas, what's once a year to an old man, who would do good in his generation? Indeed it's true, Mr Careless, it breaks my heart – I am her husband; but alas-a-day, I have no more familiarity with her person – as to that matter – than with my own mother – no indeed.[5]

A virtuosic set piece was the jewel of another production that felt, in almost every other respect, dully familiar, a matinée recycling of the museum tradition that at times felt as mummified as Sir Paul Plyant. William Gaskill's 1984 Chichester Festival production aimed at leisurely period elegance and achieved it; for energy and clarity it lagged some way behind Rachel Kavanaugh's 2012 revival at the same theatre, with Penelope Keith as Lady Wishfort (see front cover). One seasoned performance scaled the highest summit of accomplishment, however. Maggie Smith had first played Millamant at Stratford, Ontario, in 1976. By 1984 she was at least thirty years older than her character, a gap reduced to insignificance by high-definition timing and deadpan irony. It is rare in the theatre to see an audience bursting into applause at the conclusion of a mere speech, but that is what happened regularly when Smith's Millamant conceded at the end of the proviso scene, drawling out the words in a self-mocking diminuendo, that she might, by degrees, dwindle into a wife; the effect was that of a virtuoso aria being dashed off with impossible skill. As Hytner's productions attempted to capture something of the topical urgency of their originals, so these distinguished individual performances served as a reminder that Restoration plays were crafted to show off the ability of actors to peruse their misery from so a high vantage point as to transform it into giddy joy.

Actors and directors on Restoration style

The peculiar challenges and opportunities of acting in Restoration Comedy have been explored by a leading exponent of them, Simon Callow.[6] Whether there is such a thing as a dominant 'Restoration style' is one of his first questions, since genres proliferated, and Congreve – for example – is a notably more cerebral writer than even Vanbrugh, and significantly less inclined to physical farce than Behn. Settling into a series of observations about language, audience, clothes, props, dramatic conventions and scenery, Callow provides a guide not only as to how actors might approach this diverse body of work but how modern audiences could appraise productions of it.

Complicity between actor and audience is the starting point. For Callow, the scenic stages of Restoration Drama are postcard rather than panorama, a set of minimally painted signs; the performers are known to the audience and learn to cast them by type as much as they have themselves been cast. Asides are gestures of familiarity as much as inner life. There is a competition of wit, so that the main task for the actor is to think hard, to be 'ahead of each thought, in perfect command of the sequence of ideas'. He contrasts this with the support available to the Shakespearean actor, who can ride the 'emotional wave' of 'glorious word-music' and rhythmic pulse and so gain energy

from language that forms a 'sensuous, emotional lubricant'. Performance in which 'pace of thought. . .creates the pace of the playing' is not
necessarily speedy, but buoyant: exhilarated and exhilarating. Preparing to achieve this effect means, for Callow, waiting in the wings and
imagining himself slightly drunk.[7]

The same discipline applies to the actor's body. This is, to use
Callow's term, a theatre of 'self-representation' in which the actor
has to focus on the social idea of the self, on what he describes as the
silk thrown effortlessly over strong emotions.[8] Callow has in mind
productions in which performers must manage the business of bowing,
curtseying, finger kissing and fan waving armed with cuffs, breeches
and waistcoats, but the principle transfers easily to updated versions such as Hytner's, in which 'performance' was construed both
theatrically (as acting) and managerially (as visible, self-proclaiming
success). Above all, actors must learn to speak in a 'lapidary' way,
putting lines out as precious jewels; these characters, Callow concludes, are knowers rather than discoverers.[9]

The best account of how modern directors wrestle with traditions
of Restoration style is Max Stafford-Clark's *Letters to George*, written
as an accompaniment to his 1988 production of Farquhar's *The
Recruiting Officer* (1706). But Stafford-Clark was drawn to this play
precisely because it seemed untypical. In the words of William Gaskill,
who directed the 1963 National Theatre production, this was

the only Restoration play that presented a cross-section of society and which
was set outside London. It had no fops, no court intrigue, the leading
characters were in the army and even the gentry were not fashionable.[10]

The claim is diminished by Farquhar's own *The Beaux' Stratagem*, but
it is easy to see why a director of Gaskill's socialist convictions was
drawn to a play that seemed to depart from the theatrical tradition
of 'high camp, lisps, huge wigs, canes and fans' with which some
people continue to associate Restoration Drama.[11] Certainly, the play
has elements of a conventional sex farce with a new, reformed conclusion: handsome young army captain (Plume) descends on provincial
town, in love with heiress (Silvia) but distracted by comely maiden
(Rose); his friend, meanwhile (Worthy), is troubled by a rich former
fiancée (Melinda) who has turned against him and is now wooed by
another man (Brazen); Silvia disguises herself as a man, then finds
herself sharing a bed with Rose; everything is resolved when Plume,

like any good sentimental hero of the nineties and noughties, gives up his roving life for marriage to Silvia.

Letters to George shows how amenable the text is to Stanislavskian analysis of objectives and actions, and part of the charm of the book is the way it pretends to open up this modern science of acting to Farquhar. Speeches are broken up into actions using transitive verbs ('befriends', 'warns', 'pleases', 'snubs'...). The effect is to highlight the remarkable degree of intuitive interaction in Farquhar's writing. Callow's 'self-representation' emerges as less important than the characters' ability to work upon, succumb to or resist each other, and Stafford-Clark's asides about acting are endlessly revealing ('One definition of bad acting would be when an actor plays the result of his action...and not the intention itself').[12]

The core of *The Recruiting Officer*, the part that appealed most to Gaskill and that seems both original and disturbing today, is the anti-hero. Sergeant Kite is, as the name suggests, drawn from comic traditions that found their focus in the work of Ben Jonson and were remembered in the work of Dryden and Shadwell. Kite circles his prey, bribes them and feasts upon them with a comic glee reminiscent of Volpone or Subtle in *The Alchemist*. He tempts a pair of local lads, Thomas Appletree and Coster Pearmain, with promises of what army life will bring, drinking them into compliance:

KITE: Thus we soldiers live, drink, sing, dance, play; we live, as one should say – we live – 'tis impossible to tell you how we live – we're all princes – why – why you're a king – you're an emperor, and I'm a prince – now – an't we –
COSTER: No, sergeant – I'll be no emperor.
KITE: No!
COSTER: No, I'll be a Justice of the Peace.
KITE: A Justice of the Peace, man!
COSTER: Ay, wauns I will, for since this pressing Act they are greater than any emperor under the sun.[13]

Pearmain is canny enough to see which side of the fence he should be on when governments force those 'without visible support' into military life, as happened in successive Mutiny and Impressment Acts from 1703 to 1705 (this legislation produced the play's best bad joke, when it is said that miners should be forced to join up since when they're at work underground they lack visible support). But Kite

inveigles him all the same. At the chilling conclusion to Act Two,
Plume leads both young men off, singing *Over the Hills and Far Away*
and promising they will all return as 'Gentlemen'.

In private, Kite is – predictably – more cynical. Plume embodies the
easy glamour of army life, likening his escape from injury in battle to
his freedom from syphilis after a stay in London; this is the image of the
dashing heroism that had recently defeated the French at Blenheim
and put the brightest gloss on any recruitment drive. Kite's autobiog-
raphy is a cheerful memoir of crime. Worthy praises him as 'the most
useful fellow to [his] captain, admirable in your way, I find' (Kite is,
in part, the ever-willing sidekick, a Leporello or Dromio who gets into
unlikely scrapes to serve or save his master); in reply, Worthy hears
a life story steeped in heroic parody that reveals what the salt of the
earth is really made of:

KITE: I understand my business, I will say it. You must know, sir, I was born
a gypsy, and bred among that crew till I was ten year old; there I learned
canting and lying. I was bought from my mother Cleopatra by a certain
nobleman for three pistoles, who liking my beauty made me his page;
there I learned impudence and pimping. I was turned off for wearing my
lord's linen and drinking my lady's brandy, and then turned bailiff's
follower; there I learned bullying and swearing. I at last got into the
army, and there I learned whoring and drinking. So that if your worship
pleases to cast up the whole sum, *viz.* canting, lying, impudence,
pimping, bullying, swearing, whoring, drinking, and a halberd, you
will find the sum total will amount to a recruiting sergeant.
WORTHY: And pray, what induced you to turn soldier?
KITE: Hunger and ambition – the fears of starving and hopes of a truncheon
led me along to a gentleman with a fair tongue and fair periwig who
loaded me with promises; but i'gad it was the lightest load I ever felt in
my life. He promised to advance me, and indeed he did so, to a garret in
the Savoy. I asked him why he put me in prison; he called me lying dog
and said I was in garrison...[14]

Farquhar's gift for comic obsession owed something to Molière too;
his Captain Brazen has 'the most prodigious, and the most trifling,
memory in the world', a supremo at military Trivial Pursuit who recalls
how a soldier was killed in battle with a blue ribbon in his hat and
an ox tongue in his pocket. *The Recruiting Officer* ended a four-year
silence for Farquhar: it was his first play since *The Twin Rivals* (1702),
a piece conceived in the shadow of Collier's proposed reforms that

shows a pleasure-loving hunchback scheming fruitlessly against his virtuous older brother (it might be described as a simplistic take on the twinning conundrum of *The Way of the World*). Robert D. Hume categorizes *The Twin Rivals* as a 'harsh moral melodrama' that 'gives way to [the] genial realism' of *The Recruiting Officer*, and it is fair to say that, while the realism of the latter has contributed to its popularity among audiences, the extent of its geniality is its key controversy. Yet such controversy has perhaps only recently become apparent. Farquhar's play survived the reaction against Restoration 'indecency'. In each of the seventy years following its premiere it was performed in London; to those 447 known performances can be added another forty-nine by the end of the eighteenth century. The next century would see it established as a staple of provincial repertory theatres.[15]

In modern productions, shades of interpretation have often centred on the casting of Kite; the play's early reception also indicates how the success of the play was linked to the performance of a brilliant mimic, Richard Estcourt, in the role. Gaskill's 1963 production for the newly formed National Theatre featured the gritty Northern Irish actor Colin Blakely, already a veteran of the new wave of British drama mounted at the Royal Court; his persuasion of Coster and Thomas to join the army was described by the director years later as 'a demonstration of jingoism' in which the young recruits 'fall for nationalism, sentimentality and violence as readily as soldiers going to the Falklands War'.[16] In 1980 Pete Postlethwaite brought boulder-eyed psychopathy to the role in Adrian Noble's production for the Bristol Old Vic, twinned with a *Troilus and Cressida* in which he played an earthy general among generals, Ulysses. This Kite set forth his history of canting, lying, impudence, pimping, bullying, swearing, whoring and drinking as though giving his name and pack drill, and the effect was both funnier and more chilling than any self-consciously genial reading. But geniality is a tool for an actor as well as an effect. By force of personality, and in the context of a production that otherwise fell under the spell of Gaskill's, the Kite of Jim Broadbent in Max Stafford-Clark's 1988 production for the Royal Court Theatre was a wheedling clown, put upon by his master but exploiting his natural 'hail fellow' geniality to enlist recruits. A different kind of comedy – zany, youthful and pushing the boundaries charted by Pete Postlethwaite – was provided in Josie Rourke's 2012 version at the Donmar Warehouse, in which Mackenzie Crook suggested a man driven to the edge of his nerves, fanatically committed to the cause. This was a crazed, post-Iraq Kite, but still in breeches; without overt modernity, the play served its historic purpose of setting before a London audience their country's ambivalent relationship to the experience of war, with sentimentality pitched against nervous anxiety.

If *The Recruiting Officer* is atypical of Restoration Comedy because its social relevance does not have to be trumpeted to an audience, it is also highly unusual through being so evidently grounded in its author's own experience. Commissioned in 1704 as Lieutenant of Grenadiers by the Earl of Orrery, Farquhar spent time recruiting first in Lichfield and then in Shrewsbury. His dedication of the play 'To All Friends Round the Wrekin' indicates he enjoyed himself, even if his praise for Salopian hospitality sits uncomfortably with the darker tones directors such as Gaskill and Stafford-Clark have sounded in the play:

'Twas my good fortune to be ordered some time ago into the place which is made the scene of this comedy; I was a perfect stranger to everything in Salop, but its character of loyalty, the number of its inhabitants, the alacrity of the gentlemen in recruiting the army, with their generous and hospitable reception of strangers. This character I found so amply verified in every particular, that you made recruiting, which is the greatest fatigue upon earth to others, to be the greatest pleasure in the world to me.[17]

Farquhar worked from local observation ('Some little turns of humour that I met with almost within the shade of that famous hill gave the rise to this comedy') while remaining anxious not to 'make the town merry at the expense of the country gentlemen'. A later correspondence between a bishop and a Shrewsbury resident provides a full-blown reading of the play *à clef*, with the character of Justice Balance identified as the town's deputy recorder, Melinda as 'Miss Harnage of Belsadine near the Wrekin' and Plume as Farquhar himself.[18] The account is made more persuasive by the bishop's confession that Brazen's original was 'unknown' and 'the story I suppose the Poet's invention'. Farquhar's 'originals' are as much theatrical as they are Salopian, but local scenery remains conspicuous. Leigh Hunt described the play's knack of making an audience 'breathe the clear, fresh, ruddy-making air' of the country (noting also the adjacency of 'hospitable elegance'), and the effect is achieved through multiple references to rural life and through backdrops that must have had the Drury Lane painters asking Farquhar for details of 'the Market Place' and 'the Walk by the Severn Side' and the manager, Christopher Rich, feeling relieved that those novelties were punctuated with standard-issue scenes showing apartments and antechambers.[19]

Recruiting adaptations

Paradoxically, the Restoration comedy most demonstrably rooted in personal and social experience is also the one that has been most radically adapted by subsequent writers. Just as its inclusiveness has attracted theatre directors whose natural metier is not Congreve or Etherege, it has appealed to writers with a strong interest in penetrating the comfortable horizons of bourgeois life. In *Trumpets and Drums* (1955), Bertolt Brecht grafted onto Farquhar's play a recruiting drive for the American War of Independence, but still set in Shrewsbury. The marketplace speech by Kite that opens *The Recruiting Officer* serves naturally as a Brechtian chorus in which the audience is invited to join a dishonest enterprise:

> I'm Sergeant Barras Kite, now gathering a company
> To help our good King George. For across the sea
> In His Majesty's colony America
> There's rebellion such as no man ever saw...
> ...Who among you, in exchange for a handsome uniform and plenty of fodder
> Will defend our dear old England...?[20]

In Scene 2, Justice Balance enters reading, with some disgust, a draft of the Declaration of Independence:

'All men are created equal...' Where does the Bible say that? – 'Liberty and the pursuit of happiness...' So here it is in black and white; these new ideas we've heard so much about. It's base greed, that's what it is.[21]

Brecht's indignation flips from the Old World to the New: there are noble ideals Balance can't see, but there is also base greed (in Richard Nelson's War of Independence play, *The General from America*, a character exclaims, 'I have searched with great interest to discover what you Americans in fact believe in. Besides of course the freedom to cheat each other').[22]

Brecht's representation of Kite's victims is less ambiguous but calls into question the 'genial' quality so many critics have found in Farquhar's original. In *The Recruiting Officer*, Kite's first success is to

coax a compliant 'mob' into marching off to huzzas and drumrolls.
Updating Plume on his progress, Kite proudly announces that he has
'been here but a week and...recruited five', confirming that 'the mob
are so pleased...that we shall soon do our business'.[23] Did this require
Brecht's intervention to make it socially purposeful? In *Trumpets and
Drums*, Kite's five is a failure, his influence over the 'mob' negligible:

KITE: I ask this rabble, as is my bounden duty: doesn't your English blood
    boil in your veins when those American dirt farmers and fur trappers
    refuse to pay taxes to our good King George?
PLUME: Well?
KITE: Their answers weren't nice. I've been here a full week and only
    recruited five.[24]

This only rams home the point made in the previous scene, in which
Coster Pearmain answers Kite's blandishments with all the clarity of a
conscientious objector:

Look 'ere, sergeant; no coaxing and wheedling. You can't pull the wool over
my eyes. Take back your cap and your brothermanship, because I ain't in the
mood today.[25]

The willingness of Farquhar's 'mob' is arguably the more disturbing
and instructive sight.

The broader refashioning that is *Trumpets and Drums* privileges the
public lives of the characters over the private pasts explored by Farquhar.
Recruiting for war is exposed as an expression not just of false patriotism
but economic interest: Plume's friend Worthy is turned by Brecht into
a boot manufacturer supplying the army. This was entirely in tune with
the historical moment of *Trumpets and Drums*, although history
threatened to wriggle free of Brecht's analysis. In 1955 the relatively
new state of West Germany was beginning to rearm, making Kite's
opening chorus an uncomfortable experience indeed for audiences; but,
then, the communist-run East was rearming too. As he was working on
the play, Brecht was also preparing to travel to Moscow to receive that
most dubious honour, the Stalin Peace Prize. It did occur to him to
wonder whether *Trumpets and Drums* might have to be postponed.
Some of Brecht's revisions make it seem like the work of a narrowly
partisan writer, but it manifestly speaks against empires of all colours.

Empire was the foundation of Farquhar's next leap into time travel.
Robert Hughes's 1987 history of the founding of modern Australia,

The Fatal Shore, brought to light a curiosity in the stage history of Farquhar's play. The journal of a British naval lieutenant, Ralph Clark, tells how a group of transported convicts performed *The Recruiting Officer* at Sydney in 1789, and the extraordinary event was reimagined by Thomas Keneally in his own 1987 book, *The Playmaker*. Catching the tide of interest, Max Stafford-Clark commissioned the playwright Timberlake Wertenbaker to devise a 1988 adaptation of Keneally's novel (eventually entitled *Our Country's Good*) that would play in tandem with a new production of *The Recruiting Officer*. Stafford-Clark pursued the idea with a later production of *The Man of Mode* that played alongside Stephen Jeffreys's *The Libertine*, which drama-tizes the courtly travails of Etherege's presumed model, the Earl of Rochester.[26] The process might be described as one of reverse adapta-tion, in which the original text is left to its own devices but speaks in dialogue with a later text on which it has visibly cast a shadow.

The playwright Wertenbaker was more keen to cast Farquhar's achievement in a positive light than the novelist Keneally. The Ralph Clark of *The Playmaker* falls foul of what is represented as Farquhar's easy geniality, only to discover his mistake:

[A]s Ralph's version of *The Recruiting Officer* neared its end, as all the characters grew not only redeemable but worthy of congratulation, the players and the playmaker Ralph himself were left with the sense that life could be easily amended, that love was an easy ploy, and that everyone really intended the best.

Ralph considered that in the real world it might also be the case that there was always too much hidden, and too much to take into account. It was only within the circumference of a play, and particularly of a comedy, that all characters could be so deftly delivered from their meanness... [T]hough art perpetually improved itself, society went its reckless and complicated way.[27]

Lonely and separated from his wife by 12,000 miles, he falls for his Silvia, a convict called Mary Brenham (in real life he abandoned her and their daughter and sailed back to England). The chaplain of the penal colony, Dick Johnson, upbraids him fiercely in the tones of Jeremy Collier himself:

First I come to you and counsel you against a play. The play finds fornication funny, fidelity a joke and woman a fickle organ of pleasure. But it is merely an entertainment, you say. Yet now I approach you under circumstances which have made the conditions of that play incarnate in this cove, on this shore, in your very household, Ralph. Adultery is a laughing matter for you now, fidelity is a joke and woman is an organ of pleasure! The play – as I warned – has become your very life.[28]

The novel leaves Ralph crushed with guilt for his infidelity and makes the performance more of a shambles than the historical record suggests, with the sober realities of crime, punishment and colonialism providing noises off and on. This 'sputter of the European humour on the edge of a continent' would lead, Keneally posits, to the end of 'the different and serious theatre of the tribes of the hinterland' – as unlikely a consequence of Restoration Comedy as any yet devised.[29]

The text of Wertenbaker's play is prefaced with letters from contemporary convicts who, movingly, benefited from exposure to theatre. Their enthusiasm colours *Our Country's Good*, which counters Keneally's colonial pessimism with the logic of arts therapy. Ralph Clark's penultimate speech suggests that, far from obliterating the indigenous cultural landscape, *The Recruiting Officer* looks forward to the modern state idealized in the revolutionary year, 1789: 'The theatre is like a small republic,' he tells his company; 'it requires private sacrifices for the good of the whole.' Watching Stafford-Clark's production it was easy to revel in this enactment and defence of theatre while remaining oblivious to the way it sidestepped Keneally's postcolonial purpose.

When it comes to retrieving a radical social purpose from Restoration Comedy, no writer goes further than Edward Bond. In his 1981 play *Restoration*, Bond frequently nods towards Vanbrugh's *The Relapse* and *The Provok'd Wife*, but this is less an adaptation than a reinvention through a Marxist lens. Lord Are, blessed with land and pedigree, is broke and needs a rich wife, so he marries Ann Hardacre, the local iron founder's daughter. Like Sir John and Lady Brute, they bicker endlessly. She resolves to frighten him by appearing as a ghost, and he runs her through. He sets out to place the blame on his hapless servant, Bob, and succeeds. Bob is hanged and Lord Are goes on his merry way.

The farcical highpoint of the play, when Are finds it is his wife he has stabbed and not her ghost, illustrates how adeptly Bond crafts a modern language of wit that allows the actor to move between stage action and audience address with 'Restoration' authenticity. Ann falls to the ground and Are exclaims,

Why, 'tis a heavy ghost! I had thought to go whisk-whisk and – as I am a gentleman – opened the window for it and it had vanished in a puff of smoke. The ghost bleeds. (*Stoops, examines.*) 'Fore god 'tis flesh and blood. My wife. (*Steps back. His voice falls and he presses the index finger to the side of his mouth.*) Hsssssssssssss. . .here's a fine how-d'ye-do. My wife. Stretched out on the floor. With a hole in her breast. Before breakfast. How is a man to put a good face on that? An amendment is called for. It were a foolish figure I should cut. A buffoon. Murdered his wife. Got up like a ghost. Before breakfast. I break into a cold sweat when I think of how I should use it had it befallen Lord Lester. I could not put my foot in a duke's door again. Never ascend the stairs to a hall blazing with chandeliers. Or ogle the ladies from the *balcon reserve* of a pump room. My life would be over. (*Nibbles toast.*) Cold. Faw!^[30]

Are's glittering callousness sets a trap for the audience. In earlier plays, such as *Saved*, Bond modified the Brechtian tradition of detachment by shocking the audience into extreme emotional reactions, seeking indignation at social injustice through the viscera rather than the rational mind. In *Restoration*, he makes it impossible for an audience not to side with Are, as Jonson lures us into the world of Volpone or Etherege into that of Dorimant. It is partly the theatricality of the role – one of the great opportunities for an actor in late twentieth-century drama – and partly the way Bond creates an authentic period cynicism in order to point up the shallowness of everyday moral responses. Are embodies the ruthlessness of power we choose to live with because we can't help falling for it.

'We' have our stage counterpart in Are's social inferiors, not least the doomed Bob Hedges, who is complicit in his own downfall, falls for Are's false promises to save his neck, and fails. It is left to his wife Rose to reflect that 'Man is what he knows – or doesn't know', a sentiment that reflect Bond's purpose in creating his provocative, unignorable style of shock theatre. 'I would like to feel,' he said three years after *Restoration*, 'there was some way in which you can dislodge segments of belief that people have so that the whole structure of their ideology is changed.'^[31] This 'dislodging' is key to the work of adaptive reinvention that is *Restoration*. Showing us what we recognize as a familiar comic form, Bond exploits its tendency to enforce class divisions to a degree that is both joyous and intolerable. Ironically, he does this partly by dismantling any pretence that the play is merely an act of historical reconstruction. *Restoration* spans history rather than settling into it. Rejecting Brechtian rationality, Bond nonetheless enjoys Brechtian styles of presentation that turn the occasional, pastoral songs of Restoration Comedy into bitter invectives against war and nationalism viewed forward and back in time:

> When Englishmen owned half the world
> All Englishmen were brave
> And every Englishman was free
> And cursed the foreign knave
> Who meekly bowed to tyranny
> When England ruled the mighty sea
> All Englishmen learned at their mother's knee
> That England was the home of liberty...[32]

As Keneally kidnapped *The Recruiting Officer* to focus on the woes of early British colonialism, so Bond recruited a whole genre to decry one of its last endeavours, the Falklands War. Such ingenuity is rare, but the riches summoned up by Restoration plays and players will, it is hoped, inspire many more writers of the future to take up the great Restoration business of taking the old and making it new.

Endnotes

1 Cited by Robert Markley, 'The canon and its critics', in Fisk, *The Cambridge Companion to English Restoration Theatre*, 226–42, 231.

2 See Emmett L. Avery, '*The Country Wife* in the eighteenth century', *Research Studies of the State College of Washington* 10 (1942), 141–72.

3 *Daily Telegraph*, 3 March 1934; *Times*, 3 March 1934. Both are cited by B. A. Kachur, *Etherege and Wycherley* (Basingstoke: Palgrave, 2004), 183.

4 Charles Spencer, 'Review of *The Way of the World* at the Sheffield Crucible Theatre', *Daily Telegraph*, 8 February 2012.

5 Congreve, *The Double Dealer*, 37 (III.468–79).

6 Simon Callow, *Acting in Restoration Comedy* (New York: Applause Theatre Books, 1991).

7 Ibid., 13–15.

8 Ibid., 29–30.

9 Ibid., 74, 98–9.

10 William Gaskill, *A Sense of Direction: Life at The Royal Court* (London: Faber & Faber, 1988), 56.

11 Ibid.

12 Max Stafford-Clark, *Letters to George* (London: Nick Hern Books, 1989), 67.

13 Farquhar, *The Recruiting Officer*, 20 (II.iii.10–22).
14 Ibid., 27–8 (III.i.135–64).
15 John Ross, 'Introduction', Farquhar, *The Recruiting Officer*, ed. John Ross (London: Ernest Benn, 1973), xxxiii.
16 Ibid., 58.
17 George Farquhar, 'Epistle Dedicatory "To All Friends Round the Wrekin"', *The Recruiting Officer*.
18 Letter from Bishop Percy to E. Blakeway, 4 July 1765; cited by Ross, *The Recruiting Officer*, xvi.
19 Leigh Hunt; cited by Ross, *The Recruiting Officer*, xviii.
20 Bertolt Brecht, *Trumpets and Drums*, in *The Collected Plays of Bertolt Brecht*, 9 vols., trans., ed., Ralph Manheim, John Willett (New York: Random House, 1972), vol. IX, 246–326, 249.
21 Ibid., 258.
22 Richard Nelson, *The General from America* (London: Faber & Faber, 1996), 78–9.
23 Farquhar, *The Recruiting Officer*, 3–4 (I.i.94–114).
24 Brecht, *Trumpets and Drums*, 251.
25 Ibid., 250.
26 For the Out of Joint Theatre Company, 1994.
27 Thomas Keneally, *The Playmaker* (London: Hodder & Stoughton, 1987), 302–3.
28 Ibid., 329.
29 Ibid., 359.
30 Edward Bond, *Restoration: A Pastoral* (London: Methuen, 1988), 18.
31 Edward Bond; cited by David L. Hirst, *Edward Bond* (Basingstoke: Macmillan, 1985), 164.
32 Bond, *Restoration*, 32.

Further reading

Modern editions

David Womersley's *Restoration Drama: An Anthology* (Blackwell, 2000) has well-edited texts of eighteen plays, from Tuke's *The Adventures of Five Hours* to Centlivre's *The Busy Body*, with brief critical introductions. Two volumes in the Oxford English Drama series provide attractive and authoritative themed anthologies: Deborah Payne Fisk's *Four Restoration Libertine Plays* and Michael Cordner's *Four Restoration Marriage Plays* (Oxford University Press, 2005). It says something for the fluidity of such definitions that one of Cordner's plays appears in Gillian Manning's *Libertine Plays of the Restoration* (Dent, 2001). Sandra Clark's *Shakespeare Made Fit* (Dent, 1997) is a useful collection of five Restoration adaptations. The New Mermaids series contains unfailingly reliable texts of individual plays by Congreve, Dryden, Etherege, Farquhar, Vanbrugh and Wycherley.

Major scholarly editions of Restoration Drama include: Robert D. Hume and Harold Love, eds., *Plays, Poems and Miscellaneous Writings associated with George Villiers, Second Duke of Buckingham*, 2 vols. (Clarendon Press, 2007); D. F. Mackenzie, ed., *The Works of William Congreve*, 3 vols. (Clarendon Press, 2011); Janet Todd, ed., *The Works of Aphra Behn*, 7 vols. (Pickering, 1996); Arthur Friedman, ed., *The Plays of William Wycherley* (Clarendon Press, 1979); J. C. Ghosh, ed., *The Works of Thomas Otway*, 2 vols. (Clarendon Press, 1932); Robert Jordan and Harold Love, eds., *The Works of Thomas Southerne*, 2 vols. (Clarendon Press, 1988); and Edward N. Hooker *et al.*, eds., *The Works of John Dryden*, 20 vols. (University of California Press, 1956–90).

Surveys of Restoration drama

Two studies, one by Robert D. Hume, the other by Derek Hughes, stand out for their comprehensive coverage of plays. Hume's *The Development of English Drama in the Late Seventeenth Century* (Clarendon Press, 1976) is a genre-based study, rich in information about theatrical contexts, and an authoritative guide to how dramatic form changed between 1660 and 1710. Written in trenchant style, the book charts a middle course

234

between those who find Restoration Drama frivolously superficial and the others who populate the critical world hypothesized at the end of his first chapter:

As I write this, I have a horrid vision of every profundity-zealot for years to come triumphantly seizing on what I have been saying here, to 'show' that no one understands and appreciates these plays, before going on to 'prove' the seriousness, complexity, profundity, and high moral worth of whatever play he may be in the process of resurrecting.[1]

Not everyone appreciates a middle course that describes most of the plays discussed as 'conventional, imitative, and repetitive', while praising them as 'extremely effective and enjoyable entertainment'.[2] Even so, Hume's mastery of theatrical contexts is unmatched by any other scholar. Three subsequent studies offer rich enquiry into genre. Laura Brown's *English Dramatic Form, 1660–1760* (Yale University Press, 1981) is strong on the relationships between genre and politics, while Brian Corman's *Genre and Generic Change in English Comedy, 1660–1710* (University of Toronto Press, 1993) pursues fine distinctions between comic modes. Nancy Klein Maguire's *Regicide and Restoration* (Cambridge University Press, 1992) examines how Restoration dramatists exploited the mixed form of tragicomedy as a means of dealing with the contrasting histories of Charles I and Charles II.

It is a matter of debate how large Derek Hughes's *English Drama 1660–1700* (Clarendon Press, 1996) might loom in Hume's horrid vision of 'profundity-zealots'. Hughes discusses plays that Hume missed, and his emphasis is less on theatre than on ideological debate. In his hands, comedies of intrigue and tragedies of love turn into serious disquisitions on the nature of rights, on state power and on gender roles. Hume asks for recognition of the 'highly circumstantial context' of Restoration Drama, which for him means largely the context of theatrical competition. Hughes accepts the invitation but in terms of political ideology. His readings of plays are consistently more nuanced than those found in J. Douglas Canfield's complementary volumes on Restoration Tragedy and Comedy, *Heroes and States* and *Tricksters and Estates*.[3] Canfield's surveys focus on 'jewels, most of them already treasured, a few undervalued'.[4] Like an entertaining lecture, they are peppered with provocative headings such as 'Apocalypse now' or 'Tupping your enemy's wife' and grab from French theory any concept that might rescue the plays from the suspicion of antiquarianism or Hume's 'enjoyable entertainment'.

Studies of Restoration theatre

Hume's belief in the integration of plays and theatre history derives partly from his grounding in the magnificent work of Allardyce Nicoll, whose

A History of Restoration Drama 1660–1700, reprinted with revisions numerous times since its first publication by Cambridge University Press in 1923, provides clear narratives of both drama and performance practice, including invaluable extracts from primary documents and a not quite complete handlist of plays. Volume II of what became his *History of English Drama 1660–1900* deals with the early eighteenth century and went into its fourth impression in 1955, thirty years after it was first published. The spirit of Nicoll's wide command of theatre practice is evident not only in Hume's critical idiom but in David Thomas's *Restoration and Georgian England 1660–1788*, the first volume of a projected series called *Theatre in Europe: A Documentary History*, and published by Cambridge University Press in 1989. Thomas and his co-compiler, Arnold Hare, provide annotated texts of key theatrical documents and succeed in pushing the boundaries of British theatre history in this period well beyond London. What happened on the margins of the formal theatrical season is documented by William J. Burling's *Summer Theatre in London, 1661–1820* (Fairleigh Dickinson University Press, 2000).

Jocelyn Powell deals with the technologies of performance in *Restoration Theatre Production* (Routledge, 1984), but it was Peter Holland's *The Ornament of Action* (Cambridge University Press, 1979) that set a standard for the discussion of Restoration plays in the context of theatrical practice: here was a thorough treatment of the way the performance codes of acting and scenery inform interpretation. Chapters 4 and 5 of Tiffany Stern's *Rehearsal from Shakespeare to Sheridan* (Clarendon Press, 2000) offer authoritative accounts of the work that went into making those codes visible. Joseph R. Roach's *The Player's Passion* (University of Michigan Press, 1993) places Restoration acting in the context of the scientific and rhetorical theory of its period, while Elizabeth Howe's *The First English Actresses* (Cambridge University Press, 1992) considers the impact of the first generation of professional actresses on playwrights and audiences. Michael Cordner and Peter Holland's *Players, Playwrights, Playhouses* (Palgrave, 2007) has innovative essays on texts, performance practice and theatre historiography from 1660 to 1800.

Music and dance, two essential ingredients of Restoration Theatre, are expertly dealt with by Curtis Price's *Henry Purcell and the London Theatre* (Cambridge University Press, 1984) and Moira Goff's study of an actress-dancer who rose to prominence during the 1690s, *The Incomparable Hester Santlow* (Ashgate, 2007). Judith Milhous provides a detailed assessment of managerial practices in her *Thomas Betterton and the Management of Lincoln's Inn Fields, 1695–1708* (Southern Illinois University Press, 1979).

Companion volumes and collections of essays

The Cambridge Companion to English Restoration Theatre and the Blackwell *A Companion to Restoration Drama* appeared within a year of each other.[5] *Theatre* and *Drama* here do not signify fundamental differences of approach, in the sense that the Cambridge volume has an abundance of material on literary-ideological topics, while the Blackwell has fine essays on performance spaces, actresses and (a missing ingredient for Cambridge) music. Each editor contributes to the other's collection, and both are well served in terms of scholarly apparatus, with Cambridge's author-based bibliographies a particularly useful feature. Both volumes highlight neglected areas of the field: Cambridge has a fine essay by Peter Holland on farce and a useful treatment of the critical afterlife of Restoration Drama by Robert D. Markley; Blackwell sports a thought-provoking sequence of chapters in which dramatists are paired, so inviting discussion of how playwrights might be seen as both singular and part of a broader movement. If Cambridge is more likely to be used by undergraduates, Blackwell has the edge in originality and rigour.

At the ebbing of the critical movement known as New Historicism appeared a collection of essays designed to bring to Restoration Drama the animated attention to cultural context that had characterized the work of Stephen Greenblatt on Renaissance texts. J. Douglas Canfield and Deborah C. Payne's *Cultural Readings of Restoration and Eighteenth-Century English Theater* (University of Georgia Press, 1995) combines essays whose ideological engagement seems conventional with others that illuminate new areas of inquiry, such as J. S. Peters's seminal essay 'The novelty' and a bracing discussion of actors and homophobia by Kristina Straub.

Biographical and single-author studies

The best biography of anyone connected with the Restoration Theatre is James A. Winn's *John Dryden and His World* (Yale University Press, 1987), which might itself serve as a literary history of the entire period. Those daunted by its scale can sample Winn's entry on the same writer in Paula R. Backscheider's *Restoration and Eighteenth-Century Dramatists*, volume LXXX of the Dictionary of Literary Biography (Gale, 1989). Backscheider's volume also has very good short biographies of some less-studied figures, such as John Banks, Thomas D'Urfey and Nahum Tate. Aphra Behn has attracted more recent biographies than any other Restoration dramatist. See Janet Todd, *The Secret Life of Aphra Behn* (André Deutsch, 1996), Maureen Duffy, *The Passionate Shepherdess* (Methuen, 1989) and Angeline Goreau, *Reconstructing Aphra* (Oxford University Press, 1980).

Biographical treatments of Restoration actors are, with one exception, in short supply. Nell Gwyn has been the subject of numerous biographies, for reasons not entirely connected with theatre history (or, indeed, sound scholarship), but Charles Beauclerk's *Nell Gwyn* (Pan Macmillan, 2005) has the merits of readability, respect for facts and affection for a distant relative. David Roberts's *Thomas Betterton* (Cambridge University Press, 2010) offers a cultural and institutional reading of the actor's life.

Critical studies of individual Restoration dramatists include the following: Dale Underwood, *Etherege and the Seventeenth-Century Comedy of Manners* (Yale University Press, 1957); Rose A. Zimbardo, *Wycherley's Drama: A Link in the Development of English Satire* (Yale University Press, 1965); John A. Vance, *William Wycherley and the Comedy of Fear* (Associated University Press, 2000); Jessica Munns, *Restoration Politics and Drama: The Plays of Thomas Otway, 1675–1683* (University of Delaware Press, 1995); Janet Todd, ed., *Aphra Behn Studies* (Cambridge University Press, 1996); and Derek Hughes, *The Theatre of Aphra Behn* (Palgrave, 2001).

Specialist subjects

The politics of Restoration Drama receive detailed treatment in the following: Paula R. Backscheider, *Spectacular Politics* (Johns Hopkins University Press, 1993); Susan Staves, *Players' Sceptres* (University of Nebraska Press, 1979); Derek Hughes, *Dryden's Heroic Plays* (Macmillan, 1981); and Susan J. Owen, *Restoration Theatre and Crisis* (Clarendon Press, 1996), which focuses on Popish Plot drama. Political and institutional appropriation features widely in Michael Dobson's study of Restoration Shakespeare, *The Making of the National Poet* (Clarendon Press, 1992); for a reading more focused on aesthetics, see Barbara A. Murray's *Restoration Shakespeare* (Fairleigh Dickinson University Press, 2001). Pauline Kewes's *Authorship and Appropriation* (Clarendon Press, 1998) examines the rising status of the dramatist in Restoration London, with its own account of the 'Bardification' of Shakespeare. It is complemented by Julie Stone Peters's *Theatre of the Book 1480–1880* (Oxford University Press, 2000), which has fine sections on the way Restoration play texts sought to represent performance.

Mark S. Dawson's *Gentility and the Comic Theatre of Late Stuart London* (Cambridge University Press, 2005) reads class anxiety in the Restoration Theatre from a sociological perspective, while Katherine M. Quinsey's *Broken Boundaries* (University Press of Kentucky, 1996) features essays on feminist approaches to drama of the period. David Roberts's *The Ladies* (Oxford University Press, 1989) is a study of the female audience. The sexual politics of drama is the subject of Richard Braverman's *Plots and Counterplots* (Cambridge University Press, 1993) and Harold Weber's *The Restoration Rake-Hero* (University of Wisconsin Press, 1986). Cynthia

Wall's *The Literary and Cultural Spaces of Restoration London* (Cambridge University Press, 1998) provides psycho-geographical context for Restoration plays. Two useful studies of libertinism and Restoration Drama are James Grantham Turner's *Libertines and Radicals in Early Modern London* (Cambridge University Press, 2002) and Jeremy Webster's *Performing Libertinism in Charles II's Court* (Palgrave, 2005).

Research resources

The monumental databases Early English Books Online (Chadwyck Healy) and Eighteenth-Century Collections Online (Gale) offer subscribing institutions unparalleled access to primary texts from the period, with search facilities. The first two volumes of *The London Stage 1660–1800* are an invaluable guide to the calendar of performances in Restoration London (Southern Illinois University Press, 1961, 1963); volume II is updated by Robert D. Hume and Judith Milhous in an online edition. The introductions to theatre practice for each volume are available separately in paperback form and are in themselves good working introductions to Restoration Theatre culture. Hume and Milhous's two-volume *A Register of English Theatrical Documents 1660–1737* (Southern Illinois University Press, 1991) is a treasure house for serious theatre historians, and still too little consulted.

Endnotes

1 Hume, *The Development of English Drama*, 30–1.
2 Ibid., 31.
3 J. Douglas Canfield, *Heroes and States: On the Ideology of Restoration Tragedy* (Lexington: University Press of Kentucky, 2000), and *Tricksters and Estates: On the Ideology of Restoration Comedy* (Lexington: University Press of Kentucky, 1997).
4 Canfield, *Heroes and States*, 4.
5 Fisk, *The Cambridge Companion to English Restoration Theatre*; Owen, *A Companion to Restoration Drama*.

Timeline

Date	Politics	Theatre	Society and literature
1660	Charles II returns to London	Patents granted to Davenant and Killigrew	Foundation of the Royal Society
1661	Rising of Fifth Monarchy Men	Duke's Company occupies Lincoln's Inn Fields playhouse	John Bunyan imprisoned
1662	Act of Uniformity; Charles II marries Catherine of Braganza	Molière, *L'Ecole des Femmes*	Publication of *The Book of Common Prayer*
1663	Attempted impeachment of first minister, Clarendon	Tuke, *The Adventures of Five Hours*; Dryden, *The Wild Gallant*	Butler, *Hudibras, Part 2*
1664	Conventicle Act, forbidding non-Church-of-England religious assemblies of more than five people	Dryden and Howard, *The Indian Queen*	Evelyn, *Sylva*
1665	Second Dutch War	Theatres closed	Great Plague
1666	French join Dutch in the war	Theatres closed; Molière, *Le Misanthrope*	Great Fire
1667	Dutch burn the English fleet	Dryden, *Sir Martin Mar-All*; Molière, *Tartuffe*	Milton, *Paradise Lost*
1668	Protestant Alliance between England, the Dutch Republic and Sweden	Davenant dies	Dryden, *An Essay of Dramatick Poesie*

(*cont.*)

Date	Politics	Theatre	Society and literature
1669	Charles II's dispute with Parliament over his debts	Dryden, *Tyrannick Love*	Death of the Queen Mother, Henrietta Maria
1670	Charles II signs Treaty of Dover with France	Dryden, *The Conquest of Granada*, Part 1	Milton, *The History of Britain*
1671	Louise de Keroualle recognized as Charles's mistress	Duke's Company moves to Dorset Garden Theatre; Dryden, *The Conquest of Granada*, Part 2; Buckingham, *The Rehearsal*	Milton, *Paradise Regained* and *Samson Agonistes*
1672	Third Dutch War	King's Theatre in Bridges Street burns down	Bunyan freed from prison
1673	Test Act to exclude Catholics from public office; Duke of York marries Mary of Modena	Behn, *The Dutch Lover*	Davenant, *Works*
1674	Peace treaty with Dutch	King's Company moves into Theatre Royal, Drury Lane; Davenant/Dryden, *Tempest*	Rymer, translation of Rapin's *Reflections*; death of Milton
1675	Further parliamentary dispute over the king's finances	Wycherley, *The Country Wife*; Crowne, *Calisto*	Temporary order for the suppression of coffee houses
1676	Charles II's second secret treaty with Louis XIV	Etherege, *The Man of Mode*; Otway, *Don Carlos*; Wycherley, *The Plain Dealer*	Cotton, Part 2 of *The Compleat Angler*
1677	Buckingham and Shaftesbury imprisoned	Behn, *The Rover Part 1*; Lee, *The Rival Queens*	Marvell, *An Account of the Growth of Popery*

(*cont.*)

Date	Politics	Theatre	Society and literature
1678	Start of Popish Plot depositions	Dryden, *All for Love*	Bunyan, *The Pilgrim's Progress* Part 1
1679	Duke of York sent abroad for his safety; dissolution of Parliament	Behn, *The Feign'd Curtezans*; Dryden, *Troilus and Cressida*	Non-renewal of Licensing Act gives encouragement to newspapers
1680	Duke of York returns and flees again	Lee, *Lucius Junius Brutus*; Dryden, *The Spanish Fryar*	Rochester, *Poems*; Bunyan, *The Life and Death of Mr Badman*
1681	Monmouth proposed by Whig faction as heir to the throne	Tate, *King Lear*	Hobbes, *Behemoth*; Marvell, *Miscellaneous Poems*
1682	Duke of York returns again; Monmouth arrested	Merger of King's and Duke's Companies; Otway, *Venice Preserv'd*	Dryden, *The Medal, MacFlecknoe* and *Religio Laici*
1683	The Rye House Plot against the King	Death of Thomas Killigrew	Dryden, *The Vindication of the Duke of Guise*
1685	Death of Charles II and accession of his brother, James II; Monmouth's rebellion	Dryden, *Albion and Albanius*	Waller, *Divine Poems*; Behn, *Miscellany*
1686	James II appoints Catholic peers as Privy Councillors	Behn, *The Luckey Chance*	Thomas Browne, *Works*; Anne Killigrew, *Poems*
1688	Flight of James II; William of Orange installed as king	Shadwell, *The Squire of Alsatia*	Death of Bunyan; Halifax, *The Character of a Trimmer*
1690	James is defeated at the Battle of the Boyne	Dryden, *Amphitryon*	Locke, *An Essay concerning Human Understanding*
1691	Tillotson becomes Archbishop of Canterbury	Southerne, *The Wives' Excuse*	Congreve, *Incognita*

(*cont.*)

Date	Politics	Theatre	Society and literature
1692	Defeat of French fleet at Le Hogue; Glencoe massacre	Betterton and Purcell, *The Fairy Queen*	Motteux, *The Gentleman's Journal*
1693	French ambush Smyrna convoy	Congreve, *The Double Dealer*	Rymer, *A Short View of Tragedy*; Locke, *Thoughts Concerning Education*
1694	Death of Queen Mary	Dryden's final play, *Love Triumphant*	Founding of the Bank of England
1695	Commencement of the Whig Junto and, therefore, party government	Betterton splits from Rich to form new company; Congreve, *Love for Love*; Dryden/Howard/ Purcell, *The Indian Queen*	Rapid growth of newspapers after expiry of Licensing Act
1696	Jacobite plot to assassinate King William	Cibber, *Love's Last Shift*; Vanbrugh, *The Relapse*	Toland, *Christianity Not Mysterious*
1697	Parliament calls for disbandment of the army	Vanbrugh, *The Provok'd Wife*	Dryden, translation of Virgil's *Aeneid*
1698	Anglo-French Partition Treaty to resolve the Spanish succession	Collier, *A Short View*	Ward, *The London Spy*; Defoe, *The Poor Man's Plea*
1699	Break-up of Whig government	Farquhar, *The Constant Couple*	Dampier, *Voyages and Descriptions*
1700	Further Anglo-French Partition Treaty; statute against papists	Death of Dryden; Congreve, *The Way of the World*	Dryden, *Fables Ancient and Modern*; Defoe, *The Pacificator*
1702	Death of William III; accession of Queen Anne War declared on France	Rowe, *Tamerlane*; Gildon, *A Comparison Between the Two Stages*	Defoe, *The Shortest Way with the Dissenters*

(*cont.*)

Date	Politics	Theatre	Society and literature
1705	Whig election victory	Vanbrugh opens Queen's Theatre, Haymarket	Defoe, *The Consolidator*
1706	Definition of terms of union with Scotland	Farquhar, *The Recruiting Officer*	Dennis, *Opera after the Italian Manner*
1707	Ratification of Act of Union with Scotland	Farquhar, *The Beaux' Stratagem*	Thomas Brown, *Works*
1710	Trial of Henry Sacheverell for preaching against the Whig government, which falls	Death of Betterton; Congreve, *Collected Works*	Gildon, *The Life of Mr Thomas Betterton*; Swift, *A City Shower*
1714	Death of Queen Anne; accession of George I	Rowe, *Jane Shore*	Pope, *The Rape of the Lock*

Index